THE GOLDEN ASS

THE GOLDEN ASS

by
APULEIUS

Translated by
JACK LINDSAY

Indiana University Greek and Latin Classics
INDIANA UNIVERSITY PRESS
Bloomington

TO RANDALL SWINGLER

The world grows stranger as we stare,
with vortices of maddening change.
How understand what we unbare
as through the ragged scene we range?

When transformations mock control
and the split atom is our all,
what monstrous faces crowd the soul.
The seed's corrupted by our fall.

It seems that Apuleius guessed
the curious things that happen when
the gap is widening betwixt
reality and the minds of men.

Now Isis cannot save us; yet
the answer's truly here explained:
redemption from the faceless threat,
and earth regained.

J. L.

Introduction copyright 1960 by Jack Lindsay
All rights reserved
First Midland Book edition 1962

12 13 14 15 16   87 86 85 84 83 82

ISBN 0-253-20036-9

INTRODUCTION

Apuleius and his Work

WE generally know little of the life of an ancient author if he did not happen to play some part in the political scene. Apuleius, however, is one of the exceptions. He was involved in a lawsuit in which he defended himself; and the speech he then delivered has come down to us, with many details about his life. Further information may be gleaned from *Florida,* a collection of excerpts from his orations or lectures.

He lived through the mid-decades of the second century A.D. and was born in North Africa at Madaura (Mdaurusch today), a well-to-do town set on high above the Medjerda Valley. The place, he claims, was 'a Colony of the highest distinction' – that is, it had been settled many years before by veterans from the Roman army.

My father reached the rank of mayor (*duumvir*); and after filling all the municipal posts of honour he became the town's leading citizen. I, straightway after my entry into the Council, succeeded to his position in the community: no degenerate successor, I trust, but receiving a similar honour and esteem for keeping up the dignity of my rank.

This does not mean that he held the same offices as his father. Augustine says that he never at any time held any public office. But as a councillor's son he could attend council meetings and belonged to the ruling class of the town, the *Ordo.*

Madaura was close to the border between Numidia and Gaetulia, so that Apuleius calls himself semi-Numidian semi-Gaetulian. What language did he speak in his hometown? It may have been Punic; for we find his stepson Pudens speaking that tongue, which was strong (we know from Augustine) even in such a large mercantile town as

5

Carthage. But he would also certainly know Latin, even if of a provincial and vernacular kind. Later, at Rome, he had to work hard to master the metropolitan form. Greek too he would know. It was commonly used in Africa, and his wife's letter, produced at the trial, was written in it.[1] The fact that at an early age he probably knew and conversed in Punic, Latin, and Greek no doubt had an effect on his literary style, helping to bring about his experimental attitude to language, his remarkably florid and vivid style.

While he was still young, his father died, leaving him and his brother a fortune of two million sesterces – a comfortable though not an overlarge sum. Apuleius says that he used up a large part of his inheritance on his prolonged education and travels, on his gifts to friends and teachers. After an elementary grounding at Madaura, he went on to study at Carthage, Athens, Rome.

There is a famed saying of a wise man about the pleasures of the table: 'The first wine-bowl quenches thirst, the second begets jollity, the third stirs up desire, the fourth sends mad.' But the bowls of the Muses have an opposite effect. The more you drink and the stronger the draught, the better is it for the good of your soul. The first bowl, given you by the elementary teacher, rescues you from ignorance; the second, proffered by the teacher of literature, sets you up with learning; the third, brought by the rhetorician, arms you with eloquence.

These three draughts are enough for most men. But I have drunk other cups at Athens: the imaginative draught of poetry, the clear one of geometry, the sweet one of music, the austere one of dialectic, and the nectar of universal philosophy, of which one can never have enough.

He travelled farther east from Athens; for he speaks of visiting Samos and Hierapolis in Phrygia. At Cenchreae near Corinth he was initiated into the Mysteries of Isis; and on reaching Rome he was twice again initiated into those of that goddess and Osiris – if we take Book XI of *The*

[1] In the last years of the Republic the native kings, especially Juba, had encouraged Greek culture. Greek was taught by the *grammatici* in the secondary schools till the Severan age, then declined (Augustine's *Confessions* i, 13, 14 and Terentius Maurus, 1971). Apuleius assumes a knowledge of Philemon and Menander in his audience (*Flor.* xvi), though in some cases at least a Latin translation was used (*Flor.* xviii). Fronto wrote *Epistolae Graecae*. See Norden, *Die antike Kunstprosa*, p. 362 f.; F. Skutsch, *'Die lat. sprache'*, p. 547 in *Kultur und Gegenwort*, 1, viii.

Golden Ass[1] as autobiographical. The personal impact of that book is so great that we feel the experience it describes as certainly that of Apuleius himself. To meet the charges of the necessary rites he conducted cases in the law-courts and perhaps wrote his great tale.

Then he wandered off again, making for Alexandria – probably out of his devotion to Isis. But at Oea on the African coast (near modern Tripoli) he fell seriously ill. In this town was the home of a student he had known in Athens, Pontianus, who was on the look-out for a husband for his widowed mother Pudentilla. His father Sicinius Amicus had died fourteen years before, leaving Pudentilla with two young sons to rear. Recently her father-in-law had been threatening to cut her sons out of his will unless she married his other son, Sicinius Clarus, an old and ailing man; he was keen to keep the money in the family. Before, however, the marriage was solemnized, he died and Pudentilla broke off with Clarus. She wrote to her elder son that she wanted to make a more suitable marriage, and Pontianus decided that it would be best to see her united with someone who wouldn't grab the family fortune of four million sesterces.

He hurried home and learned at Oea that his friend Apuleius was lying ill at the house of some friends, the Appii. At once he insisted on a transfer to the family residence, where Apuleius stayed, convalescing, for a year. Then, restored to health, the latter gave a public lecture, which was received with much applause. Pontianus proposed that he should marry Pudentilla and settle at Oea. Apuleius says that he had meant to continue his travels, and hints that he was not so keen to marry a woman much older than himself – she was over forty. But he had grown to have a high regard for her good qualities, and gave way before Pontianus' insistence.

The marriage was celebrated at a country villa – to save expenses, he declared later when the quiet nature of the event was described as suspicious. The real reason may well have been that there was already a certain amount of unfriendly gossip and family dissension. Pontianus was himself now married, and had become hostile to his old friend

[1] 'The Golden Ass': The epithet is mere laudatory, 'The Golden Tale of the Ass'.

under the influence of his father-in-law, Herennius Rufinus – though he finally, says Apuleius, apologized for his behaviour. However, he soon died; and the field was left open to the malevolent Rufinus, whom Apuleius calls a gormandizer and debauchee, with a fraudulent bankrupt of a father and a harlot of a wife. He describes the daughter who married Pontianus:

Cast off by her previous lover, she brought the marriage the name but not the pure fact of a maiden. She was borne in a litter by eight slaves. Those of you who were there saw how boldly she flirted with her eyes at all the young men and how shamelessly she flaunted her charms. Who did not recognize the mother's pupil when they beheld her rouged lips, her carmined cheeks, her lewd eyes? Every copper of her dowry was borrowed on the eve of the wedding.

Rufinus worked on the surviving son Pudens and a charge was brought against Apuleius of having murdered Pontianus and of winning Pudentilla by magical practices. The murder charge, which lacked any evidence, was dropped; but the second charge went forward. Apuleius was tried at Sabrata (now Zowara), some forty miles west of Oea, in a court presided over by the proconsul Claudius Maximus. He acted as his own lawyer, and we have his speech of self-defence.

His account gives us a lively picture of philistine and voracious small-town provincials, vulgar and venal, ready for any dirty trick in their hunger for money. Pontianus, having found his wife out, 'did not make her a decent legacy. He bequeathed her as an insult linen worth 200 denars, to show he had neither forgotten nor ignored her, but that he expressed his resentment by such a low valuation of her.' As heirs he appointed his mother and brother. Rufinus promptly inveighed the lad Pudens 'by pushing on to his embraces the girl who was much his elder and who had been such a short while back his brother's wife.' Now the demoralized Pudens gave up his studies:

He is a familiar visitor of the Gladiatorial School, and there, as a boy of rank should! he learns from the school's keeper the names of the gladiators, the fights they've fought, the wounds they've received. He speaks no tongue now but Punic; and though he may now and then drop a Greek word picked up from his mother, Latin he will not and cannot use. You heard, Maximus, a little while ago, you heard

8

my stepson — O the shame of it — the brother of that eloquent young man Pontianus, hardly capable of stammering single syllables when you asked him if his mother had given him and his brother the gifts which, as I told you just now, she in fact gave them with my hearty assent.

The evidence for his magical practices Apuleius treats with scorn and tears to shreds with much display of wit and learning. He had bought fish and dissected them; he had taken a boy to a secret place with a small altar and a lantern, and so bewitched the boy that he fell to the ground and awoke out of his wits; he kept some wrapped-up objects of mysterious importance; he had done something wicked that left feathers and soot in a house's hall. Such accusations he discredited with a mocking humour. He was an ichthyologist, he said, interested like Aristotle in 'the generation, the anatomy, the history of animals;' the boy who fell down was Thallus, a sufferer from epilepsy; the covered objects he revered were 'certain talismans' associated with the mysteries into which he had been initiated. And so on. He admitted that he had written amorous poems.

But so vilely and coarsely did they read them out as to leave no effect but that of disgust. Now what has it to do with the malpractices of the Black Art if I write poems in praise of the boys of my friend Scribonius Laetus? Does the mere fact of being a poet turn me into a magician? Who ever heard any orator trot out such plausible grounds for suspicion, such apt conjectures, such closely-reasoned argument? Apuleius has written verses! If they're bad, that's a mark against him as poet, but not as philosopher. But they were frivolous verses of an erotic nature! So that's your charge against me? and it was just a slip of the tongue when you indicted me for practising the Black Art? Yet many other men have written such verses, though you may be ignorant of the fact.

He admitted also that he owned a mirror. 'Pudens nearly exploded in the violence of his declamation against the horrific character of my offence. The philosopher owns a mirror, the philosopher actually possesses a mirror of his own!' He laughs:

Grant that I do have a mirror. If I denied you, you might really think you had struck home with your accusation. Still it is by no means a necessary inference that I am in the habit of adorning myself before the mirror. Suppose I owned a theatrical wardrobe, would you have the face to argue thence that I am in the continual habit of wearing

9

the trailing robes of tragedy, the saffron cloak of the mime-dance, the patchwork dress of the harlequinade? I think not . . .

But come, let me admit that I have looked into the mirror . . .

He then goes on to claim an interest in the scientific problems of light-refraction, the nature of prismatic colours, the effects of concave and convex mirrors.[1] He agrees that he came to Oea with only one slave, and asks why then do his accusers bring up the fact that at Oea he 'gave three slaves their freedom on the same day.'

The one bit of apparently solid evidence his opponents had was a letter written by Pudentilla in which she exclaimed that Apuleius had bewitched her. He demolished this by insisting that her words be read in their context. Her letter to Pontianus had run:

As I wanted to marry for the reasons I adduced to you, you urged me to choose Apuleius before all others since you admired him greatly and were eager through me to become yet more intimate with him. Now that certain ill-natured persons have started accusing us and attempting to dissuade you, Apuleius has all of a sudden become a magician and has bewitched me to love him. Come to me then while I am still in my senses.

At this point the oration had taken on a serious tone, and Apuleius vehemently rebutted the charges of being a careerist who married for money. He had received only a moderate dowry of 300,000 sesterces, which was to revert to Pontianus and Pudens if he got no children on Pudentilla,

[1]Mirrors were used magically, e.g. for bringing influence to bear on the moon or for crystal-gazing: Abt, *Die Apol. des Apul. und die antike Zauberei*. The *magus* was a familiar figure in Africa, in spite of the enactments from the time of Tiberius to that of the Digests. Augustine describes three classes: astrologers, fortune-tellers and horoscope-compilers who acted as confessors (*Conf.* iv, 3, 4); quacks with spells and incantations; diviners and clairvoyants, who cast children into trances, called up the dead, or themselves spoke in a state of possession — they recovered lost property, detected robberies, read thoughts, found water-springs. (African water-diviners had a high repute all over the empire, *Cassiod.* iii, 53; cf. *Sid. Apol.* viii, II.) Fear of the evil eye was specially strong (Pliny, *N.H.* vii, 2, 4). Jailers took steps to stop prisoners' escape by magic: *Act. perpet.* xvi. Love-spells and curses were common. Under Constantine, Sopater, a philosopher was condemned for a spell on the winds to stop African cornships bound for Italy, and a proconsul of Africa was exiled for consulting wizards: *Amm.* xxviii, 7, 19 and E. S. Bouchier, *Life and Letters in Roman Africa* (1913), 54-6.

or to be divided between the two sets of offspring if he did. He had prevented his wife from disinheriting Pudens; and he had not spent her money. A farm costing 60,000 s. had been acquired by her in her own name.

We feel throughout the speech a keen pleasure in the display of superior sophistication and culture. We can see how he might well have dazzled the rich citizens of Oea for a while and how he would also soon arouse deep suspicions and hostilities. Particularly one feels that he is of a divided mind about the accusation of wizardry. He deals with the actual charges in tones of amused contempt, yet seems not averse from being considered one of the great magicians of the world.

He may have rewritten or touched up his speech for publication; but as a whole it has the effect of a genuine court-document, revealing him as an able pleader with a thorough grasp of Roman law. We do not know if the case was dismissed as unproven or if Apuleius won a clear acquittal. In any event he would not have wanted to stay on among the embittered feuds at Oea. Augustine mentions a quarrel with the citizens there over some statue that was to be set up in his honour, so that he seems to have had his partisans as well as his enemies. He himself returned to Carthage, where he carried on his work of lecturing in Latin and Greek, with extempore displays of sophistic brilliance. Statues were erected to him and he was made a priest of the healing saviour-god Aesculapius, an office of some prestige, during his term of which he gave gladiatorial games.

The date of his trial had been 155-8 – certainly not later than 161 when the emperor Antonius Pius, who is mentioned in the speech, died. In *Florida* we can date some pieces: a panegyric of the proconsul Scipio Orfitus, 163; another on Severianus, during the joint rule of Marcus Antonius and Lucius Verus, 161-9; a passage mentioning Aemilanus Strabo (consul in 156), probably before 166 or at most a little later.

Pudentilla had presumably left Oea with him; for in the mid-fifth century Sidonius Apollinaris cites her as one of the model wives who felt a keen interest in their husbands' work. 'Pudentilla was for Apuleius what Marcia was for Hortensius, Terentia for Cicero, Calpurnia for Piso.

11

Rusticiana for Symmachus: these noble women held the lamp while their husbands read and meditated.' She may have borne him a son, for the second book of his treatise on Plato is dedicated *To my Son Faustinus* – unless he is there thinking of a disciple, a spiritual son. When he died we do not know.

He gives varying pictures of himself. At one moment he appears as an unkempt philosopher, haggard with study, his hair as matted as a lump of tow. At the next he is the debonaire and handsome youth who bewitches the affluent widow of Oea. Then again he is the priest of Isis, one of the Egyptian *pastophori*, moving meditatively through the streets of Rome with shaven head and linen stole. All the various aspects of his personality indeed merge in his work: the man-of-the-world's sophistication, the Madauran boy's fascination with language, the scholar's awareness of all the most up-to-date theories, the lover's obsession with the sensuous and rhythmic essence of women's bodies, the devotee's quest for redemption in a new life.

His world, that of the Antonine emperors, shows the Roman State at the height of its expansive power and prosperity. The period was that which Gibbon rated as the happiest known by men. In fact the rot had long set in and the world rang hollow to a knock. By the end of the century the cracking-up of the State built by Augustus was going violently on. Apuleius is thus the man of a world in which there is much apparent stability. The empire has spread over practically all that is known of the civilized world; there has been a steady growth of urbanization, trade, money-economy; local and tribal ways have gone down before the extension of Roman law with its strong basis in personal property. There have been some threats on the northern frontiers, but there is no reason to think that they cannot be met. The Roman power seems indeed eternal, its name inscribed on enduring bronze. Yet under the impressive surfaces the corrosion was busily at work, sapping the urban bases, increasing instead of decreasing the differences between town and country, strengthening the big landlords and preparing the series of upheavals through the peasant-based army which led to the general crisis of the third century and finally issued in the Constantinean State.

Apuleius, needless to say, is no political prophet who fore-sees the coming crisis; but he is a great and sensitive artist who feels the subterranean tremors in the human sphere. He is aware in his own way of the growing fissure between social reality and people's ideas of themselves. And in the last resort his whole artistic method is based on this realiza-tion with its sense of furious contradictions, of dark and dangerous fissures of betrayal yawning under the com-fortable surfaces of everyday life and the assumptions of State-power. In his *Metamorphoses* (generally known as *The Golden Ass – golden* being merely an adjective of praise) he tells a tale which is simultaneously realism and fantasy, directly related to the life of the times and continually moving into a symbolic interpretation.

His book is one of the three great works of imaginative prose narrative that we own from the ancient world. Petronius' *Satyricon* is the first, with its turbulent realistic ironic and poetic picture of the successful philistine world of the first century A.D. with its expanding money-economy. The second is *The Golden Ass*. The third is Longus' *Daphnis and Chloe,* a slighter but wholly delightful work in which the Greek spirit looks nostalgically back over its lost chances and creates an image of 'paradise regained', of restored innocence and happiness, out of the poetic essences of the fertility-cults.

Apuleius tells the story of one Lucius who through his overweening curiosity and magic-dabbling is turned into an ass. Lucius goes through an odyssey of misfortunes and sufferings, till at last he eats the redeeming rose-petals and regains his human form. The theme of the tormented man-inside-the-ass (the beast of burden bearing the weight of the unintelligible world, as Christian bore a crushing burden till he reached the foot of the Cross) is one that enables Apuleius to achieve a new and startling focus from which to look out on human activities and judge them. Lucius has been avid to grasp the forbidden lores and prac-tices that will enable him to get behind the appearances of things; as a result he becomes the victim of the dark forces he has invoked. His odyssey is a long struggle towards a new level, a new integration of life, in which his old hungers and compulsions are overcome.

The tale seems to have been written in Rome. Apuleius seems speaking through Lucius' mouth when in Book I he says that he learned to write Latin at Rome under no teacher, but with much toil, so that his style must still have some tang of his speeches in the law-courts. Many allusions show a location at Rome: the *metae Murciae*, the fines for being late at the Senate, the law about slaves, the marriage-laws. And in the last Book the narrative seems to make a leap into the openly autobiographical. Lucius of Corinth becomes the young man from Madaura, and the experiences set out in Book XI correspond with what we learn of Apuleius' life in Rome from his Sabrata speech. We may then assume that *The Golden Ass* was a work of his youth, written during his residence in Rome; and though this view has been combated, I feel that it is correct. The tale has a youthful effervescence which suits better the enthusiast convert of Rome than the worldly-wise and flowery orator of Carthage.

Apuleius himself classifies his work among the Milesian tales. We possess little of the *Milesiaka* of Aristides; but we know they were a collection of short stories, many at least not much longer than anecdotes, with amatory themes predominating and a bawdy note recurring – a sort of slighter and more primitive form of the genre that begot the *Decameron*. Apuleius, however, though using the tale within the tale, has welded his material in a highly original way that bears no relation to the Milesian tales. (In the inset of *Cupid and Psyche* the parents of Psyche consult the oracle of Apollo at Miletus, and Apollo answers in Latin – in order, Apuleius mentions with a grin, not to embarrass the author, Apuleius himself. The touch suggests that he was elaborating a Milesian tale.)

In some of the insets he seems to have drawn rather hastily on some such collection as the *Milesiaka*. Thus in Book IX there are four tales on the theme of faithless wives; in two cases the lover fools the husband, in two he is found out. In the last two instances the parallelism is clearly intentional; but it is hard to find any such compositional reason for the first two with their repetition of the theme. In Book VIII the ass tells how his master the miller was murdered at his wife's instigation and how the miller's ghost appeared to his daughter. Later we learn that the girl was not the woman's daughter but her step-daughter, *noverca*. This sort of thing may represent careless copying from some lost original or it may be meant to give the casualness of a real narrative of daily life. The same double-edged reasoning may be applied to the fact that the ass omits any reference to the arrest of the murderess.

A more pressing problem of origins is raised by the existence of a tale, *Lucius or the Ass,* among writings attributed to Lucian. (The style is hardly that of Lucian, however.) This is a very much plainer account of a man changed into an ass, which lacks Apuleius' rich variety and poetic overtones. There seems also to have been a third version, written by one Lucius of Patrae. The Lucianic tale has a mild vein of comedy, with no hint of the Isis-redemption that sets the seal on Apuleius' symbolism. Its hero regains his humanity by mere accident; the conclusion is farcical. Lucius calls on the woman with whom he had copulated as an ass.

I thought that I'd appear more handsome in my human form. Indeed she welcomed me, enraptured, it seemed, by my odd adventure. She even invited me to dine and pass the night with her. I accepted, considering that it would be unseemly if, after having been loved in my ass's skin, I showed disdain on becoming once more a man and scorned my old mistress. So I dined with her, soaked in scents and crowned with those beloved roses to which I owed my return to the world of men. When the hour grew late and the time came for bed, I rose, and thinking to do a pretty act, I threw off my clothes and made myself quite naked, imagining that I would please the woman far more when she compared me with the ass. But she, seeing that I was really a man, threw a glance of scorn on me and cried out, 'Go and kick up your heels far away from me and my house. Go and make your bed where you will, but not here.'

'What crime then have I committed?' I answered her.

'By the Lord on high,' she said, 'it wasn't you, it was the ass, that I fell in love with. It was with him, not with you, that I lay. I thought you'd have kept the magnificent handsome what's-it that distinguished my ass. But I see that instead of that charming and useful animal you've been changed into an absurd ape.'

She at once called her slaves and bid them raise me on their shoulders and throw me out of doors. So there I was, carried out of the house, naked, with a splendid show of scents and garlands, forced to embrace the bare earth and repose on its bosom.

When day came, without having been able to regain my clothes, I ran to the ship and laughingly told my misfortune to my brother. A favourable wind began to blow and we left the town with sails aloft and in some days arrived in my homeland. There I sacrificed to the Saviour-Gods and made them an offering for having emerged— not from the dog's bottom, as the saying goes – but from the ass's

15

skin where my curiosity had imprisoned me so long, and for having returned at last safe and sound to my home.

Our knowledge of Lucius of Patrae comes from the *Bibliotheca* of Photius, Patriarch of Byzantium in the ninth century, who records the reading of a collection of tales of miraculous transformation made by this Lucius. The first two books, he says, give the impression of an almost literal copy of *Lucius or the Ass* of Lucian; but he inclines to think Lucian imitated Lucius and not Lucius Lucian.

> For Lucian seems to have cut down the longer story of Lucius and removed all that was necessary for his own purpose, and then, keeping the original phrases and sentences, to have welded what he had left into a consecutive story . . . [Also] whereas Lucius writes as one who believes in the possibility of such transformations, Lucian writes as one who derides the extravagances of superstition.

Photius is perhaps reading into the Lucianic tale what he knows of Lucian's irony; for it is only the conclusion that could be said to have any clear satirical intention.

Much argument has gone on about the relation of the three works. It has even been suggested that Apuleius wrote both the Greek and Latin *Metamorphoses,* and that the Lucianic text is an epitome of them.[1] The most convincing thesis, however, is that both the Lucianic author and Apuleius drew on Lucius of Patrae – the first cutting the tale down into a concise sarcastic narrative, the second expanding in his characteristic style and introducing his own deeper meanings. (Thus, when the ass tries to carry off the captive girl, in *The Golden Ass* there is a struggle between the girl and ass when they reach the cross-roads; for the ass knows that if the girl has her way they'll run into the robbers. In *Lucius or the Ass* they merely happen to meet the robbers at cross-roads. We may infer that Apuleius embodied the original incident, while the epitomizer through carelessness or desire for brevity has retained the vestigial reference to cross-roads without their reason-for-existence in the tale). Photius describes the work of Lucius of Patrae as sweet in style, with a love of portentous incidents; and such writing may well have inspired Apuleius to write his masterpiece.

[1] Rohde (*Klein. Schrift.* ii 70) thinks Apul. copies the Lucianic tale.

Attempts have been made to explain his style as purely African, owing its rich colours to the Punic element with its roots in the Mediterranean East. But though there is no need to dispute the point that something in his use of words derives from his Madauran origins, we cannot reduce his style as a whole to African influences. His mixture of ornate invention and rhetorical ingenuity with archaic and colloquial forms marks him rather as a man of his epoch, in which the classical heritage is being transformed by a welter of new forces.

Fronto, an elder contemporary of Apuleius, was born at Cirta and studied at Carthage. At Rome he became a pleader and rose high in the political world, though his African birth made the arrogant Italian nobles antagonistic to him. His orations gained him fame and he became the head of a group of disciples who joined in attempting to revitalize Latin style, mainly by a return to archaic forms of the Republican period. He failed to distinguish between old words which had often survived vigorously among the populace, and others that were temporary innovations and had never taken root in the language. But his antiquarian effort links with the elements of archaism and colloquialism in Apuleius, and shows that they were not merely a personal deviation of the latter.

With all its idiosyncrasies, Aupleius' style clearly belongs to its period; and we can scarcely doubt that at Rome he had listened to Fronto.

The part played by Africa in the intellectual life of the Latin West from the days of Fronto to the invasion of the Vandals was of the greatest importance. Fronto and Apuleius were the creators of the *elocutio novella;* and following them came the great patristic literature of Tertullian, Cyprian, Lactantius and Augustine – while Italy and Rome had practically nothing to offer. In the literary field we may select as characteristic of the new African school a love of extreme colour-richness, a tendency to allegory, and a predilection for realism even in grotesque terms. Apuleius' *Cupid and Psyche* may be linked with Fronto's *Creation of Sleep;* and indeed even the lesser African poets give a new life to the old myths with their profusion of warm colours, their pictorial fantasy, their eye-on-the-object—

as the scene in Nemesianus (*Eclogue* iii) where the young Bacchus playfully plucks out hairs from the shaggy chest of his guardian Silenus, the medical consultation in the *Aegritudo Perdicae*, or the account Dracontius gives of Cupid feathering an arrow from his own wing. Another example on a more serious subject may be sought in Tertullian's fearful vision of the future torments of the heathen: philosophers burning with the disciples whom they had taught to disbelieve in God, charioteers red-hot on fiery wheels, tragic actors shrieking louder than they had ever done in life, and many more. (Bouchier).

But we must beware of seeing such attitudes as specifically African. They belong to a general trend, partly based on the development of regional cultures now asserting themselves against the breaking-up 'classical' systems; and they have their counterparts in Spain, Gaul and in Egypt. This new trend of the provincial cultures that displace the metropolitan culture of Rome is highly 'romantic' in that it seeks local colour and the precise contours of the particular instead of the old generalities. In Apuleius, despite his rhetorical training, the old schemes of antithesis, emphasis and amplification have collapsed; in their place appear vehement and complicated sentences with their own forms of fluid antithesis and with heaped-up epithets, or else short symmetrical clauses, ready to use rhyme or alliteration for dynamic effects. The forms of Ciceronian clause-subordination are thrown aside.

Under the Antonines, the eastern and western sections of the empire had again been drawn closely together; the emperors followed the philhellenistic line of Hadrian. One result was the revival of Greek literature itself – in Plutarch, Aristides, Dion of the Golden Mouth, Appian, Lucian and others. But while these Greeks tended to seek an Attic discipline of style, the Africans and other provincials delighted in the extravagances of the Asiatic school.

So the academics are loud in denouncing Apuleius' style: antithesis, isokolon with homoioteleuton [equality of clauses and jingling likeness of endings], play upon words, the complete transfusion of prosaic and poetical expression, the frivolous method of using language as the subject of an experiment in the coinage of new words with an occasional mixture of archaisms.' So writes Norden, condemning Apuleius for his virtues.

More correct is it to note that the litany to Isis in Book

18

XI has a rich ground-swell of musical power and expressiveness, which already embodies the organic harmonies of the medieval world. 'This is a rhythmical poem, anticipating or foreshadowing the poetry of the future, which was to spring from the manifold suggestions conveyed by those who wielded this rhetorical prose more boldly than others. The language of this novel of Apuleius stands on the border line between prose and poetry. It was the precept of the schools that prose must borrow from poetry the ornaments that poetry has always possessed. And it was now to give back to poetry the more questionable gift of those borrowings added to and transmuted in the course of centuries.'[1]

Let us glance at some of the details of Apuleius' style and it will become clear that English translators have not even tried to preserve and carry over the least tincture of his manner – the manner which is the man. Thus, 'Tell me the whole story from the beginning' is a poor rendering of *ordine mihi singula retexe;* yet that is the sort of thing we are offered. Apuleius is obviously aware of the metaphor in *retexe* (unravel), which is close to that in our phrase 'spin a tale'. The imagery implicit and explicit in his use of words must be brought out by the translator, or the delicate and vivid colours fade out. The reader does not need to know any Latin to feel that a jingle (with an archaic flavour) like *oppido formido* cannot be turned into 'I greatly fear'.

This prose is a mosaic of internal rhymes and assonances. Alliteration is frequent. Phrases like *habitus et habitudo* or *voluptatem veneriam et scortum scorteum Lari et liberis* litter his pages. There is also something of a Meredithian excess of abstract terms. But it is the tumultuous eagerness of the sounds that constitute the chief problem, the omnipresent sense of tension, anxiety, and hurry, which is defined by the rhythm, the word-order, the texture. Take the description of the baker's wife: *saeva scaeva virosa ebriosa pervicax pertinax* . . . The nagging clashing effect of the rhymes gives us half the meaning. I quote two well-known versions: 'She was crabbed, cruel, cursed, drunken, obstinate, niggish.' 'She was mischievous, malignant, addicted to men and wine, froward and stubborn.' And here is the most recent one (by R. Graves): 'She was

[1] F. J. Raby, *A Hist. of Secular Latin Poetry* (1934), i, 24. (Norden, *Kuntsprosa*, 601).

19

malicious, cruel, spiteful, lecherous, drunken, selfish, obstinate.' Read again the merry and expressive doggerel of Apuleius and it will be seen how little of his vision of life has been transferred into English.

There are also his punning tricks, which often show a remarkable virtuosity. Thus he describes Charite after the death of Tlepolemus as wishing to die but 'unwillingly remaining alive: *invita remansit in vita*. The identity of sound between the terms for the unwillingness and the aliveness of the girl, with the split inside one term in the form in which it is written, has a sharp, concise, violent impression like the shock it expresses; and the compact *invita* against the split *in vita* has further an effect of broken life divided against itself.

This may seem an over-nice analysis of a verbal trick; but Apuleius' creative energy resides precisely in this sort of thing – which reveals a refraction of his whole outlook, his world view, in the smallest possible patterns of emotional or sensuous significance.

The pervasive symbolism thus appears both in the major design and in small details. In saying this, we are not agreeing with those who have, for instance, tried to reduce *Cupid and Psyche* to a frigid allegorical construction. Apuleius' meaning is first of all broadly defined by the thesis-antithesis and resolution of the three main stages of the story. The first stage when Lucius fondly imagines himself human, but keeps probing into all that is anti-human, lured by the forbidden. The second stage, when, trapped by the regressive forces he has made part of himself, he becomes an undeniable beast, thereby discovering his humanity. The third stage when he is able to overcome the conflict of beast-level and human aspiration.

The tale of *Cupid and Psyche* repeats this fundamental theme in a variant form. The act of disobedience, which is an act of betrayal, throws Psyche, the Soul, into a sphere of loss and suffering; but by successfully passing through the ordeals, by an unbroken devotion and love, she regains her happiness, now on a securer level of consciousness. Innocence has renewed itself by becoming Experience, yet cleaving all the while to that which is truly human.

The tale here is at root a folk tale. It belongs to the tale type of the Beast-Lover, but it has gone through several changes of level before it reaches the form given it by Apuleius. The innocence of the folk tale, close to a ritual-myth of death and rebirth, has been polished away by the erotic focus of the Milesian bawdy story, and has then been regained by the poetic insight of Apuleius. In a sense the stages of development in the tale itself thus correspond to the stages of development in Psyche, in Apuleius' symbolism of the soul's progress.

In Book XI we find the only full testimony of religious experience left by an adherent of ancient paganism. That it reflected a widespread experience, felt in one degree or another by all the devotees of mystery-cults, of the cults of the saviour-gods, is shown by numerous inscriptions and other fragments of evidence. But without this extended statement we should have been left in part guessing, tentatively reconstructing a difficult and obscure sphere of emotional experience. We can judge by it how deep was the sense of self-dedication that the mystery-cults could beget in a worshipper, and how strong the sense of being a new man integrated in the god, with a new all-enveloping moral purpose.

Commentators have often asked if there was an anti-Christian polemic involved. But they have been unable to answer this question satisfactorily because they have failed to understand Apuleius' artistic method, which is one with his moral aims. In my opinion there was a strong under-lying anti-Christian polemic, though for Apuleius the main thing was the positive expression of devotion to Isis and of the possibility of renewing one's personality through know-ledge of her suffering and her love, and of the resurrection of Osiris. Christianity had not by the Antonine period such an impressive air of challenging the creeds of the empire that he would concentrate on the polemical positions; but at the same time he could not, at this period, have been unaware of the existence of the Christian groups. He classed them, it seems to me, with what he considered other degene-rate mystery-groups, such as the self-castrating Galli of the Great Mother.

We must base our judgement in this matter on his total picture and definition, not on incidental points of satire. Quite probably the phrase about the Virgin triumphing on the Ass in Book VII and the picture of the vile baker's wife with her one-and-only god are meant to glance at the Christians; but these are not the decisive points. (It is also possible that in choosing the ass for his symbolic beast he was partly thinking of the belief that the Jews worshipped an ass and of the representation of Christ in ass-form. It is of interest also that the Arabic Gospel of the Infancy tells of a man transformed into a mule who becomes human again by having the Christ-child placed on his back.)

Another important aspect of the symbolism is brought out by the episode of the bakery. Here the beast-of-burden is revealed as one with the slave-worker; and Apuleius' criticism penetrates to the heart of the social problem of antiquity. Without this experience the 'fall' of Lucius would remain abstract; with it, it is seen to express the totality of the inner contradictions and conflicts of the ancient world. How is man to 'rise' out of this hell of exploitation? By individual efforts to better his condition and to walk on the faces of his fellows? The logic of Apuleius' tale answers that the 'escape' is only by a total transformation, which is both possible and necessary for one and all if men are to keep on struggling to become human. The lonely progress of Ass-Lucius thus becomes that of all men; it reflects and defines the processes by which they exist, and, existing, move forward. (Incidentally, with the account given by Diodoros of the Egyptian gold-mines, the bakery-episode is the only passage in the whole of ancient literature which realistically looks at and examines the conditions of slave-exploitation on which the culture of the ancient world rested. And since Apuleius, unlike Diodoros, is depicting the hellish state from within, he may claim the proud position of being the only ancient writer with the courage, insight and humanity to look clearly and unflinchingly at the ugly thing.)

Florida is a disappointing collection after *The Golden Ass* or the *Apology*. The excerpts show the skilled and learned sophist, who knows how to dazzle an audience he could not really have respected, but not a flash or a gleam from the world of the *Ass*. They consist of encomia of great men and great cities, mythological and historical anecdotes, fables, scientific disquisitions (on themes from ethnography, geograpny, natural history), and discourses on the sophistic art. True to the ideals of the Second Sophistic, but ignoring the standards of his romance with its demand that art cut deep into life, he chatters away:

> The reputation I have won, your kind anticipations, do not allow any careless utterance, rather they demand my most whole-souled work. Who of you would forgive me for one solecism? Who would permit me one barbarously-pronounced syllable? Who would assent to my babbling as madmen may ill-starred and ill-chosen words? Such diction, indeed, you lightly and rightly overlook in others. But with me, every single word I utter you closely scrutinize, you diligently consider, you test with file and plumb-line, you insist on the polish of the lathe and the grandeur of the stage.

Even the theme of the god Aesculapius stirs nothing of the poet in him:

> Everywhere I boast myself the nursling of your city of Carthage, everywhere and all ways I sing your praises, I zealously honour your learning, give glory to your wealth and reverent worship to your gods. Now therefore I shall begin by speaking of the god Aesculapius. With what more auspicious theme could I engage your ears? For he honours the citadel of our Carthage with the shield of his undeniable presence. See, I shall sing to you in both Greek and Latin a hymn I composed to his glory and long past dedicated to him. For I am well known as a haunter of his ceremonies, my worship of him is no new thing, my priesthood has been vouchsafed the smile of his favour, and before today I have uttered my veneration of him in prose and verse alike. Even so I shall chant a hymn to his glory in both Greek and Latin. I have prefaced it with a dialogue, also in both tongues, in which Sabidius Severus and Julius Persius shall speak together . . .

He tells us that he wrote dialogues, hymns, history and satire. Three poems of his are cited in the *Apology*; a translation of a passage from Menander once existed in a now-lost manuscript of Beauvais; and he wrote a verse-panegyric on Orfitus. We have his treatises *The God of Socrates,* which deals with the doctrine of intermediary spirits, and *Plato and his Creed (dogma),* a popular abridgement of Plato's teachings. The latter work attempts to describe Plato's world-picture, but does not deal with such philosophical problems as those raised by the doctrines of Ideas. A third treatise, *On Dialectic,* is missing from the manuscripts; and a fourth one, which treats formal logic, bears his name but is certainly by a later grammarian. *The*

Universe is a translation of a pseudo-Aristotelean work (which like a book of his *Plato* is dedicated to his son Faustinus). Among the lost books was a version of Plato's *Phaedo*, an Epitome of History, and the scientific *Natural Questions*, writings in both Greek and Latin on Fish, Trees, Agriculture, Music.[1]

At least these works testify to his enthusiasm for Plato and his untiring curiosity. But the one we most regret is another novel named *Hermagoras*. We have no clue as to what its theme was and whether he developed further on the style of *The Golden Ass*. (Of persons hearing the name Hermagoras we know two rhetoricians and a Stoic philosopher.)

The texts of *The Golden Ass*, the *Apology*, and the *Florida*, have come down to us through one manuscript, now in the Laurentian Library of Florence, which also holds parts of Tacitus. This manuscript, in Lombardic characters, was written about the eleventh century and is thought to have been in the monastery of Monte Cassino; Boccaccio may have been responsible for its coming to Florence. It goes back to an archetypal manuscript at least as old as the fourth century; for a subscription to Book IX of the *Ass* shows that one Sallustius worked on it at that period. Poggio Bacciolini came across the manuscript in 1427 in the possession of Nicolo del Niccoli; the latter bequeathed it to the Convent of St. Mark, whence it went to the Laurentian Library. The manuscripts we have of the philosophical writings belong generally to the twelfth and thirteenth centuries; but one (B of Brussels) seems written early in the eleventh.

Apuleius was among the first authors printed in Italy. The first press there was set up in 1465 at the monastery of Subiaco in the Sabine mountains by two Germans. Two years later these men moved to Rome, where in 1469 they produced their edition of Apuleius under the editorship of Giovanni Andrea de Bussi, a pupil of Vittorino da Feltre.

The earliest known reference to Apuleius in ancient writings occurs in the work of Lactantius, a professor of

[1] An *Asclepius* is ascribed to him apparently on the strength of his devotion to Aesculapius; it is an Hermetic work, not his. (T. Whittaker, *Macrobius*, 8f).

rhetoric who wrote a manual of Christian doctrine and who cites Apuleius in company with Apollonius of Tyana as a famous magician. His account shows that he knew Apuleius' remarks about demons in *The God of Socrates*. Apuleius was thus early launched on tradition as himself a wizard – a reputation that was not, we have noticed, entirely undeserved, despite his urbane denials in the *Apology*. But in the form that the tradition takes he is himself identified with his Lucius, not only as a devotee of Isis; but as a man who had undergone the same transformations.

Julius Capitolinus, one of the compilers of the Augustan Histories, knew the *Ass*, for he wrote that Clodius Albinus occupied himself with old wives' tales and grew senile over the Punic Milesian stories of Apuleius and literary trifles. Ausonius, the Gaulish poet, refers to Apuleius in his *Marriage Patchwork, cento nuptialis*, in the year 368 – a poem made up wholly of quotations from Virgil. In the last section where he describes with warm detail the consummation in bed, he requests that no inferences about his own life be drawn from his verses, and bids the reader recall that Apuleius was a philosopher in life, but an amorist in his poems. Macrobius, Sidonius, Priscianus, Cassiodorus, also mention Apuleius, and John Lydus in Byzantium knew him.[1]

Martianus Capella, a native of Madaura like Apuleius, wrote in the early fifth century an encyclopaedia of the seven liberal arts, which he tried to brighten up by introducing the arts at the Marriage of Philologia and Mercury. This allegory in verse and prose is a frigidly dull imitation of *Cupid and Psyche*, turning into an elaborate mechanical form what is poetically defined by Apuleius. Its interest lies in showing that the latter's method, however individual in its working out, was part of a general trend. (The treatise which Martianus wrote for his son, to introduce him to the arts without tears, became a textbook in medieval days and

[1] Macrobius, proconsul at Carthage 409-10, was probably an African: Schanz, *Gesch. d. röm Litt.* (3rd. ed.) iv, 2, 191; Monceaux, *Les Africains*, 426 ff. Raby, i, 100 ff. for Martianus' allegory; Monceaux, 453. C. Weyman, *Stud. zu Apul. (Sitzungsb. . . . zu Munchen* ii, 321-92) 1893, puts too much on Apul. in influencing Tertullian, Zeno of Verona, etc. and underestimates general trends.

was seriously annotated by scholars like John the Scot, Dunchad, and Remigius of Auxerre – while Notker Labeo, a monk of S. Gall in the tenth century, translated it into German.) Fulgentius Planciades attempted directly to allegorize *Cupid and Psyche*.

Apuleius' effect on the Christian Fathers is even more interesting. Jerome knew him, and Augustine (a fellow African) has much to say on the man and his works. He knew *The Golden Ass* (he uses this name), the *Apology*, and *The God of Socrates*. He looked on their author as *Platonicus nobilis*, couples him with Apollonius, and is inclined to believe that both men did perform miracles – though with the aid of demons, not angels – and that Apuleius had experienced an ass-transformation. He is horrified that the followers of Apuleius and Apollonius compare their miracles with those of Christ, and he feels it necessary to produce long arguments to prove that Apuleius did not really have very great magical powers. For all his magic, Augustine says, he never reached any political office though he was obviously ambitious. He defended himself against the charge of magical practices, 'only wishing to show his innocence by denying such things as cannot be innocently committed.' If he had truly believed in magic, he should have been ready to suffer martyrdom for it. If he practised magic, he must have done it with the aid of demons, who, on his own admission, are for ever agitated and given to angers. Such demons are therefore evil spirits and should not be used by good men as intermediaries between themselves and the gods.

The fact that Apuleius like the thaumaturge Apollonius had become regarded as a magician to be set up against Christ gives a tangential support to the thesis that *The Golden Ass* is from one angle an anti-Christian polemic. In any event Apuleius became for the Christians a most controversial figure.

In the fourth and fifth centuries . . . the Christians, upheld by the imperial authority and the magistrates, sought to compel the final suppressions of paganism. Obliged by their own dogmas to believe in the marvellous, they admitted the reality of the miracles of Apuleius and took his novel's inventions seriously. But that made them combat his popularity with all the more fury . . .

Apuleius, orator and priest, was in the eyes of the Africans the most brilliant representative of the ancient civilization at the moment when the apostles set out to make Carthage one of the capitals of Christianity. Foes and friends alike personified in him pagan society. The conquered gods had been relegated by the conquerors to the train of devils: Apuleius, their priest and their prophet, was changed into sorcerer . . .

The legend's success is explained by the religious struggles that convulsed Roman Africa. Everyone believed in the miracles of Apuleius. The pagans opposed him to Christ as the great wonderworker; the Christians assailed in him a sorcerer and an Antichrist.[1]

He continued to be known through the medieval period. In the sixth century, as the elegiacs of Cristodoros tell us, a statue of him was set up at Byzantium; and Psellus there in the twelfth century refers to his magic powers. In Italy in the eleventh century Alphanus I of the great medical centre of Salerno refers to *The God of Socrates* and cites a passage not found in this or any other known work of Apuleius; Waiferius of the same place cites the *Florida*. In the twelfth century Bernard Silvester of Tours based his *Of the Universe* on Apuleius' *De Mundo*; and Geoffrey of Monmouth in England refers to *The God of Socrates* in relation to Merlin's birth. Alexander Neckham, Bartholomew of England, and Albertus Magnus also knew *The God of Socrates* (of which a twelfth century manuscript is in the Harleian collection of the British Museum).

There is no need to discuss here the wide influence of Apuleius on later literature and art, but we may note that Boccaccio in his *Decameron* translated two of his tales into Italian (Nov. 10, 5th day; Nov. 2, 7th day). The latter tale was used again by Morlini, a sixteenth century Neapolitan and by La Fontaine in his poem, *Le Cuvier*, which in the eighteenth century inspired three French comic-operas and one English musical-entertainment. Don Quixote's battle with the wineskins is drawn from Lucius' encounter with the wineskins in Books II and III of the *Ass*; and Gil Blas's experiences in the robbers' cave take their setting from Apuleius' cave. Boiardo translated in 1549 the *Ass* of a Latin version of the Lucianic tale and *The Golden Ass*; then Firenzuola translated the latter book, while about the same time Machiavelli wrote a poem in *terza rima* which tells how a Florentine, changed into an

[1] Monceau, *Apuleé magicien (Rev. des deux mondes,* lxxxv 607f, 1888); E. H. Haight, *Apuleius and his Influence,* 1927, 99.

ass, suffers in his wanderings over the world in order to work out his salvation; a macaronic poem by Teophilus Folenghus, 1521, used the theme with a certain amount of satire; and Pontano's political dialogue depicted the Duke of Calabria as a foolish old man devoted to an ungrateful ass. Praises of the ass were written, e.g. by E. C. Agrippa; and the theme was taken up importantly by Giordano Bruno, in whose work the symbolism of the Ass plays a recurrent and significant part. For instance, in the second dialogue of the *Cabala,* Onorio tells of his changes from ass to wandering spirit, then to winged ass, then man – learning that there are no vital differences between men and beasts. In the *Asino cillenico* at the end of this work an ass petitions to be admitted to the Academy; and when the Academicians point out the difficult requirements and curriculum, the ass feels capable of achieving entry since he believes that he was once a man. With Mercury's aid, he does get in, transformed into a dogmatic pedant. *L'asinità* is a concept that plays a key-part in Bruno's thinking, and it certainly looks in part towards Apuleius.[1]

The tale of *Cupid and Psyche* again has played a considerable part in inspiring poets and artists, from Boccaccio, Da Correggio, Udine, Marino and others to Keats.[2]

The Golden Ass is a great work with perennial interest. It sums up its epoch and at the same time remains a timeless fantasy to which men can always return for images and symbols of their earthly life. In one sense it records the breakdown of Graeco-Roman civilization; in another it prophetically looks to the reconstruction of the fourth century in which the Constantinean State, with its acceptance of Christianity as the official religion, was to give a new start to things. But beyond all such points of reference, it has an inner vitality which makes it symbolic of the life of man here and now, in the twentieth or any other century. As with the *Satyricon,* though from a very different angle, it has

[1] See Haight for much more information on imitations and adaptations. In the *Cabala* Bruno shows that his meditations on 'transformation' have led him to an organic notion of the relation of form and substance, mind and body. If a snake could change into a man, he says, it would *be* a man. (The Medieval Prose of the Ass plays a part in the Renascence jokes and praises.)

[2] The versions by William Morris and Robert Bridges are not successes.

a surprising air of modernity, which sets it abreast of each age that reads it. The mocking scepticism of the author is merged with a deep and reverential love for life; and his odd style is so closely linked with his love, his eager curiosity, that it refuses to seem precious or obscure.

JACK LINDSAY

PREFACE

In this Milesian Tale,[1] reader, I shall string together a medley of stories, and titillate your agreeable ears with a merrily whispered narrative, if you will not refuse to scan this Egyptian paper written with a subtle pen of Nilotic reeds. It tells how the forms and fortunes of men were converted into alien natures, and then back again by the twist of fate into their first selves. Read and wonder; but first I shall answer your query: Who is this man?

A few words will explain. Hymettus of Attica, the Isthmus of Ephyre,[2] Taenarus of Sparta (famous lands mirrored in even more indestructibly famous books) are my old nurseries. There as a lad I went to school and learned the Attic tongue. Soon after, a stranger in the Latian city, with headsplitting effort and with no pedagogic fingerposts, I acquired the native speech of the Romans. So I prelude with an apology lest I should annoy the reader with any unfamiliar or harsh constructions in what is to me a foreign tongue. Yet this very change of language suits a tale of magical metamorphoses, such as you are here to read. We begin then, reader, a Grecian tale. Attend, and pleasure is yours.

---

[1] 'Milesian Tale': Miletus was famed for luxury and gaiety and early produced sets of the light tales that went by this name.
[2] 'Ephyre': The old name for Corinth.

BOOK THE FIRST

Business directed me into Thessaly. For it was from
Thessaly that my mother's family originated, the line being
traced back to Plutarchus,[1]– that notable man, and Sextus,
his philosophic nephew – a genealogy highly honourable to
us. After I had traversed the tops of mountains and the
slides of valleys, the dews of the grass and the furrows of
the fields, I noticed that my horse, a milk-white thorough-
bred of the country, was somewhat blown. Feeling sore
from the ride myself, I leaped out of the saddle, to shake the
stiffness from my limbs by walking. I carefully wiped the
sweat from the horse with a handful of greenery, and
stroked his ears, and unbridled him, and walked him along
at a quiet pace to give nature a chance to muster her usual
resources.

And now while the horse, bending down his head and
sideways crunching the grass, was engaged in this ambling
breakfast, I saw a short way ahead two fellow-travellers,
with whom I presently made a third. I pricked up my ears
to learn the theme of their conversation, when one of
them with a pointed laugh explained, 'Enough of this.
Please don't tell me any more such ridiculous monstrous
lies.'

At this I, always thirsty for every sip of novelty, interrupted, 'Excuse me, but I should like very much to be informed
what you are discussing – not because I mean to pry, but
because I want to know everything in the world . . . or at
least a good part of it. Besides, a light gay-tale will carry
us more smoothly over the ruggedness of this hill that we
are just ascending.'

The man who had laughed answered me, 'This fabrica-

[1] 'Plutarchus': Plutarch the historian was a Boeotian, and his
nephew Sextus seems to have been later than Apuleius. The reference
is therefore to some other Plutarch, unless Sextus has crept in through
a gloss.

tion is about as true as if a man should choose to assert that mutterings of magic can make swift rivers run backwards, the ripples be flattened out of the sea, the winds dribble and die, the sun stop dead, the moon drop her venomfoam[1] upon the earth, the stars be plucked-out, day vanish, and night fall over all things.'

I replied to this in rather a confident tone, 'Come on, you the story-teller, don't feel sorry you've started, and don't flinch at going on.' And turning to the other, I said, 'But for you, sir, with the dense ears and the firm prejudice, you are rejecting a story which may very well be true. By Hercules, you are ignorant that man's debased intelligence calls all those matters lies which are either seldom seen or heard, or which exist on heights beyond the narrow cast of his reason. And yet if you probe these matters closely, you will find them not only understandable and clear, but even easily beheld. Why, last evening I was trying to out-eat the others who were with me at supper, and I took a large bite at a barley-cheesecake in my hurry. It was so soft and glutinous that it stuck in the bottom of my windpipe and all but choked me. And yet not long ago at Athens, before the Porch named the Poecile, I saw with these identical two eyes a juggler who swallowed a horseman's sharp double-edged broadsword, tip-first, right down to the hilt – and then, for a few miserable coppers, he rammed home a hunting-spear until he had the point with all its deadly threat buried deep in his entrails. But you should have seen our gapes of surprise when over the spear blade, about the place towards the back of the head where the weapon had been shoved in down his throat, there climbed a pretty little boy, who wriggled and turned about as if he hadn't any bone or gristle in his body. He looked like that noble Serpent which clings with slippery coils to the knotted staff, with its half-clipped twigs, that the God of Physic bears. So, you that were telling the story, begin anew. I shall believe you, even if your friend won't, and in return for your trouble I should like you to dine with me at the first inn we encounter.'

The man replied, 'Thanks. It's a fair offer and I'll be pleased to begin my story all over again for you. And

[1] 'Venomfoam': There was a superstition that the moon dropped a venomous dew.

first I swear to you by the light of this Sun, the all-seeing God, that every word I relate is my true experience. Indeed, you won't have any doubt left when you come to the next Thessalian city. You'll find the tale on everybody's lips there, for the events are publicly known.'

The Tale of Aristomenes

F I R S T, as to who and what I am – I am from Aegina – and as to my business, I travel the country in every direction through Thessaly and Aetolia and Boeotia, to buy honey and cheese and other foodstuffs for retail to the shopkeepers. Now, hearing that at Hypata,[1] the capital of Thessaly, there were available fresh cheeses of a particularly fine flavour at a very moderate rate, I dashed off to see if I couldn't snap up the whole market.

But – the usual bad luck – I'd put my worst foot[2] forward, for Lupus, a wholesale merchant, had cleared the stock on the day before. I was fatigued by the unprofitable speed of my journey; and so, early in the evening, I proceeded to the baths. There, whom did I see but my old comrade Socrates. He was sitting on the ground, barely covered with a ragged apology for a cloak, almost wanned into another man, and so disfigured by emaciation that he looked like one of those parings of fortune who whine for alms at street corners. I was still in doubt as I approached him, although he had once been a bosom friend and daily companion.

'My Socrates,' I cried, 'what does this mean? this change! What is your sin? Lord, how you've been lamented at home. You're counted as dead. The provincial magistrate has appointed guardians for your children; and now that your wife has completed her mourning-period – wasted away she was by grievous and continual sorrow, and her eyes all but wept into utter blindness – she is being solicited by her parents to brighten up the benighted house with the pleasures of a new marriage. And here you rise up like a ghastly ghost to the unseemly confusion of our plans.'

[1] 'Hypata': A well-known Thessalian city on the banks of the Spercheius.
[1] 'Worst foot': To start with the left foot represented bad luck.

'Aristomenes,' he answered, 'now I see indeed that you are unaware of the sliddery twists, the freakish whirligigs, the ceaseless vicissitudes of Fortune.'

And with that he hid his face, which was blushing for shame, in his darned patch-work cloak, leaving his body naked from the navel downwards. I couldn't bear to see this spectacle of calamitous misery another moment – I caught hold of him and tried to lift him from the ground. But, with his face still hidden, he wailed, 'Leave me alone, leave me alone. Let Fortune still gloat over the trophy she has erected.'

However, I compelled him to follow me. I pulled off one of my two garments and clothed – or rather covered him – and haled him at once to a bath. There I took on myself the jobs of anointing and scrubbing him. Diligently I peeled off the scurf of dirt; and then, having tended him properly, tottering with my own weariness, I supported his debilitated steps till we reached my inn. I laid him to rest on a bed, I filled him with food, I slaked him with wine, and I soothed him with the news. At last our conversation began to flow freely, and we bandied jests and witticisms. Our banter was going fast and furious, when he fetched a tormented sigh from the depths of his breast and beat his forehead with demented fist.

'Wretch that I am,' he cried, 'I rushed eagerly to see some widely canvassed Gladiatorial Games, and I fell into this Misfortune. For as you know very well, I had gone on a business-trip to Macedonia, and I was on my way back, flush with cash, after having been detained there some ten months. Well, just before I came to Larissa, while making a detour to bring these games into my itinerary, I was suddenly beset by a ravening horde of robbers in a wild and broken valley. I escaped with my life, but lost everything else. Left in this sad fix, I had recourse to one Meroe, who kept a tavern – an old woman, but not without a charming touch. I told her the whole tale of my lengthy journey, of my harassed home-coming, and of my recent unfortunate robbery. She treated me very consolingly, provided a fine supper gratis – and then, pricked by carnal heat, laid me in her own bed. And I, unhappy man, lay there acquiescent, and after that one intercourse with her I succumbed to the pestilential drag of a hag. I gave her even such

36

clothes as the robbers had been kind enough to leave me
to hide my nakedness, and what small earnings I was able
to make, while still sound, by carrying bags – till at last
this good woman and bad luck harried me into that
decrepitude and rags in which you have just now found
me.'

'In good faith,' I answered, 'you deserve the worst you
can get, if there is anything worse than this, for preferring
the festivals of the flesh and the wrinkles of a whore to your
fame and your family.'

'Hush, hush,' he exclaimed, placing his forefinger on his
lips and sitting stupefied. Then he looked about for any
eavesdroppers. 'Beware how you get up against so inspired
a woman, or you'll be hurt yourself with your rash tongue.'

'What's this?' I asked. 'What kind of a woman is this
redoubtable Queen of a tavernkeeper?'

'She is a witch,' he said. 'She is superhuman, able to drag
down the heavens or to lift up the earth, to harden running
water or to dissolve mountains, to raise the dead or to
tumble down the gods, to poke out the stars or to light up
the darkness of hell.'

'Now, now,' said I, 'please draw the tragic curtain, and
dispense with the drop-scene, and speak plainly.'

'Would you like,' he asked, 'to hear one or two, yes, or a
long list of her practices? As for drawing not only the whole
countryside flockmell sniffing after her, but also the Indians
and Ethiopians and even the Antipodeans, such tricks are
but the merest sprigs and flim-flams of her art. For listen,
and I'll tell you what many witnesses can deliver.

'A lover of hers who had rashly ravished another woman,
she changed with a single word into a beaver – because
when that beast fears captivity, he frees himself from his
pursuers by self-castration, and she wished that penalty to
slash the man for his enjoyment of another than herself.

'In the same way she bewitched a neighbouring inn-
keeper, who was her rival in trade, into a frog; and now the
poor old man swims about in one of his own winecasks, or
ensconced in the dregs he calls out at his previous customers
with a hoarse croak, quite in the way of business.

'Another man, a lawyer of the Forum, who had pleaded
in a case against her, she turned into a horned ram; and
you can still see him as a ram butting and rebutting.

37

'Again, she laid a spell on the wife of one of her lovers, because the woman had propagated some scandal about her. This woman was baggaged with a child, and the witch barricaded her womb and doomed her to a perpetual pregnancy. By the general calculation, it's now eight years since the poor woman began to swell with the load, as if she were bringing an elephant[1] to birth.

'After this outrage and many others, public indignation was noisily excited, and the townsfolk resolved next day to execute condign judgement upon her by stoning her to death. But by the power of her enchantments she foiled this decision. For as Medea, after being granted one day's truce by Creon before her departure, burned in the garlanding flames his whole house, his daughter, and the old man himself, so here by conjurations and by raising of the dead in a ditch – she told me the full story a few days back in a burst of drunken talk – this witch used the noiseless bulk of her demons to block everybody up in their own houses. And for two days the inhabitants could not break through the barriers, or open the doors, or even make holes in the walls. So at last, after exhorting each other, the citizens with one voice besought her mercy and swore by all the most sacred oaths that they would never molest her with so much as a little-finger, and that if anyone should conceive such an assault they would all rally to her aid.

'So they propitiated her, and she unloosed the whole city. But about midnight she swung aloft the chief instigator of the plot, and all his house – I mean the very ground and all the foundations – and carried it, with all its doors shut, a hundred miles away to another town situated on the top of a rocky mountain and consequently lacking all water-supplies. And the buildings there were all packed so tightly together that there was no room left for the new house; so she dropped it down in front of the city gate and departed.'

'A strange story,' I replied, 'and a cruel one, dear Socrates, is this you tell me. In fact, you have stricken me with no small anxiety. I might even call it panic – and not a mere thorn-scratch but a bad spear-jab – that this old woman might use the deputed ears of some demon to learn our conversation. So let us lie down to sleep, early as it is, and

[1] 'Elephant': Pliny says that the elephant goes ten years with young.

after a night's rest has cleared away the worst of our weariness, let us get out before dawn as far as we can.'

In the midst of my advice the worthy Socrates fell fast asleep, and snored aloud, succumbing to the unusually plenteous wine and the day's exertions. I closed the door of the room, and drove home the bolts; I pushed my bed hard against the hinges, and heaped it up; and then I lay down to rest. At first the fear that kept buzzing in my mind gripped me awake; but as midnight came on, I dozed fitfully.

At last I was dropping into heavy slumber, when suddenly the door crashed open with greater violence than any robbers' shoulders could have produced. The hinges snapped with a crack and were torn out, and the door was flung flat. The bedstead, which was rather narrow, lame of one foot and rotten, was knocked upside-down by the furious impact. I went topsy-turvy, hurled upon the floor; and the bed, rolling over, neatly covered and muffled me in the wreckage.

At that moment I experienced the truth that, under great strain, Nature expresses herself by contradictions. Just as tears are oft shed for joy, so in this extremity of terror I could not restrain a peal of laughter at finding myself, Aristomenes, become a tortoise. And while I lay where I had been pitched, I peeped out under the rim of the enveloping bed to see what was the matter.

I saw two women of advanced age – one bearing a flashing lantern, the other a sponge and naked sword. Thus charactered, they took their stand about Socrates, who had slept peaceably through the whole commotion. The woman with the sword spoke first.

'Look at him, sister Panthia. Look at my beloved Endymion, my sweet Catamite,[1] who day and night has abused my youthful body. Look at him who sets my love beneath him, who not only defames me scandalously but also prepares for wriggling out of my clutch. And I shall be deserted by this Ulysses in his craftiness. I shall be a Calypso wailing in eternal desolation.'

Then she lifted her right hand and pointed me out to her friend Panthia. 'And look at that fine fellow, his counsellor Aristomenes, who suggested this defalcation and who

[1] 'Catamite': Ganymede.

39

now quakes himself to death, flung prostrate beneath his bedstead. He is spying on all our movements and thinks to get off with his insults unrevenged. But I will make him repent someday, soon – in fact, at once – for his late reckless speeches and his present peeping-eye.'

When I heard this, cornered as I was, a cold sweat broke out all over me, and my bowels quavered and opened, till the very bed shook and rattled above my palpitating spine.

'But why not rip him,' remarked Panthia, 'to shreds as the bacchanals do, or let us set up the mark of his manhood and knock it off?'

But Meroe[1] (for this was clearly the heroine of Socrates' story) answered, 'No, he must survive to dump the corpse of this wretch under a sprinkle of earth.'

Then she laid Socrates' head over on one side, and drove the sword into the left part of his throat up to the hilt, and caught the spout of blood in a leathern bottle which she held ready, so carefully that not a single drop was left visible. And more, I saw Meroe – to omit no correct detail of the sacrificial rite, I suppose – thrust her hand down through the wound into the very entrails, and, after groping about, finally wrench out the heart of my unhappy comrade. And he, with his gullet slit by the impact of the blade, uttered a cry through the wound (or rather a broken gurgle), and bubbled out his ghost.

Then Panthia stopped the big wound in his throat with a sponge, and cried, 'Beware O sponge born of the salt-sea, beware that you pass not through a running stream.'

After this declaration they raised up the bed and straddled above my body, emptying their bladders till I was drenched to the skin with filth.

That done, they flittered across the threshold. The door swung up, and leaped into its former position. The hinges settled back into their sockets. The posts hopped back to the bars. The bolts shot back into the stanchions. But I still lay flat upon the floor, nerveless, naked, chilled, and wringing-wet with urine, like a child just discharged from the mother's womb – gasping indeed as if in death-throes, yet (as it were) surviving and soliloquizing posthumously –

[1] 'Meroe': There is a pun on *merum* 'pure' — the adjective used with *vinum* for 'unmixed wine'.

or at the very least like a candidate for crucifixion[1] (to which fate I seemed devoted).

'What will become of me,' I meditated, 'when a man is found here tomorrow with his throat cut? Who will think my story truthful if I speak truly? They will reply "Even if you, stout fellow that you are, were unable to resist the woman, you should have at least shouted for succour. A man's throat is cut before your eyes, and you don't raise a murmur. And how is it that she didn't annihilate you as well? How did these atrocious butchers spare you, a witness of the murder, to give evidence against them? Ho, you escaped death in the night, but you will find it again in the morning." '

I revolved these cross-questions unceasingly, till night began to merge into day. Then I considered that the best course would be to leave stealthily before daybreak and to push ahead on my journey, shaken as I was. So I took up my bundle, unlocked and unbolted the door – only to find that this staunch and upright door, which had collapsed of its own accord during the night, creaked and stuck fast, however often I inserted and turned the key.

At last I called out, 'Hey there, ostler, where are you? Open the pub-door. I want to leave before daybreak.'

The ostler, who was sleeping behind the front door of the inn, replied still half-asleep, 'What's that? Don't you know the roads are thick with robbers? Why do you want to leave at this time of night? And if you're tired of life because you're plagued with a bad conscience, I'm not so pumpkin-headed as to want to die for you.'

'It's almost day,' I called, 'and anyhow what could they take from a poverty-stricken traveller? Don't you know, you bumpkin, that ten prize-fighters can't strip a naked man?'

But the sleepyheaded ostler muttered in a drowsy drawl as he turned over on his other side, 'How do I know you haven't strangled the other chap you brought in last night, and now you want to skedaddle?'

---

[1] 'Crucifixion': The cross was the penalty for slaves and foreigners. I have tried to retain some of the metaphorical uses of the cross in the common Latin phrases for anxiety. For us, a strange religiously-haloed term, it was close to the everyday experience of the ancient citizen.

I remember that, when he said that, I felt the earth yawning under my feet and I saw the depths of hell and the jaws of Cerberus gaping to swallow me; and it came into my mind that Meroe had not spared my gullet through pity, but through a malicious intention to preserve me for the cross. So I turned back into the chamber and cast about for some rapid means of suicide. But as Fortune had furnished me with no death-dealing weapons, except the bedstead, I cried, 'Bed, Bed, beloved of my soul, that have felt with me the strain of this terrible night, you know and can judge of all that has transpired. You alone can I cite in the court as witness of my innocence – then furnish me with a serviceable weapon, for I am hungry for the shades of death.'

With his I began to undo the rope that corded the bed, and to throw and fasten one end of it over a rafter jutting out above the window. I made a strong slip-knot at the other end, and climbed upon the bed. Having elevated myself thus as first step towards the fatal way out, I thrust my head into the noose. Then I gave a kick at the sustaining platform, meaning that the rope, tightening as my weight jerked at it, should put an end to the offices of breath. But the rope was old and worm-eaten, and it broke. I tumbled down heavily upon Socrates who lay stretched beneath, and sprawled with him on the ground.

At that very moment the ostler burst into the room, vociferating, 'Where are you? You that was raving with hurry in the middle of the night -- you, snoring now in that heap of bedclothes!'

And now Socrates, awoken either by the collision or by the ostler's raucous hail, extricated himself first, and answered, 'I can see there's good cause for the bad name that travellers give ostlers. Here this poke-nose thumps in – I wouldn't be surprised if he hoped to steal something – and he bellows until he scares me out of a sound sleep, tired as I was.'

At this welcome sound I jumped smartly, in a sweat of incredulous joy. 'Trustiest of ostlers!' I cried, 'here is my friend – my father, my brother – that you lyingly said I'd murdered last night in your drunkenness.' And I embraced Socrates with a warmth of kisses.

But he, overcome by the stench with which the loathly

vampires had wetted me, shoved me away indignantly. 'Avaunt,' he said, 'with your smell like the dregs of a sewer.' And then he made some friendly inquiries as to how I had become afflicted with this aroma.

I invented some silly joke on the spur of the moment to cover my confusion, then diverted our conversation into another channel. Taking him by the hand, I said, 'Why don't we go? Let us enjoy the freshness of the morning-road.'

So I lifted my bundle, and settled with the proprietor for the night's lodgings; and then the pair of us set off.

We had not proceeded far before all objects were reflecting the full brilliancy of the risen sun, and I kept inspecting my comrade's gullet with unabated curiosity, looking for the spot where I had seen the sword glide in, and saying to myself, 'Lunatic, buried in your winecups, you have dreamed the maddest things. Here is Socrates safe and sound, without a scratch showing. Where is the wound? Where is the sponge? Where is the scar of the wound, so recent and so deep?'

At length I addressed him, 'Without a doubt experienced physicians aver the truth when they say that those who cram themselves with food and spirituous liquor evoke horrible ominous dreams. Take myself, for instance, I overdid things in my evening-cups, and I passed a dreadful night full of such cruel visions that I still feel polluted and wet with human blood.'

Socrates laughed at this. 'No,' he replied, 'It's not blood that wets you, but chamberlye. Yet seriously, I dreamed myself last night that my throat was cut. I felt a pain in my neck, and I thought that my heart was plucked out. Why, even now my knees are shaky; and I feel giddy as I walk, and weak from the need of some reviving food.'

'Your breakfast is all ready,' I said, and divesting myself of the scrip that hung about my shoulder I handed him some bread and cheese. 'Let us take a seat,' I continued, 'near that plane-tree.'

We seated ourselves, and both started on a snack. Socrates was gobbling greedily; but as I looked at him more attentively, I saw that he was turning faint, and as pale as boxwood. Indeed the hues of life were in such pell-mell flight that my terrified imagination conjured up those Furies of

43

the night; and the first morsel of bread, tiny as it was, that I put into my mouth, lodged in the middle of my throat, and I could neither gulp it down nor urge it up. Moreover, the number of the passers-by intensified my fear for when one of two companions dies suddenly, who believes that the other is not somehow responsible?

But when Socrates had gnawed sufficiently at the bread, he grew impatiently thirsty. For he had hastily swallowed a fair portion of a very good cheese; and not far from the roots of the plane-tree a smooth stream wound sluggishly along, rather like a placid lake, lustrously rivalling silver or glass.

'Come here,' I cried. 'Drink your fill of this spring-water like milk.'

He rose and searched about awhile till he found a flat space on the river bank. Then sinking on his knees he inclined himself down to take a draught. But he had no sooner touched the dewy sparkle of the water with the tips of his lips, when the wound in his throat gaped open wide, and the sponge suddenly sprang out, a little gush of blood accompanying it. And his body, now void of life, would have collapsed into the stream had I not gripped him by the leg and dragged him with difficulty higher up the bank. There I lamented over my hapless comrade as well as time would allow, and then buried him in the sandy soil that bordered the river, to lie there for ever.

That done, trembling, terrified, I rode through many strange and desert places, as if driven by the guilt of murder. I abandoned my country and my home. I exiled myself and came to Aetolia, where I have married again.

.   .   .   .   .

Here ended the tale of Aristomenes; and his fellow-traveller who from the beginning had with stubborn incredulity rejected the story, commented, 'Never have I heard an account less accountable, or lies more far-fetched.'

Then he turned and appealed to me, 'You, sir – your bearing and the clothes you're wearing show you to be a cut above the ordinary – do you credit this account?'

'Certainly,' I answered, 'I consider nothing impossible. As

the Fates have predestined, so unwinds all human action. For you and I and every other man alive have had experiences so curious as to be outside reality, and which when described carry no conviction to those who have not shared them. But, by Hercules, I truly believe what I have heard, and I offer the story-teller my greatest gratitude for having entertained us so pleasantly. For myself, I have concluded a rough and interminable journey without effort or tedium. Indeed, I am sure that my nag must be as delighted as I am with this good turn; for I have been borne without fatiguing him right up to the city gate – not so much by virtue of his back as by that of my ears.'

This was the end both of our conversation and of our companionship; for my two fellow-travellers turned off to a nearby village on the left, while I rode on and stopped at the first inn I sighted. There I accosted the old woman who conducted the house.

'Is this the city of Hypata?' I asked.

'Yes,' she nodded.

'Do you know Milo, one of the first men of the city?'

She laughed. 'There's good cause for calling him one of the first men in the city, for you come upon his house in the Pomerium,[1] even before you enter the city's bounds.'

'All jokes apart,' I answered, 'my good mother, tell me what kind of man he is, and which is his house.'

'Look over there,' she said, 'at those last windows that face on this side towards the city, and that door on the other side opening upon a blind-alley in front. There lodges Milo, a man with heaps of money and other good things besides. But he's got a bad name for miserliness and dirty griping ways. For he spends all his time in usury and in making advances on pledges of gold and silver. And there, shut up in that poky house, poring over his hoard, he lives with a wife that shares his miserable lot. He won't have another servant than a single wench, and he stalks about as ragged as a common beggar.'

When I heard this, I smiled to myself. 'Very particular consideration for my comfort,' I mused, 'my friend Demeas

[1] 'Pomerium': The space adjoining the city walls, within which the city's auspices were taken. Milo is a first citizen because his house is met with first.

45

had when he recommended me a stranger to the care of such a man. While I am under his roof, I need not fear to be stifled with smoke and kitchen-steam.'

But I rode on a little way, and reached the door, which was strongly barred; and there I knocked and halloaed. At last a girl appeared.

'Hey,' she exclaimed, 'why have you been drubbing our door in such a frenzy? What's the pledge you want to borrow on? Are you the only person who doesn't know that we accept no security but gold and silver?'

'Have a better guess,' I replied, 'and tell me whether I have caught your master at home.'

'You have,' she said. 'But why do you ask?'

'I bring a letter of introduction,' I told her, 'from Demeas of Corinth.'

'Twiddle your thumbs here a moment,' she said, 'till I tell him so.' And barricading the door again, she retired.

After a while she came back and re-opening the door let me in. 'He'll see you,' she said.

I entered and found him lying down on a very scanty couch, on the point of starting to sup. His wife was seated at his feet, but there was next to nothing on the table. He indicated the meagrely set boards.

'Your entertainment,' he said.

'Excellent,' I answered, and straightaway delivered Demeas' letter.

He skipped through it, then remarked, 'I thank my friend Demeas for introducing into my house so worthy a guest.' Then he bade his wife vacate her place, and begged me to sit down instead; and while I was making some courteous excuses, he seized me by my garment and pulled me towards the seat.

'Sit down there,' he insisted. 'From precaution against thieves we haven't been able to provide the stools and other bits of furniture that would come in handy.'

I obeyed, and he continued, 'By your handsome appearance and your coy way of self-deprecation, I am safe in conjecturing that you are a gentleman born. Moreover, my friend Demeas declares that that's what you are, in his letter. Consequently I ask you not to think slightingly of the straitened circumstances of our poor cottage – for, sir, look you, you shall have the small bedroom opening out of

46

here, and a choice little snuggery it is. Make yourself freely at home with us. You will magnify our poor house by such a mark of esteem; and you will appropriate a deal of flattering reports by showing yourself as nobly contented with a humble hearth as your good father's namesake Theseus was when he didn't turn up his nose at the hospitality of the aged Hecale.'[1]

Then he called to the servant girl, 'Fotis, take our guest's baggage and see it safely stowed in the spare bedroom, and hurry back with some oil from the store-cupboard to anoint him – and a towel as well, to dry him – and any other necessary thingumbobs. And then show him the way to the nearest Baths, for he must be worn-out after his long and racking journey.'

Listening to these orders, I computed the character and meanness of Milo; and wishing to earn even more of his favour, I answered, 'Sir, these attentions are unnecessary. When travelling, I carry such articles along with me; and I can easily inquire in the street for the Baths. But my chief anxiety is for my horse who has had a strenuous job with me on his back; and so, Fotis, take these odd coins and buy hay and oats for him.'

When this was settled and my luggage deposited in my room, I strolled out to find the Baths. But first I went to the Provision Markets, meaning to provide something eatable for supper. There I saw some gorgeous fish for sale; and investigating the price, I was told one hundred pieces. But after some haggling I brought the dealer down to twenty coppers. As I was leaving the market, Pythias, a fellow student of mine at the Attic Athens, followed me out; and after reconnoitring me affectionately for some time, he rushed up embraced me, and saluted me with comradely kisses

'Dear Lucius,' he cried, 'by the Twins! What an age since we looked into each other's eyes. Hercules! not since we said good-bye to our professor Vestius. Now what is the reason for your journey?'

'Tomorrow you shall hear,' I replied. 'But what do I see? My congratulations. For I perceive attendants, and rods of office, and a dress that utters the magistrate.'

[1] 'Hecale': A poor old woman who gave Theseus refuge during his wanderings. There was a festival in her honour.

'I am aedile,' said Pythias, 'and market-inspector; and if you wish to do some catering, I am at your convenience.'

I declined with thanks, as I had already bought sufficient fish for supper. But Pythias, seeing my basket, took it from me and shook up the fish to inspect them more thoroughly.

'And what,' he asked, 'was the charge for these sprats?'

'After a squabble,' I said, 'I got them from the man for twenty coppers.'

On hearing this, he caught my hand, and, earnest to see me righted, led me back into the Forum.

'From which of these salesmen,' he asked, 'did you obtain that trash?'

I pointed him out a little old man who was squatting in a corner; and Pythias, assuming all the terrors of aedileship, rebuked him in a severe voice.

'Here now, here now,' he said, 'have you no mercy on our friends – not to mention strangers – that you ticket your paltry fish with such exorbitant prices, and reduce this town, the Flower of the Province of Thessaly, to the level of a Desert and a Mere Crag by the premium you put on victuals? But not unscathed! I'll teach you how rogues are kept in their places while I'm the Magistrate.'

Then he emptied the fish out of my basket, and ordered one of the minor officials to jump on them and to trample them to smithereens. After which, this friend of mine, Pythias, smiling complacently at the rigour with which he fulfilled his duties, motioned me to depart.

'I am satisfied, Lucius,' he said. 'That is enough reproof for the old scoundrel.'

Speechless and flabbergasted, I wandered off to the Baths, bereft of both food and money through this high-handed procedure of my judicious fellow student. I bathed and refreshed myself, and then returned to Milo's house, and went into my bedroom.

But Fotis the servant girl looked in. 'Supper time, master says,' she announced. Already, however, conversant with Milo's parsimony, I sent my best excuses, protesting that I wished to repair my tired body with sleep more than with food. When she had conveyed this apology, he came in person, and taking my hand mildly attempted to draw me from the room. I hung back and made some polite denials.

'I refuse to go,' he said, 'unless you come with me.' And

48

reinforcing his words with an oath, he drew me, reluctant but no longer able to resist his persistence, to his meagre couch.

I seated myself. 'How is our friend Demeas prospering?' he at once asked me. 'How is his wife? And his children? And the rest of the household?' I answered each inquiry. He then pried minutely into the reasons for my journey. I informed him in full. He then interrogated me inquisitively about my district and the principal inhabitants, and went on to ask after the prefect. But he was forced to perceive that, fatigued by my heavy travelling and dazed with the effort of speaking, I kept drowsing and halting in the middle of a sentence, and stammering and floundering in a jog-trot of incoherent phrases. So he finally allowed me to withdraw to my bedroom.

Thus I escaped at last from the garrulous and starveling entertainment of the nasty old man, weighted with sleep and not by good cheer, having dined on nothing but words. I re-entered my chamber and there gave myself up to the repose that I so much wanted.

BOOK THE SECOND

As soon as the darkness was dispersed by the beams of the
newborn Sun, I threw off sleep and my bedclothes, and
leaped from bed. I am normally eager and only too inclined
to ferret out the Rare and the Marvellous and now,
reflecting that I was located in the very heart of Thessaly,
which is universally acclaimed as the aboriginal crucible
of the Art of Magic – that I stood in the very city which
had set the scene for the story of my worthy fellow-traveller
Aristomenes – I was so agog with desire and zeal and I
savoured every detail with gleeful curiosity.

In fact, there was nothing that I saw as I walked about
the city which I did not believe to be something other than
it was. Everything seemed to me to have been just struck
by some fatal incantation into a quite contrary image. I
thought that the stones on which I trod were petrified men,
that the birds twittering in my ears were enchanted men
with plumes, that the trees surrounding the Pomerium were
men magically spirting into leaves, and that the waters of
the fountains were flowing human bodies. I thought that
the statues would step down and walk, that the pictures
would move, that the walls would speak, that the oxen and
other cattle would tell me strange news, and that the
heavens and the sun's orb of glory would make a sudden
annunciation.

Thus bewildered (or rather stunned) with the cruel
intensity of my search, though I found not the slightest
vestige or footprint of what my curiosity sought, I strayed
round and round the city. At length, while promenading
from door to door like some well-to-do idler, I found myself
unexpectedly turning into the market-place; and there my
eyes alighted on a woman who was making her way across
the square, accompanied by a large train of domestics.
Quickening my steps, I caught up with her and noted that
the jewels set in gold, and the broidered gown embossed

and crossed with gold, proclaimed her at a glance as a lady of position.

Trotting close at her side was an old man bowed under his years, who exclaimed as soon as he looked at me. 'Hercules! Here's Lucius.' And in the same breath he embraced me. Then turning to the lady he whispered into her ear some hoarse remark I could not catch.

'Won't you approach,' he continued, addressing me, 'and welcome your loving aunt?'

'How can I?' I answered. 'I do not know the lady.' And I stood, blushing hotly with averted eyes, while she regarded me closely.

'Just like his noble mother Salvia,' she murmured. 'He has the same air of birth and breeding, and all his physical attributes are inexpressibly like hers. He and she are as like as two peas – his stature tall but graceful; his form slender but plump; his skin rosy but delicate; his hair gold but uncrimped by fopperies; his eyes grey but keen and kindling as an eagle's; his face, altogether a natural bloom, his bearing comely and unaffected.'

Then she added, 'O Lucius, I have nursed you in these very arms. Of course I have. For I was not only kindred to your mother: I shared a nipple with her. We are both descendants of the house of Plutarchus, and we sucked the same nurse, one to each pap, and we grew side by side in the ties of sisterhood. There is no difference between us but our stations in life. She married splendidly: I married like anybody else.

'I am that Byrrhaena whose name you have perhaps heard repeated as belonging to one of your nurses. Then come and entrust yourself to my roof – or rather, call it your own, and use it accordingly.'

Her speech afforded me an interval for the dispersal of my blushes. 'Heaven forbid, cousin,' I answered, 'that I should desert my host Milo unless he gave me cause. But I shall take advantage of your offer as much as I can without breach of my position as his guest. As often as I find occasion to pass your way, I shall not fail to call upon you.'

We had gone on walking as we talked, and it needed but a few steps to bring us to Byrrhaena's house. The hall was particularly handsome. There were columns erected at each of the four corners, with statues (representations of the

Palm-bearing Goddess) set on the tops. The wings were outspread, but did not stir; and the dewy feet skimmed the tremulous rim of a rolling sphere, on which they seemed to float rather than rest.

There too stood Diana, carved in Parian marble, on a level space in the middle of the hall. A gloriously executed figure, with garments windblown, poised swinging forward full in face of those who entered. She awed you by the majesty of her divine nature.

Dogs guarded each side of the goddess, and these dogs were also of stone. Their eyes glared fiercely, their ears were erect, their nostrils snorted wide, their jaws slavered, and if some barking outside had assailed the neighbourhood you would have sworn that it came from these throats of stone. Here too the distinguished sculptor had exemplified consummately the craft with which he used his chisel; for he had carved the dogs in mid-chase, their hind feet thrusting at the ground, their forefeet lifted as high as their chests.

At the back of the goddess there rose a stone shaped into a grotto profusely clustered with moss, grass, leaves, and twigs, and entangled with vine tendrils and bosky-shrubs; and the reflection of the statue glistened back from the smoothed marble within the grotto. Over the edge of the rock depended apples and grapes polished with great virtuosity. Art (life's flattering rival) had deployed these with such cunning effect that you would have thought 'I have but to wait till mellowing autumn has breathed upon them the hues of ripeness, and I shall then be able to pluck and eat.' And if you bent forward and looked at the stream which sprang out in crinkling waves from under the feet of the goddess, you would have thought the waves were as vividly endowed with the essences of movement as the swelling grape clusters.

Finally, in the midst of the branches of stone Actaeon was staring hungrily at the goddess, the horns up-curling from his brow; and both in the marble and in its reflections in the stream he was to be seen ambushed, waiting for Diana to strip for her bath.

While I was exploring these objects with fascinated pleasure, Byrrhaena said to me, 'Everything you see here is yours.' Then she privately entreated all the others to leave us alone. When they had disappeared, she went on,

'My dearest Lucius, by the goddess beside us, I fear deeply for your safety, and I wish to put you on your guard as if you were my child of my own womb. Beware, I tell you. Beware with might and main of the wicked arts and vicious seductions of this Pamphile who is married to the Milo whose guest you say you are. She is a witch of the first rank, and is accounted Mistress of every Necromantic Chant. By merely breathing on twigs and pebbles and suchlike ineffectual things she knows how to drown the whole light of the starry universe in the depths of hell, back in its ancient chaos. For as soon as she sees an attractive youth, she is on tenterhooks of admiration, and she rivets her eyes and her lustful mind upon him. She sows her blandishment, she invades his spirit, she snares him in unbreakable bonds of bottomless love.

'And those who do not comply at once she loathes, and in a flash she whisks them into stones or cattle or any animal she chooses – or else she simply wipes them out. That is why I am alarmed for you, and consider that you ought to beware. For she inflames a man beyond redemption; and you, young and handsome as you are, are an apt victim.'

Thus Byrrhaena warned me, apprehensively enough, but she merely excited my interest. For as soon as I heard her mention the Art of Magic, than which nothing was nearer to my heart's desire, I was so far from shuddering at Pamphile that a strong compulsion made me yearn to attain the described mastery, though I should have to pay heavy fees for it, though I should fling myself with a running jump into the very Abyss.

Trembling with distracted haste, I extricated myself from Byrrhaena's grasp as if from shackles, blushed, and bidding her farewell dashed excitedly off to the house of my host Milo. And while I scurried along like a madman, I was saying to myself, 'Come now, Lucius, keep your wits about you, and look alive-O. Here is the desired chance. Put out your hand and take the thing you've prayed for so long. Satiate your heart with Marvels. Discard all puerile fears. Grapple as if you meant business. But renounce all amorous connexion wheresoever with your hostess, and respect the nuptial sofa of the upright Milo. On the other hand sue and woo the servant girl Fotis strenuously. For she is charmingly shaped, sportive in her ways, and decidedly talkative.

53

Last evening when you retired to rest, she conducted you obligingly into the bedroom, and laid you soothingly in bed, and rather lovingly drew up the bedclothes. And then her reluctant face showed how little she liked leaving only that one goodnight kiss upon your brow. And on the doorstep she turned her head, and smiled again, and could not go. Good luck and speed to your need, my lad; and come what may, a breach must be made through Fotis.'

Debating these matters, I reached Milo's front door and entered, with the question answered (as the saying goes) overwhelmingly in the affirmative. I did not, however, find Milo or his wife at home. My darling Fotis was alone in charge. She was preparing the stuffing for some black pudding, and was mincing the pigs' tripes, some of which stood finely shredded on the sideboard, ready for mixing with a gravy that tickled my nostrils with its succulently wafted steam.

She was neatly clad in a linen apron, with a shining scarlet stomacher which gathered her dress up high under her meeting breasts; and she was stirring the stock-pot with her rosy little hands moving round and round above it. As she stirred and turned the meat, she herself stirred and vibrated congruously all over her supple body. Her loins softly undulated, and her agile spine swayed and rippled in time, as she placidly stirred the pot.

I was entranced by the sight, and stood in mute admiration – as did that part of me which so far had not intruded. At last I addressed the girl, 'How finely, my dear Fotis, how gaily you stir your buttocks as you stand over the pot. What a honeyed relish I see you getting ready. A happy man, a blessed man, is he that you will let dip finger there.'

'Be off, you poor fellow,' answered the young chatterbox, never at a loss for a repartee. 'Be off from my fireplace. Keep your distance. For if the tiniest spark of that heat grazes you, you'll be scorched to the gizzard, and no one will be able to quench you but myself. For I'm very good at putting choice spice into pot or bed, and making them both equally stirring.'

Chattering thus, she glanced at me and smiled; and I did not leave the room until I had diligently scrutinized every angle of her charm. But why divagate into detail? It has always been the prime concern of my life to observe in public the heads and tresses of beautiful women, and then to conjure up the image at home for leisurely enjoyment. This procedure is based on a clear and rationally determined proposition. Firstly, that Hair is the most important (visible) portion of the body, and that from its prominent position it provokes attention first. Secondly, that Hair by its natural hues provides that comeliness for the head which the gay tints of flowering dresses provide for the other limbs.

Moreover, most women, to commend their natural charms and graces, discard all mufflers, throw open their cloaks, and proudly delight in exhibiting their naked breasts, knowing that there is more delectation in the rosy gloss of the skin than in the golden sheen of a dress.

On the contrary (though even the supposition is irreligious, and I pray that there may never be an instance of so horrible a monstrosity) if you despoil the most surprisingly beautiful woman of her Hair, and denude her face of its natural accommodation – though she were dropped down from heaven, conceived of the sea foam, cradled among the waves – though she (I say) were Venus herself, though she were ringed-round by the three Graces, and environed with the whole mob of Cupids, and laced with her love-girdle, fragrant as cinnamon, and dewy with balsamum – yet if she came out bald, she would not be able to seduce even her own husband.

What satisfying hues and tangled lustres burn in woman's Hair. Sometimes it briskly repels the flash of the sun; sometimes it is absorbed into a softer penumbra, or glistens with varying toilettes of light. Now it coruscates with gold; now it deepens into honey-coloured shadows; now it is raven black; now it reflects the blue flower-tints of a dove's throat. And then when it has been anointed with Arabian nard, or parted by the fine teeth of the artful comb, or looped up at the nape of the neck, the lover looks upon it and sees there his own face, as in a mirror, enhanced by delight. O what beauty in Hair, whether in braided luxuriance it is twisted together and built up upon the head, or whether it is allowed to tumble in prolix curls down the back. Such, I conclude, is the dignity of Hair that no woman whosoever, though dressed-up with gold, tissues, gems, and all other cosmetical apparatus, could be described, unless she had duly arranged her hair, as dressed at all.

But as far as my Fotis was concerned, it was not toilet-care but ringleted freedom that crowned her charms. Her plentiful hair, thrown loosely back and hanging down to her nape, was scattered over her shoulders and rested softly upon the swelling fringe of her dress, till at last it was gently collected and fastened up by a knot on the top of her head.

I could no longer bear the excruciation of such exquisite pleasure, and bending forwards I impressed a most delicious kiss on the spot where the hair was heaped on the crown of her head. She twisted away, and looked at me over her shoulder with sidelong and marrow-sucking glances.

'Hey now, my scholar,' she said, 'sweet and bitter is the sauce you lick. Take care that the sweetness of an overdose of honey doesn't choke you bitterly with bile for many a fine day.'

'How is that, my Merriment?' I asked, 'for I am ready to be laid flat for basting above that fire as long as I am recruited every while by a tiny kiss.' And, as good as my word, I embraced her more straitly and began kissing her.

With that her own desires kindled, and a mutually waxing ardour twined our bodies akin in love. Cinnamon was the exhalation of her opening mouth; and she succumbed to my kiss, while her quickening tongue ravished me nectarously.

'I am going,' I said. 'No, I'm a gone man already, unless you take pity on me.'

Repeating the exploit of her kiss, she answered, 'Raise up your spirits, man. I am fettered to you by the same leg-cuff of desire, and our pleasures won't be delayed very much longer. At the first flicker of torchtime I shall be in your bedroom. So be off, and gird yourself ready, for I mean to have a nightlong bone to pick with you, and there'll be no flinching on my side.' And after some further (similarly pointed) remarks we separated.

About the hour of noon Byrrhaena sent me some guest-gifts[1]—a fattened pig, five hens, and a winecask of choice vintage. I at once called Fotis.

[1] 'Guest-gifts': *Xeniola*: Tokens of hospitality sent to strangers in their lodgings.

'Look here,' I said. 'Bacchus, the abettor and squire of Venus, has arrived of his own accord. Let us quaff all this wine today, so that we may lull the cowardice of shame in ourselves, and prick awake the lively courage of desire. For the voyage of Venus needs no other cargo than this – plenty of oil for the lamps through all the wakeful night, and plenty of wine for the cups.'

I spent the rest of the day in the bathing-tubs, and then at supper. For I had been invited to share the neat tabloid meal of the worthy Milo. Mindful of Byrrhaena's counsel, I took my seat as safely sheltered from the gaze of his wife as possible, and turned my apprehensive eyes seldom towards her face – and then only as if towards the gulf of Avernus. But I kept looking round the room after the assiduously ministering Fotis, and by that means lifted up my heart.

Evening was already on us; and Pamphile, peering into a lamp, asserted, 'It will rain heavily tomorrow.' Her husband asked her how she could foretell the weather, and she replied that the lamp had thus prophesied.

When Milo heard this, he laughed and said, 'So we are feeding a mighty Sibyl in this lamp which looks out from its socket as from a watch-tower on all the business of the Heavens and the Sun himself.'

I interrupted here. 'This is my first experience of this type of divination – though it is not so very mysterious that this Flamelet, trivial as it is, and produced by human agency, should yet possess an awareness of that greater and celestial Flame as of its Sire, and that it should know and announce to us by divine intuition what the latter will be doing up on the crest of the sky.

'Among us at Corith there is a certain Chaldean stranger who is agitating the whole city with his marvellous responses, and exposing to any comer the Secrets of Fate for cash down. He declares to some what day strengthens the marriage twine, to others what day makes the foundations of buildings endure, what day is profitable for business, or best resorted-to for travel, or opportune for a sea-voyage. To me, when I consulted him as to the outcome of this journey of mine, he gave several answers curious in sooth, and sufficiently different.

'For he told me that I would win some fine bouquets of

57

Fame, and also that I'd provide a great Tale, an incredible Plot, and material for Books.'

'With what kind of appearance,' asked Milo, guffawing again, 'is this Chaldean blessed? and what is the name that he's ticketed with?'

'He's tall,' I said, 'and duskyish. Diophanes by name.'

'That's the man,' said Milo. 'The very man. He gave the same sort of responses here, lots of them to lots of people – and at a good price too. Indeed he made an excellent thing out of it, till Fortune handed him a trick – or as I might rather say, landed him a kick.'

The Tale of Diophanes

ONE day when he was the centre of a jostling crowd, and busy ladling out the Fates to the onlookers, a certain merchant by the name of Cerdo approached him with a query as to the most favourable day for a journey. After Diophanes had particularized a likely date, Cerdo lugged out his money-bag, emptied out the money, and counted a hundred denars which he meant to leave as the prophesying fee. At this moment a youth of the upper-class tiptoed up behind Diophanes and grasped him by the garment.

Diophanes swung round, and found himself clasped and kissed most dearly. Returning the salute, he desired the newcomer to take a seat at his side, for he was so blankly astonished at this sudden aparition that he forgot the business transaction in which he was engaged.

'Well now, I am glad to see you,' he said. 'How long ago did you arrive?'

'Jogged-in early last evening,' the other answered. 'But tell me in your turn, my dear friend, how you have sailed so rapidly to this city from the island of Euboea, and how you got along on land and sea.'

Then Diophanes, this egregious Chaldean and scatter-brain, forgetting who he was, declared, 'May all my enemies and ill-wishers light on such a chapter of accidents – as bad as the Odyssey! For the ship in which we embarked was smashed about by the veering cyclonic blasts. The rudders were carried away, and no sooner had we brought the hulk near to the farther shore than she sank like a stone. We saved our lives by swimming to land, but lost all else. And then whatever oddments we scraped together through the charity of strangers or the kindness of friends were stripped from us by a mob of robbers. My brother Arignotus was the only man to put up a resistance, and him they murdered before my very eyes.'

While Diophanes was mournfully recounting his mishaps, the merchant Cerdo snatched up the money which he had paid out as fee for the prophecy, and showed the prophet a clean pair of heels. Then at last Diophanes collected his faculties and realized how he had blundered, while all of us that had stood round listening burst into salvoes of helpless laughter.

.　　.　　.　　.　　.

'However, Master Lucius, I trust that the Chaldean hit on the truth in your case, if in no one else's, and that you may be fortunate and find nothing to mar your journey.'

Thus Milo went on lengthily discoursing, while I sat silent, groaning internally and not a little irritated at myself for having started off a series of unseasonable anecdotes which threatened to lay waste a good part of the evening and its delectable fruits. But at last I gulped down my shame and said to Milo:

'Let Diophanes carry on with his Fortune, or miscarry with his ill-gotten gains again on land or sea. I am still sore from the exertions of yesterday. So please excuse me for going to bed rather early.'

As I spoke, I rose and went straight out, and reaching my bedroom I discovered there a pleasant spread of toothsome tidbits. The servant-boys' bed was removed outside the door on the ground a fair distance away – to prevent them from eavesdropping, I suppose, on our night-long babble.

Beside my bed a table was ranged, packed with the best of the supper remnants, and generous cups already stained half-full with wine that awaited only the tempering water, and a flagon near by with gradually distending orifice to let the wine gurgle out more freely – the whole advance guard of gladiatorial Venus.

No sooner was I laid in bed than lo! Fotis. Her mistress

had now retired for the night; and the girl had come to me gaily garlanded with roses and with one rose in full blosso. opening between her breasts. She embraced me with fas kisses, and tied a wreath about my head, and strewed flowers over me; and then she snatched a cup, and pouring warm water into it she proffered me a draught; and before I had finished, she indulgently took the cup away from my lips, and sipped the remainder of the wine with little dainty birdlike sips, keeping her eyes intently upon me all the while.

Another cup, and then a third, we shared thus, passing the cup to and fro, until I was drenched in wine and every inch of my body partook of my perturbed desire. I felt ticklishly elevated, with all my energies keyed up; and now with one tweak I demonstrated incontestably to my Fotis my straightforward intention.

'Pity me,' I said, 'come to my succour on the spot. For you can see that I am nervously taut with expectation of this pitched battle to which you challenged me without any go-between of a herald. Ever since the first arrow of pitiless Cupid twanged in my vitals, I have been standing to arms, and now I'm fairly scared that the bow-strings should snap with over-tension. But if you would humour me more richly, let down your wild hair, and while it falls about your shoulders undulatingly utter lovely embraces.'

In less than a heartbeat she had pushed away with one sweep all the plates and dishes, and stripped herself of every stitch. Her hair tumbled down in blithe wantonness, and she stood before me metamorphosed into a Venus who rose beautifully from the trough of the sea – for a moment of coquettish craft shadowing (it could hardly be called modestly protecting) her depilated femininity with rosy palm.

'Fight,' she said, 'and fight stoutly. For I won't budge a hair's-breadth, nor turn my back. Face to face, I say, if you are a man, strike home, manœuvre into position busily, and die the death. Today the battle is waged without quarter.'

With these words she leaped into bed, and saddling and bridling me she rode agilely into pleasure. In the process she showed herself to possess a spine of pliant lubricity, and she satiated me with the enjoyment of Venus-on-a-swing, until stretched at the last gasp of ecstasy with languid bodies we fell twined in a warm and mortal embrace, pouring out our souls.

In these and like entanglements, without a sigh of sleep, we came up to the confines of light, charming away moments of lassitude with the winecup, once more awakening desire and replenishing delight. And a good many more nights we spent in devices similarly pleasant.

One day Byrrhaena was unusually urgent in inviting me to a supper-party; and no matter how lavishly I excused myself she refused to listen. There was nothing for it but to approach Fotis and obtain her advice as from the godhead of my life. She was unwilling that I should remove myself from her by a nail's-breadth, yet she ended by giving me a brief leave-of-absence from the campaigns of love.

'On one condition,' she said. 'Take care to retreat at an early hour from the party. For a rampageous set of young aristocratic bloods have been terrorizing the public. You will see slaughtered men in the middle of the high-streets, and the troops of the Prefect are stationed too far away to relieve the city of this menace. You too are all the more likely to be bludgeoned through envy of your fine ways and contempt of you as an alien.'

'Toss away your fears, my Fotis,' I said, 'I not only prefer my own pleasures to the luxuries of someone else's table, but I shall hurry back so as to stop your fears. And it is not as if I go unaccompanied. For I have my trusty blade dangling at my side as a protection against all dangers.'

Thus accoutred I resigned myself to the supper. There was a bustling roomful of guests: the élite of the city, as the hostess was a social leader. The tables glittered sumptuously with citronwood and ivory. The couches were covered with golden wraps. The copious cups, varied attractively in design, were richly alike in value.

Some were of glass ingeniously adorned with figures; some were of flawless crystal; some again were of polished silver, and of flashing gold, and of amber delicately hollowed and jewels made to drink from. Anything you conceived impossible was there to be found.

The carvers, more numerous than usual, waited elegantly in gorgeous liveries. The dishes were endless; and the lads, their heads fresh from the curling-tongs and their tunics finely silken, stood offering to the guests old wines in gems for goblets.

At last lights were brought in, and the supper conversation became prevalent. Abounding laughter, liberal jokes, and rogueries arose on all sides. Then Byrrhaena spoke to me:

'Does your time pass pleasantly in this country of ours? In our own opinion we easily excel all other cities in Temples, Baths, and other Public Works. Moreover the necessaries of life are produced in super-abundance. There is freedom for the man who likes quiet, while there is the hustle of Rome for the commercial visitor and the retirement of a country manor for the peaceable tourist. In short, our city is the resort of the whole province's pleasure-seekers.'

'Your sketch is correct,' I answered. 'Among no other people have I felt myself so free as here. But I feel a deadly dread for the blind and unavoidable Lurking-holes of the Guild of Witches. For I hear that even the dead are unsafe in their sepulchres, and that odd pieces and collops of corpses are stolen from the mounds and pyres to work mortal harms on the living. And they tell me that the witch-hags are so eager when they hear of a stranger's burial that they beat the funeral procession in the race to the grave.'

'Altogether true,' one of the guests remarked, 'and they do not spare the living a whit more. I know a man – no names – who found himself so badly torn that his own mother wouldn't know his spoiled face.'

At this speech the whole company broke out in uncurbed laughter, and the eyes and interest of one and all turned upon a man sitting apart in a corner. This man, confused by the prolonged merriment, rose to go out, muttering indignantly. But Byrrhaena interposed.

'Please, dear Telephron,' she said, 'do stay with us a little longer, and with your usual good nature recount that adventure of yours. I want my dear child Lucius to have the pleasure of hearing the story you tell so well.'

'You, madam,' answered the man, 'never fail your own high standard of good manners; but the insolence of certain others is intolerable.'

This he spoke with deep emotion. But Byrrhaena would not relent; she begged him as he set a value on her life to proceed with his tale; she forced him willynilly to assent. So tugging his couch rugs into a heap to make a rest for his elbow, he raised himself a little on his couch and extended his right hand. Then (the orator's gesture) he turned in the two lower fingers, stretched straight out the other two, and pointed the thumb upwards. Then with an introductory smile, he began:

The Tale of Telephron

WHEN I was an orphan, I went from Miletus to visit the Olympian Shows, and on the way I meant to see the chief parts of this far-famed province. I traversed Thessaly, and came at last on an unlucky trail to Larissa. While I was taking a look round, I racked my wits for some means of nourishing my lean purse – for my travel funds were all but used up – and I saw an old man standing in the middle of the Forum. He was standing on a stone and proclaiming in a loud voice:

'Man Wanted to Guard Corpse. Good Fee.'

So I inquired of one of the pedestrians, 'What's the meaning of this? Do dead men grow wings in this land?'

'Shut up,' the man replied. 'It's pretty evident you're very young and a stranger not to know that your foot's on Thessalian earth where the wise-women make a habit of gnawing off dead men's faces as ingredients for some Magic Spell.'

'And what,' I asked, 'are the duties of this sepulchral guard?'

'Well, first of all,' he told me, 'you must keep the strictest watch every moment of the night with wide-open unblinking eyes firmly glued on the corpse. You mustn't shift your line of vision on any account, not even for one sidelong wink; for these abandoned slidder-skins can change themselves into any beast and creep up so secretly as to cheat the eyes of the Sun and of Justice as soon as look at you. They disguise themselves as birds, and sometimes as dogs or mice or even – true it is – as flies. Then they raise their dread psalms and plunge the guard deep into slumber – but there's no end to the tale of pit-falls which these wicked women trustfully contrive to bait. And yet the pay that's offered for this dangerous job is no better than four or six goldpieces. Well, well – and there's another point I almost missed. If the corpse is not restored unblemished in the morning, the guard is compelled to yield from his own face whatever strips are necessary to patch the scars or teeth-furrows in the corpse.'

On receiving this information, I called up my courage and strode straight across to the crier. 'Leave off your calls,' I said. 'The guard is here. What's the pay?'

'A thousand pence will be handed out to you,' he answered. 'But come, my lad, keep a lively eye on the corpse and don't let the villainous harpies get at it. It's the son of one of the first citizens.'

'You're talking nonsense to me,' I said. 'Wasting air. You see in me a man of iron that never sleeps. I'm sharper-eyed than Lynceus, or Argus, I'm eyes all over.'

Before I'd done speaking he took my hand and led me away to a certain house where the doors were barred up. He showed me in through a narrow back door and into a darkened chamber with closed shutters. Here he indicated a matron vestured in mourning, who was weeping.

He accosted her. 'Here is the man hired to guard your husband faithfully.'

At these words she parted and threw back the hair that hung over her face, and looked at me – the rays of her beauty unquenched by her woe.

'Mind, I beg you,' she said, 'to be vigilant in your task.'

'Have no worry,' I answered, 'beyond thinking out some suitable present to throw-in with the fee.'

She agreed, and rising hurriedly conducted me into another bedroom where lay the corpse close-shrouded in white sheets. Next she called in seven witnesses, and in their presence uncovered the body with her own hand. Then after a long burst of tears she adjured them all to testify, solicitously pointing out each detail of the dead features and making this set speech which was taken down on tablets by a secretary:

'See here. Nose entire. Eyes intact. Ears undamaged. Lips

64

immaculate. Chin unflawed. Do you, good fellow-citizens, bear witness hereunto.'

After that, each man subscribed the deposition, and she turned to go. 'Madam,' I called, 'please give orders for all necessaries to be supplied.'

'And what are they?' she asked.

'A lamp,' I said, 'a huge lamp, and sufficient oil to stoke it with light till daybreak. Warm water, with wine-holders and a cup. And a dish decked with some of the dinner-scraps.'

But she shook her head. 'Get out, you fool!' she replied. 'Do you think to find in a house of mourning dinners or portions of dinners when for these many days not so much as kitchen-smoke has been seen? Did you plan to come here for a carouse? Rather, set yourself down to grief and tears, the right fare for this house.'

After this rebuke she turned to her maidservant. 'Myrrhine,' she said, 'fetch a lamp and oil directly, and then lock the guard in and leave the room at once.'

Thus I found myself left alone to console the corpse. I rubbed my eyes and fortified them against drowsiness, while I rocked my mind in the cradle of some songs. Soon dusk was upon me. Night fell. Deeper night; and then the silence as the others slept; and then the dead of night. My stress (I confess) was growing unbearable, when suddenly a weasel crept in and halting close before me fixed me with a needling eye. The strange confidence shown by this mite of a beast threw me into confusion, till I finally addressed it:

'Get away from here, you dirty beast. Crawl down among the baby-mice that are your own size, before you get a down-right swipe from me. Get away from here.'

The weasel turned tail and scampered out of the room; and at that moment I fell headlong down to the bottom of the deep dark sea of sleep, and the Delphic God himself could not have discerned without some trouble which was the deader man of the two there laid out. For I lay insensible, myself needing a guard, and to all intents not there.

No sooner had the clarion of the red-combed cohort sounded the night's armistice than I at last blinked awake. Struck with sickening terror I ran to the corpse and held the light above it but all the parts were correctly in place. Then in burst the doleful wife anxiously wailing at the

65

head of yesterday's witnesses; and immediately flung herself upon the dead body; she kissed it as if she would never stop, and submitted every detail to the scrutiny of the lamp.

Then turning she called Philodespotus, her steward, and bade him pay over the settled sum without delay to the worthy watchman. When this was forthwith done, she said to me, 'We give you our deepest thanks, young man; and by Hercules! you have carried out this task so dutifully that we henceforth enrol you among our household.'

This offer, beyond my hopes of preferment, dazzled my delighted wits. I stood wonderstruck staring at the gleaming goldpieces which I kept tossing up and down in my palm.

'Madam,' I said, 'I ask nothing better than to be one of your servants; and every time you desire my services in this capacity, call on me confidently.'

I had hardly finished speaking before the servants, execrating me for my ill-omened speech, had snatched up any weapons handy and assaulted me. One man smacked me in the cheek with his fist; a second dug his elbows into my back; a third punched me in the ribs; a fourth lashed out at me with his feet; a fifth tugged at my hair; a sixth tore my clothes. Thus I was propelled out of the house, as mangled and dismantled as ever was the proud young man Adonis or Orpheus poet of the Muses.

While I stood in the next roadway, pulling myself together, I reflected on my late inauspicious and unadvised compliment and could not but admit that I had deserved even worse buffetings. After a while the dead man was borne out for the last time with sobs and screams of grief; and according to the local ritual, as he was one of the ruling class, he had a public funeral which paraded through the Forum.

Seeing the procession, an old man stumbled after it, his sorrow vented in tears while he tore his venerable grey hair. With his two hands he clasped the bier and cried in a high-pitched voice broken by incessant sobs:

'On your honours, fellow Roman citizens, on your duty to the State, rally round your assassinated brother. Take severe vengeance on this wickedly plotting woman for her vile crime. For she and no other has put her husband out of the way. She poisoned the hapless youth, my sister's son, to please her lover and to grab the estate.'

66

Thus the old man shrilly lamented and complained to all in turn. Meanwhile the mob grew restive, excited into crediting the charge on mere grounds of probability. They shouted for firebrands; they looked for stones; they encouraged the lads to lynch the woman. She replied to these demonstrations with counterfeited tears, swore most sanctimoniously by all the gods in heaven, and protested herself guiltless of so foul a deed.

To this the old man answered, 'Then let us commit to divine providence the judgement of the truth. Here is Zatchlas the Egyptian, a first-class prophet, who has already agreed at heavy cost to recall the spirit for a space from the shadows and to animate the corpse from behind the threshold of death.'

So saying, he led forward a young man clad in linen raiment, his feet shod in palm-leaf sandals and the crown of his head shaven; and he kissed the hands of this man for some time, and embraced his knees.

'Pity me, Priest,' he begged, 'pity me, by the Stars of the Heavens, by the Gods of Death, by the Elements of Nature, by the Silence of Night, by the Enclosures of Coptos,[1] by the Spilth of Nile, by the Mysteries of Memphis, by the Isis-rattles of Pharos, grant to this corpse a momentary relish of the sun and infuse some dregs of light into eyes that are sealed eternally. We bow to death's law; we do not grudge the earth her own; we beseech only a fleeting return of life for the assuagement of just revenge.'

The prophet, thus placated, laid a certain herb thrice on the dead man's mouth, and another on his breast. Then he turned towards the East, and offered a silent prayer to the ascending bulk of the August Sun. A hush of interest attended this awe-inspiring rite, and all present eagerly craned to view the miracle. I had mixed with the crowd and obtained a stand close behind the bier, on a raised stone; and I was gazing curiously at the whole scene.

Soon the breast of the dead man heaved up at the puff of life; the veins throbbed vigorously; and breath began to fill the whole body. The corpse sat up and spoke in a young man's voice:

1 'Enclosures of Coptos': There was an island near Coptos which was sacred to Isis. The swallows were said to throw up embankments at the risk of their own lives to save it from the overflowing Nile.

'O why do you call me back to the business of a transitory life, after I have drunk the waters of Lethe and floated on the swamp of Styx? Let me go, I implore, let me go. O let me return to my peace.'

Thus spoke the voice out of the dead body. But the prophet, showing considerable signs of strain, answered, 'I bid you tell all unto the people. I bid you unveil the secrets of your death. Do you doubt that I have curses which can call up the Furies, which can torture your weary limbs?'

The dead man lifted his head from the couch, and after deeply groaning addressed the crowd:

'Wickedly was I cut off by my newly wedded wife. Evicted by a venomed cup I made way for her lover in my yet-warm bed.'

At this the paragon of a wife called all her strength of mind to aid, and sacrilegiously contradicted and nagged back at her denouncing husband. The crowd stormily took sides. Some said that the abominable woman should be burned alive with the husband's corpse; others insisted that no credit could be placed in the fictions of a dead man.

The next announcement made by the young man's voice, however, settled the altercation. Once again the body was racked with a groan. 'I shall give you,' the voice said, 'I shall give you indisputable proof of my statement. I shall reveal to you what is known to no one save myself.'

The dead man paused and pointed his finger at me. 'When this fellow, the keen-scented guardian of my corpse, kept his meritorious watch over me, the witch-hags that were lurking about to plunder me changed themselves vainly into various shapes. And when they failed in their effort to beguile his business-like stare, they finally cast over him a Cloud of Sleep and buried him in profound unconsciousness. Then they at once began persistently to call on me by name, till my grating joints and chilled limbs strove with heavy twitches to show obedience to their magic lure. But this man, who though still alive was slumbering dead to the world, chancing to be designated by the same name as myself, rose up in a trance and glided about of his own accord like a senseless ghost. Thereupon, although the doors of the bedroom had been carefully bolted, the witches slipped in through a crack. They snipped his nose off first, and then his ears, so that he suffered the mutilation meant

68

for me; and then, that they might keep their trickery up to the end, they moulded some ears like those they had snipped, and fitted them painstakingly to his head and they provided him also with an imitation nose of wax. And here now stands the wretched fellow, clutching the fee received for turning himself not into a nightwatchman but into a scarecrow.'

Aghast at this disclosure, I immediately made a test of my fate. I clapped my hand to my nose and pulled; and the nose came away. I rubbed my ears; and the ears dropped to the ground.

Everybody by this time was derisively pointing fingers or nodding heads at me, while laughter bubbled out riotously. Dripping with a cold sweat, I crawled out through the ranks of the crowd and ran off. Nor could I in my cicatrised and ridiculous state return to my native city; so I trained my hair to fall down on either side and hide the ear-scars, and I made a decent excuse for my degraded nose by means of this piece of glued-down linen.

.   .   .   .   .

As soon as Telephron had given his version of the mishap, the carousers, well-soaked in the winecups, burst once more into unimpaired merriment; and while they followed the custom in demanding a toast to Laughter, Byrrhaena remarked to me:

'Tomorrow is an All-Fools-Day, observed from the very cradle-times of the city, when we, alone of mankind, propitiate the most sacred God Laughter[1] with jolly rites of festival. Your presence will make the ceremonies more enjoyable. And I hope that you will use your natural wit to invent something suitably cheerful in the god's honour, and thus help us to tickle the favour of so mighty a divinity.'

'Fine!' I exclaimed. 'Your orders shall be obeyed. And by Hercules, I hope I may stumble on some theme that will abundantly do honour to so great a god.'

At this point I was warned by my servant that night had now fallen; and feeling somewhat wine-soused, I forthwith arose and hurriedly bade Byrrhaena farewell. Then with tottering steps I traced my way homewards.

[1] 'God Laughter': Pausanias mentions this rite of Hypata.

But in the very first main street that we entered, a sudden swoop of wind blew out the light on which we were depending, and it was only with difficulty that we got free from the shroud of unexpected darkness. Stubbing our toes on all the stones, we plodded on wearily towards our lodgings and had come to the last turning when three men of hefty build were seen briskly rushing with might and main against our door. They did not show the remotest alarm at our approach; rather, they heaved and kicked at the door with speeded-up zeal and fury. In consequence I naturally concluded that they were brigands, and of the most violent brand.

I therefore at once grasped the sword which I was carrying under my cloak ready for any such emergency, whipped it out, and charged headlong into the brigands. As each man sought to grapple with me, I struck at him and plunged my sword into his body up to the hilt, till at last, riddled thickly with gaping wounds, the men coughed out their spirits before my very feet.

The battle ended; and Fotis, aroused by the tumult, opened the door. Panting and laved with sweat, I crept inside. Fagged-out by the fight with the three robbers as if I had slaughtered three-bodied Geryon,[1] I at once fell abed asleep.

[1] 'Geryon': The three-bodied king of Spain whom Hercules slew. This episode clearly suggested to Cervantes the adventure of Don Quixote at the inn where that hero combats with wineskins

BOOK THE THIRD

A s soon as Dawn had lifted her rosy arm to urge on her
coursers with their crimsoning caparisons through the
heavens, Night took from me my sheltering slumbers and
left me to harsh Day. Remorse leaped into my mind as I
recollected my deed of the evening. I sat up on my haunches
in bed, my feet tucked beneath me and my fingers inter-
locked across my knees; and I wept fluently. Already I could
picture the Forum and the trial, the sentence, and finally
the executioner in person.

'What judge,' I cried, 'could I meet so lenient and benign
as to declare me guiltless when I am imbued with the gore
of a triple murder and besmeared with the life-blood of so
many citizens? Is this the glorious journey that the
Chaldean Diophanes foretold me with such assurance?'

I was turning these thoughts over and over, larding them
with 'ahs' and 'ohs' for my sad fate, when there was a knock
at the door and a hubbub broke out at the gate. In a
moment the entrance was thrown open and a crowd
swarmed in. The whole house was packed with magistrates
and their servants and a nondescript herd of people. At
once two of the lictors clapped me on the shoulder 'In the
Name of the Law', and began to hale me off. I for my part
decided to go quietly. By the time we had reached the end
of the alley-way, we came up against such a huge con-
course that it seemed the whole city had turned out. And
while I walked sadly along with head bent towards the
ground (or rather to the hell beneath), I took a side-glance
and saw what affected me with the greatest astonishment.
For all the many thousands who stood noisily around, there
was not a single man who was not splitting his ribs with
laughter.

At length, after we had traversed every street and turned
every corner like the victim of a lustral sacrifice led all

round the city to appease the Wrath threatened by omens, I was brought before the tribunal in the Forum. The magistrates took their seats on an elevated stage, and the public crier shouted for silence; but the crowd, swarming so rapidly that lives were being endangered by the dense pressure, howled out their unanimous demand that this leading case should be tried in the Theatre. No sooner said than they all streamed out and filled the pit of the theatre in a twinkle to bursting. Even the entrances and all the roofs were packed like sardines. Numbers clung to the columns. Some hoisted themselves on to statues. Fragments of many others could be glimpsed through windows or between the rafters. One and all, mad for a good view, paid no attention to their personal safety.

Then the public officers led me forward through the proscenium as though I were a victim, and stood me in the centre of the orchestra. The accusers were again cited by the bull-throated roar of the crier, and an elderly man arose. After water had been poured into a globe which, perforated like a cullender, regulated the drip of speaking-time, the latter thus addressed the assemblage:

'This is no trifle, my reverent fellow-citizens. It involves the whole question of law-abiding citizenship, and it will provide an important precedent. Wherefore it is all the more earnestly expedient for each and every one of you, in your wish to uphold the dignity of the State, to see to it that this wicked homicide does not get away scot-free after the shambles which he has so brutally and bloodily made of our streets. And do not think that I am motivated by any private grudge, or that my anger is based on personal animosity. For I am prefect of the night-watch, and I believe that till today no one has been able to disparage my dutiful vigilance. I shall accordingly give you a faithful report of the crime and all the operations of the night. It was about the third watch, while I was going my rounds from door to door and inspecting every nook throughout the city with unremitting attention, that I saw this ruthless young man with a drawn sword dealing destruction all about him. Victims (to the number of three) had already fallen before his frenzy and lay convulsively at his feet in pools of blood breathing their last. Instantly conscience-stricken at his horrid deed – and no wonder – he fled, and protected by the darkness escaped into a certain house where he lay in hiding the live long night. But by the providence of the gods, which allows no evil to go unpunished, I arrested him this morning before he could slip away clandestinely, and I guarded him hither to face the heavy hand of your honourable tribunal.

'You consequently see before you a man defiled with many murders, a man caught in the very act, a man who is an alien. Wherefore, resolutely pass judgement on this alien who has committed a crime for which you would exact grievous retribution from one of your own citizens.'

Continuing thus relentlessly my accuser reached the end of his frightful charge. The crier at once bade me begin my reply if I wished to make one. But I at that moment could utter nothing more eloquent than tears – not, by Hercules, so much on account of this truculent accusation as out of the anguish of my own conscience. Some breath, however, of heaven-sent boldness filled me, and I spoke:

'I know very well, when the corpses of three citizens are on view, how arduous it is for a man charged with the murders to persuade so vast an assembly that he is innocent, when he speaks the truth and admits that he did the deed. But if your humanity will publicly grant me a brief hearing, I shall readily convince you that I stand here on a capital charge undeservedly; that through no fault of mine I have attracted the opprobrium of this crime, but through a chance-impulse of justifiable indignation.

'Listen. As I was returning home from dinner slightly later than usual and a trifle the worse for drink – which indeed I shall not disguise was my only real offence – before the very door of my house (for I am lodging with your worthy fellow-citizen Milo) what did I see but some ravening brigands assaulting the panels and seeking to wrench the doors off their hinges! The bars, which had been firmly fixed, were all torn violently out, and the men were menacing all the inmates with sudden death. One of them, the biggest man and wildest wrecker, was egging on the others with words like these:

'Hey now, lads! keep up your hearts, and let swing with your fists! Rush on 'em sleeping. Away with all hesitations, away with all cowardly compunctions! Let slaughter stalk with naked blade throughout the house! Stab 'em if they lie

73

snoring. Knock 'em down if they show fight. Save our own skins entire by sieving the others.

'I confess, gentlemen, that, considering it my duty as a peaceful individual, and frightened at the same time both for my hosts and myself, I drew the small sword which I carried against just such dangers, and I hurled myself at these villainous brigands with the aim of scattering or scaring them.

'But this savage set of monsters were far from running away. On the contrary, though they saw that I was armed, they resisted boldly. They drew together and awaited my onset. Indeed, the ringleader who was giving the orders attacked me with extreme violence, caught hold of my hair with both his hands, and tried to bend me back to bash my head with a stone. But while he was yelling for one to be handed to him, I luckily laid him low with a well-aimed thrust; and in a few moments I stuck the second man between the shoulder-blades, while he was clinging to my legs and biting me, and stabbed the third through the chest as he charged wildly at me.

'And so, having avenged this breach of the peace and protected the house of my host and the public safety, I supposed that I was not only free from prosecution but even liable for some civic credit, being a man who has never had his character in any way impugned, who is highly respected in his own city, and who has always preferred clean hands to every material profit. Nor can I understand why I am now standing trial as a criminal because of this just requital which I was moved to inflict on some ruffianly brigands; for no one can possibly show that there was any private feud between us, or that I even knew who on earth the brigands were. At the least produce some stolen object to establish a motive for my alleged enormity.'

So far I spoke, when I was interrupted by a gush of tears; and lifting up my suppliant hands, I turned in anguish from man to man, appealing to their common mercy and the love which they bore their offspring. When I considered that they must all now have felt their withers wrung and their pity stirred by my tears, calling the Eye of the Sun and of Justice to witness and commending my sad lot to the providence of the gods, I raised my head a little and looked out on the people. And they were every man

74

doubled-up and weak with laughter – Milo my noble host and well-wisher the most helplessly overcome of them all.

At this sight I said to myself: 'So this is faith! this is conscience! For the sake of his house I have slain men and now stand on a capital charge; but he is not satisfied with withholding the comfort of his aid. On top of that, he grins at my destruction.'

Meanwhile a woman came running down the mid-aisle of the theatre, weeping and lamenting, dressed in deepest mourning, bearing a baby on her bosom. After her trotted an old woman, wrapped in dirty rags, uttering the same moans of misery. Both women were waving olive-sprigs. Hovering over the bier on which the bodies of the slain were stretched under sheets, they beat their breasts and howled lugrubriously.

'In the name of common pity, of the universal law of mankind,' they cried, 'take thought of these young men so unworthily cut-off, and afford the solace of revenge to our widowed and lorn lives. At least take sides with this unlucky babe, left destitute in the cradle, and offer up to your outraged laws and civic order the blood of this brigand.'

At this appeal the senior magistrate rose and spoke to the people: 'That this crime needs a heavy penalty not even he who committed it can deny. Therefore a point of routine alone remains to be unravelled, and that of secondary importance: the question whether this man had any accomplices in his heinous deed. For it is not likely that a man single-handed could dispose of three such sterling specimens of youth. The truth must consequently be extracted by means of torture, for the slave-boy that accompanied him has hugger-mugger fled away. So our only course is to put the accused to the question, and thereby learn the names of his abettors, so that we may root out this gang and the dread which they instil.'

Without more ado the instruments used for torture among the Greeks were produced: fire, and wheel, and every variety of scourge. Then my sufferings were intensified infinitely by the realization that I was not even to die with sound limbs. But the old woman, who had aggravated the whole proceeding with her howls, exclaimed:

'Most worthy citizens, before you hoist up to the cross

75

this plundering murderer of my unhappy children, allow the bodies of his victims to be uncovered. For the contemplation of the dead, once so young, so beautiful, will move you more and more to a just wrath, and you will pronounce a sentence angrily proportionate to this man's villainy.'

The suggestion was enthusiastically received, and the magistrate instantly ordered me in person to unshroud the bodies which were laid out on the bier. I shrank back and refused for a while to re-stage yesternight's tragedy by this exposition of myself among the slain. But the lictors peremptorily compelled me to accede to the magistrate's order; and at length by main force they dragged my hand away from my side and raised it, to its own undoing, above the bodies. Then, gripped by necessity, I succumbed. Repressing a shudder, I snatched at the pall and revealed what lay beneath.

Good gods! O what a sight was there! What an incredible joy! What an abrupt reversal of my fortunes! I, who had already felt myself enrolled on Proserpine's ledgers, one of Death's chattels – I, stupefied at the seesawing of fate, gaped, unable to explain, or even to express intelligibly, the unexpected spectacle.

The bodies of butchered men were three winebladders slashed and apertured variously – the scars corresponding in position (as far as my memory of last night's combat extended) to the wounds that I had given the brigands. Then did the laughter, which till now had been kept somewhat hushed by the leaders, swell into an irrepressible roar. Some congratulated me in the excess of their high-spirits; others sat with palms pressed on their aching bellies; all were bogged in merriment, as with their eyes turned on me they trooped from the theatre.

But I, from the moment I removed the coverlet, stood fixed and frozen into stone, not a pulse different from the other statues and columns in the place. Nor did I emerge from the land of shades until my host Milo approached and laid his hand upon me. Even then I struggled, and wept unstaunchably, and sobbed all the way, as he drew me along with kindly force. He avoided all the frequented thoroughfares and led me through various by-ways to his house, doing his best to distract me from my misery and persistent trepidation by rambling remarks. But he failed

76

altogether to soften the rankling sense of injury which was lodged deeply in my breast.

Close on my heels arrived the magistrates in full-dress uniform. They entered and set themselves to pacifying me with speeches of this sort:

'Of your high social standing and your pedigree, Master Lucius, we are not uninformed; for the noble name of your renowned family echoes throughout the province. Nor was it an ignominy to which you have been submitted, though you take it so grievously to heart. Uproot therefore all this afflicting melancholy. Banish your depression. For this Festival in honour of the jolly God Laughter, which we solemnly celebrate in public as each year returns, is always crowned with some new Diversion. The god will henceforth accompany you everywhere, propitiously and lovingly considering you his exponent. Never will he permit grief to touch your mind. No. He will smooth your brow with a gay serenity for ever. The whole state moreover confers upon you its most distinguished privileges in return for your services. It has adopted you as Patron, and voted that a statue of you be cast in brass.'

To this address I made reply: 'To you, representatives of this most splendidly pre-eminent of the cities of Thessaly, I render thanks equal to the honours that are pressed upon me. I recommend, however, that you should keep your statues and tokens for men of dignity and length of service exceeding mine.'

I spoke this with an air of modesty and a brief constraint of features into a cheerful smile. Then, assuming as much lightness of manner as my faculties allowed, I ushered the magistrates courteously out. No sooner were they gone than a servant thrust in.

'Byrrhaena, your near relation,' he said, 'reminds you of the dinner party which you promised last night to attend. Time to be there soon.'

Chilled at these words and shivering at the very mention of Byrrhaena's house, I answered, 'Tell your mistress that I would be only too glad to accept. But my host Milo has conjured me by the God of the Day to stay here. I've pledged myself to his meal, and neither is he going out nor will he let me go. I must therefore postpone my engagement with your mistress.'

While I spoke, Milo held me firmly by the hand; and having ordered the toilet-materials to be brought, he led me to the nearest bathing establishment. Dodging the glances of everybody, and wincing at the general laughter (at which I painfully felt myself the butt), I tried to crouch out of view behind Milo as I slunk along. And how I washed, how I dried, how I managed to return home, was all obliterated by my daze of shame; for I was aware of nothing but a world of inquisitive eyes, nodding heads, and pointing fingers.

At last, having wolfed a famishing snack with Milo, I alleged a splitting headache left as the dregs of my constant drip of tears, and was readily given leave to depart to my room. There, throwing myself on the bed, I miserably summoned up every detail of the day's event, until finally my Fotis, having attended her mistress duly to rest, came to me. But how unlike her normal self! She offered no dimpling smiles, no sweet babble, but a gloomy brow and lowering wrinkles. At length, after a timid delay, she murmured, 'I freely confess that I, yes I, was at the bottom of all your vexation.'

With these words she drew out a sort of lash from between her breasts and put it in my hands. 'O, please,' she said, 'take your revenge on a wicked woman. Yes, do. Make me undergo any punishment you like to impose. But please don't think that I have knotted this trouble for you intentionally. May the gods have more pity on me than ever to make you suffer one twinge of pain on my account. No, I pray that if any danger is hanging over your head my blood may ransom you. It was something else altogether that I was bidden to do, and only my bad luck could have made it turn out to your detriment.

Swayed by my usual curiosity, and eager to strip the whole affair to the buff, I pressed her thus:

'This most vicious and profligate of all lashes, which you destined for your scourging, shall itself be sliced and torn to shreds before it touches your milky swan-soft skin. But recount to me faithfully what act of yours handed malign Fate so deadly an instrument against me. I assure you by that dearest face of yours that there is no one, no, not even yourself, who could convince you might harm me in a moment's thought. And what is more, no gusty flaw of chance can turn an innocent intention into guilt.'

By the end of my speech I saw that the eyes of my Fotis were moist and tremulous and misty with indrawn desire and heavy-lidded; and I touched my lips thirstily against them and sip-sipped with dove's kisses.

Her gay self returned. 'First let me carefully close the bedroom door,' she replied, 'lest the slipshod profanity of my runaway tongue involve me in an awful sin.'

Thereupon she drove the bolts in, and latched the door securely; and coming back to me she threw both her arms about my neck, and continued in a tiny cautious whisper. 'I'm afraid. I'm all of a tremble at disclosing the secrets of this house and the hidden goings-on of my mistress. But I know you and your upbringing too well to fear betrayal – not only because of your inborn sense of honour and your highminded way of regarding things, but because you have been initiated into several of the Mysteries and learned the holy rite of Silence. Whatever then I entrust to the sanctuary of your godfearing breast I beg you to keep closely concealed there. Reward by the strictest seals of silence the frankness of my story.

'It is the love I bear you which compels me to narrate what is known to no other living person but myself. You will now hear the whole truth of this household. You will hear the wonderful secret powers of my lady, by which she bosses the spirits of the dead, disturbs the stars, dominates the deities, and enslaves the elements. Never does she exercise her magic force so ardently as when her mouth has watered at the sight of some well-timbered young fellow; and she's in that state of watering, on and off, most of the time. Just now she's in the throes of desire for a comely young Boeotian, and she is bringing into play every engine and finesse of her craft. I heard last night with these very ears, I say, I heard her curse the Sun and threaten she'd smudge him out with a cloud of dust and make things dark for ever, if he didn't hurry and clear out of the sky so that Night could take his place and let her start working her wanton spell.

'As she was coming back yesterday from the Baths, she happened to see this youth sitting in the barber's shop; and she instructed me to collect surreptitiously some of

79

his hairs, which were lying on the floor, scattered by the barber's snipping. But despite all my care, when I stooped to gather them, the barber spied me. He grabbed hold of me – for our household's blacklisted already as a den of spell-binders – and he barked at me nastily:

' "So you won't leave off, eh, you worthless bit, purloining the hairs of all the handsome young men! If you don't drop your game from now on, I'll take you before the magistrate by the scruff of your neck."

'Then, following up his threat, he thrust his hand into my blouse and furiously snatched out the hid hairs from between my teats. I was badly upset by this treatment and went away brooding over the habits of my mistress, who when amorously thwarted is always thrown into a rage which she expends in beating me like mad. There seemed nothing for it save flight; but the instant I thought of you, I put that plan aside. I was coming home forebodingly when I saw a man clipping some goatskins with a pair of shears. The skins were inflated, tightly fastened, and hanging up; and as I watched them it struck me that here was a chance to avoid returning empty-handed. For the hairs that lay on the ground were yellow, not unlike the young Boeotian's. So I took away a handful and delivered them to my mistress as the required article.

'As soon as night came, before you returned from your party, my lady Pamphile, blind with excitement, climbed up into the shingled loft which she secretly inhabits as being particularly fitted for her practices. It is exposed to every waft of air and commands every point of the compass, east and west and all the rest.

'First she prepared in this deadly workshop all her usual Tools: every kind of aromatic herb, metal plates engraved with hieroglyphs, bones of ominous birds, assorted oddments from the graves of men who had died and who had been wept and buried – here, noses and fingers; there, the blooded nails of the crucified; and there, the phialed blood of slaughtered men or the mumbled skulls removed from the jaws of wild beasts.

'Chanting over yet-palpitating entrails, she made libation with various liquids – now with spring water; now with cow's milk; now with mountain-honey and mead. Then she plaited the goat's hairs, and twined them into a love-knot, and burned them odorously on live coals together with many perfumes. In that flash the bodies, of which the hairs were smoking and crackling, received human breath through the irresistible power of magic craft and the blind energy of compelled deities. They were possessed with feeling, and they heard, and they walked. They followed the trail of their own burning excrement, and instead of that Boeotian youth it was they that came barging at the door, trying to enter.

'Then you appeared, well-tippled and deceived by the thickness of the disconcerting dark. You drew your sword boldly; and wielding it like a mad Ajax you began your massacre – but not of the whole herd of living cattle that he slew in his frenzy – for with greater valiancy you exterminated three puffed-up goatskins. You laid low your enemies without shedding a drop of blood; and the lover I embrace is not a homicide but a skinicide.'

Thus Fotis chatted lightly, and I in turn took up the jesting tone: 'I certainly can pair off this first achievement of my prowess with one of Hercules' twelve labours, standing my three slaughtered wineskins with the threefold body of Geryon or the triple heads of Cerberus. But to win my heartfelt and complete pardon for the mistake that implicated me in such suffering, abet me in the profoundest aspiration of my life. Help me to spy on your mistress when next she looses some of her superhuman powers, so that when she invokes the gods my own eyes may see her slough her present form. For I am most enthusiastically bent on a closer acquaintance with Magic, though, now I think of it, you don't seem altogether so uninstructed a neophyte yourself. I know this. Look, I experience it. I, that have already turned down the perfumed bodies of ladies, stand here a slave, freely fettered and enthralled – and all owing to your bright eyes, and your ruddied cheeks, and your glistening hair, and your open kisses, and your scented breasts. Look at me. I am neither returning home nor making any preparations to go. I see nothing beyond or above this night.'

'How I wish I could oblige you, Lucius,' she answered, 'but on account of the invidious nature of the pursuit she always withdraws into solitude, and takes care that nobody is near, before she performs her dark rites. But I shall regard your request rather than the danger I run; and if I find any opening, you shall see as you desire. Only, as I begged you at the beginning, be trusty and silent about so momentous a matter.'

At this point of our conversation a mutual desire roused us emotionally and physically. Discarding all covers, we trusted to nakedness and held a bacchanal in honour of Venus. And when I was tired out, Fotis on her own generous motion earned the lad's-gratuity. Then at last slumber filtered through our overwatched eyes and drowned us till broad daylight.

The next few nights passed in agreeably similar methods, till one day Fotis came hurrying to me in a state of eager timidity. She informed me that her mistress, having made no advance in her love affair by other means, intended on the following night to feather herself as a bird and to wing off to her desired, and that I must now take my measures for privily witnessing this unusual procedure.

So about the first watch of the night she conducted me, while I trod noiselessly tiptoe, to the upper chamber which she had mentioned; and there she bade me clap my eye to a chink in the door-panel and see what was to be seen.

I looked. First of all Pamphile divested herself of all her clothes, and opening a certain coffer she fetched out several small boxes. Taking off the lid of one of these, she squeezed out some ointment and rubbed herself all over with it, till she was smeared from the ends of her toenails to the hairs on the crown of her head. Then she muttered a series of hushed charms over a lamp, and twitched her body and jerked it shiveringly.

Gradually downy plumes began to jet and flutter out. These thickened into regular wings; her nose hooked itself hornily outwards; her nails bunched together crookedly; and Pamphile became an owl. Uttering a mournful hoot, she tested out her new shape, making little leaps and runs, and soon, soaring aloft, she swooped wide-winged out of the house.

Thus by her magic craft she changed herself at will; and I, enchanted by no spell, remained in such a rooted amazement at her act that I seemed anybody rather than Lucius. So beguiled out of my own mind was I, so full of delirious wonder, that I stood dreaming with open eyes. Indeed, I rubbed my lids for a while to make sure that I was awake after all.

At length, realizing the truth of my experience, I grasped the hand of Fotis, and laying it upon my eyes I said, 'Please let me enjoy a great and singular proof of your affection towards me, while the chance beckons. Get me a little of that same ointment. Please, by these your nipples, my honey-darling, do this and bind me your eternal slave with a debt of gratitude beyond redemption. Do this, and I shall stand at your side a winged Cupid by my Venus.'

'What's this?' she cried. 'A fox's trick, my duckie! You'd have me chop my own leg instead of the tree. As things stand, it's all I can do to keep the wolf-bitches of Thessaly away from you. Where shall I find you roosting when you're changed into a bird? When will you nest with me?'

'The heavenly ones avert such villainy!' I answered. 'Though all the roads of heaven would then be open to my lofty eagle-soar, though I should then be Jove's unerring angel and blithe squire, would I yet not circle, after I had been thus dignified with wings, back to my own snug eyrie? I swear to you, by that ravishing little knot of your hair, in which you have enwound my spirit, that I hold my Fotis above all other women. And further it occurs to me that when once I have anointed myself into a bird, I must keep aloof from all human habitation. Think what a merry pretty lover ladies would clasp in the person of an owl. For when these nightbirds blunder into any house, we see that they are hastily caught and nailed to the doorposts that they may redeem by their crucifixion the evil that their ominous flight portends the family. But I've almost overlooked an important point. What is the charm or act necessary for moulting the wings and making Lucius again?'

'Have no fear as to that part of the process,' she said. 'For my mistress has taught me every charm that brings metamorphosed humans back to their proper shape. Don't imagine, however, that she told me out of any kindly impulse. She did it so that I could assist her with the correct countercharms on her return. Just think what a mighty work trivial and common herbs can accomplish. I give her a sprinkle of anise with some bay-leaves infused in spring water, and she drinks and washes herself.'

Having given this assurance again and again, she tiptoed

shivering into the room and lifted a box out of the coffer. This box I hugged and kissed; and then, praying that the ointment would be so good as to give me a prosperous flight, I quickly tore off all my garments, greedily dipped into the box, and took out a large handful, with which I plastered every limb. And then, flapping my arms up and down, I stood waiting and trying to feel birdlike.

But no down appeared; no wings burst out. Rather, it was obvious that my hair was hardening into bristles, my tender skin was roughening to a hide. My toes and fingers lost their distinctness and clotted into solid hoofs; and from the end of my spine a long tail whisked out. My face became enormous; my mouth widened; my nostrils gaped open; my lips grew pendulous; and my ears shot hairily aloft. I could see no consolation in this calamitous change save that I was (in every respect) enlarged even beyond the capacity of Fotis.

I was now past all help; and considering my shape I saw that I was not a bird but an ass. My first impulse was to upbraid Fotis; but I had lost my human voice and gesture together, so that all I could do was to look at her sideways with dropping underlip and watering eyes, and to expostulate with her mutely.

As soon as she saw what had happened, she struck her face with angry hands. 'Wretch that I am,' she cried, 'I'm done for. In my hurry and fear I made a mistake and took a wrong box that looked the same. One good thing, however: the countercharm for this metamorphosis is easily procured. You only have to chew a few rose petals, and then you'll cease to be an ass – you will instantaneously become my Lucius again. If only I had prepared some garlands for you and me last night as I generally do! Then you wouldn't have had to drag this hide about for even one night. But I'll get the remedy at the first glimmer of light.'

Thus Fotis lamented; and, although a Complete Ass, a beast of burden, and no longer Lucius, I yet had the feelings of a man. Long and deep I meditated whether I ought to assault this deceitful whore and do her to death with a good back-kick or a bite. But better thoughts intervened, and I abandoned my rash design; for if I amerced her of life, I might trample out my own best means of assistance.

So, drooping my head and flicking my ears, I gulped down

84

my sense of injury for the nonce and submitted to the heavy pack of Fate. I withdrew to the shed where my good old nag, that had borne me so well, was stabled; and there I found another ass enstalled, belonging to my quondam host Milo.

Ah now, I thought, if there is any voiceless but instinctive sense of gratitude in animals, my horse, by an intuitional recognition and compassion, will afford me lodging and a proper welcome.[1]

But alas for Jupiter, Lord of Hospitality and the invisible deities of Faith! That estimable nag and the ass laid their heads together and forthwith schemed to take me down. Seeing me near the manger, they were afraid for their provender; and laying back their ears and snorting with rage they stamped at me with their hoofs. I retreated as far as I could from the barley which my own hands had measured out earlier in the evening to regale a grateful dependant.

Thus disposed of and relegated to obscurity, I slunk into a corner of the stable. While I there brooded over the insolence of my companions and elaborated plans of the vengeance to be taken on my perfidious steed when next morning with the aid of roses I became Lucius once more, I noticed, against the central pillar which supported the stable-beam, an image of the goddess Epona. It stood within a small shrine, daintily decorated with wreaths of roses, with freshly gathered roses.

Mad with hope when I perceived the instrument of my salvation, I boldly reached up as far as my forelegs enabled me. I strained my neck out; I smacked my lips extensively; I did my best to crop the wreath. But by a miserable chance my serving-lad, who had been put in charge of the horse, caught me stretching up. He jumped to his feet in a bad temper.

'How long,' he cried, 'are we going to let this cursed quadruped try to make havoc here – first of the nags' food, and then of the gods' images! See me if I don't tame and lame the sacrilegious beast.'

Rummaging about for some weapon, he stumbled over

1 'Proper welcome': *Lautiae:* The entertainments provided by the quaestors at Rome for foreign ambassadors. There is the same joke later when Lucius is bought by the baker.

a bundle of firewood that someone had pitched down. He selected a nobbly faggot, the weightiest of the heap, and started whacking at my poor ribs – till a vehement clang and uproar at the outer door, and the neighbours' screams of 'Thieves,' flabbergasted him and sent him running for his life.

No sooner was he gone than the doors were crashed down, and a hurly-burly of robbers rushed in, armed to the teeth. They surrounded the house from every aspect, and beat off the people who flocked to its defence. They were all brandishing swords and torches, and filled the night with glare. Flame and sword gleamed together like dawn-rays.

Then with heavy axes they attacked and split open the heavily barred and bolted strongroom which Milo had had built in the centre of the house to hold his hoard. This room they ransacked from floor to rafter; and then hastily sharing the booty they made it into separate parcels.

But the number of bags exceeded that of the backs which were to bear them. So, at their wit's end before such a superfluity of wealth, they brought my horse and us two asses out of the stable, and loaded us with as many packages as we could carry without breaking our spines. Then they drove us away from the pillaged house, urging us on with sticks. Leaving one of the band behind to act as spy and to bring information as to what steps were taken by the authorities, they whacked us fiercely up and down the mountain-trails.

What with the weight piled on my back, the steepness of the crags, and the unending winding way, I was little better than a dead donkey. The last but not least of my decisions was to appeal to the Civic Arm, and to liberate myself from so desperate a snare by calling on the awful name of the Emperor.

Accordingly, when in broad daylight we were passing through a village full of people thronging to the Fair, amid a loud group of villagers I attempted to invoke with a correct Greek accent the august name of Caesar. I brayed out 'O' with sonorous fluency, but the name itself I could not enunciate.

Irritated at my discordant noise, the robbers whanged my wretched hide left and right, till it was fit for nothing but a corn-sieve. At length, however, Jupiter in heaven provided an unsuspected chance of release. For when we were passing a collection of small farms and fair-sized country-houses, I saw a rather charming garden in which besides several other delightful blossoms there grew some virgin roses bright with morning-dew.

Jaw-dropped and brisk with hope of salvation I drew joyfully nearer; but while my lips slobbered open to crunch the flowers, it struck me that the act was ill-advised. For if I threw off my ass's hide and stood up Lucius once more while in the hands of the robbers, I would be asking to be bumped-off. They would then either suspect me to be a magician, or wish to eliminate me as a future witness.

Therefore I abstained from the roses, yielding to circumstance; and accepting my lot I gnawed my hay like any other ass.

BOOK THE FOURTH

IT was almost noon, and the sun was laying the landscape waste with his flails of heat. We turned aside in a village, stopping at the house of some old men who were mates and allies of the robbers. Ass as I was, I gathered that much from the welcome, the hurry of conversation, the salutations. A number of the packages which I was carrying on my back were removed and handed over as gifts, and the guarded whispers confessed that the objects were stolen property.

At last we were unladen of all the baggage and turned out to pasture at pleasure in the next meadow. This pasturing-party, however, did not reconcile me to the other ass and my horse, nor was I yet inured to dining on hay. But as I was perishing with hunger I confidently invaded a small market-garden that caught my eye, behind the stable, and gobbled up a bellyful of vegetables, raw as they were. I besought all the gods and poked around everywhere to see if I might light on a rosebush glowing in the adjacent gardens. For the deserted nature of the spot afforded me a fair safeguard that, if on swallowing the remedy I should discard the shambling amble of a four-legged beast-of-burden and straighten myself into humanity again, I might effect my resurrection unobserved.

While I was tossed about on these waves of speculation, I saw a little farther on a dingle shaded by a leafy clump of trees; and among its chequered growths and joyous verdures glittered the damask hues of roses.

In my imagination, which was not wholly brutish, I regarded this nook as a grove of Venus and the Graces where in shadowy secrecy beamed forth the queenly tinctures of that bridal flower. Invoking the gay God of Good-Luck,[1] I galloped along so fast that by Hercules! I felt

[1] 'God of Good-Luck': Good Event: This god had a statue in the Capitol (Pliny) and was one of the Dii Consentes (Varro).

myself no ass but at least a dashing racehorse. Yet, remarkable as my speed was, it was not so quick off the mark as my adverse fortune. For as I neared the grove I saw that what I was charging at was certainly not roses delicate and enchanting, wetted with heavenly dew and nectar – roses which happy brambles beget out of their blessed spines. It was not even a dingle; it was merely the bank of a running river lined with thickets.

The trees had long leaves like bay-leaves, and they produced a kind of scentless, cup-like reddish blossom. The ignorant herd have in their bumpkin idiom nicknamed these savourless buds rose-laurels – to graze on which is certain death to all cattle. But I felt myself so tangled in destiny's trammels and so regardless of salvation that I decided to take a suicidal bite at the venomed roses.

However, as I dilatorily drew near to crop my perdition, a young fellow (the market gardener whose greens I had devastated) perceived the damage and ran after me in a rage with a thick cudgel. Laying hold of me, he belaboured me so sorely that I was in peril of my life. But I at last had the sense to stick up for myself. I threw up my rump and lashed out persistently with my hind legs till I had given him his due and a good bit over. I laid him out flatly on the hill slope, and saved my skin by flight.

At once, however, a woman (his wife, I suppose) noticing him from higher-up as he lay prostrate and half dead, came leaping down towards him with a hullabaloo of grief – all her howls of course meant only to encompass me with immediate destruction. The village population, roused by her lamentation, instantly called out their dogs and from every side loosed them into a frenzy, inciting them to attack and tear me to rags.

I had no doubt whatever that I was near my end when I saw the dogs whistled up and urged against me; for they were a hulking breed, suitable matches for bears and lions, and there was a whole pack of them. I could perceive only one feasible plan of escape. Instead of trying to run away, I turned and trotted back to the public-house where we had put up.

But there the men, staving off the dogs with difficulty, grabbed and fastened me by an extra-thick thong to a staple. They would have flogged me straightaway to death, had it not been that my belly, contracted with the pain of the blows and afflicted with colic on account of the raw vegetables that crammed it, suddenly let loose its burden. The liquid effusion squirted out rearwards and created a stinking barrage that effectively drove away the men from my battered ribs, sprinkling some with drops of ordure and choking-off the others with the filthy stench.

Not long after, when the sun was coming down the slopes of afternoon, the robbers once more led us, all three heavily laden, out of the stable; but my load was the heaviest. A fair part of the journey was now done; and I was exhausted by the length of the road, bowed under the weight of the packages, debilitated by the cudgel-blows, and lamed and stumbling with hooves worn to the quick. Therefore, as I was dragging myself along the twists of a stream that babbled quietly through the fields, I was considering that I would make cunning use of this fortunate situation to collapse with crumpled legs and refuse obstinately to scramble back on to my feet, however they should bang me. I determined that, once down, I would not budge for any clubbing – or even for the prick of a cutlass.

For I thought that, since I was already little more than an enfeebled carcass, I should receive an honourable discharge as being on the sick-list – or that at least the robbers, chafing at the delay and obsessed with the desire for a speedy retreat, would distribute the load which I bore on my back between the two other beasts-of-burden – or that if they wanted some sharper revenge they would leave me to be devoured by the wolves and vultures.

But my relentless destiny foiled me also in this well-conceived plan. For the other ass, forestalling me through some thought-transference, forthwith assumed a tottering gait and went sprawling, baggage and all. He lay on the ground like dead; and he refused to rise, though they struck him and goaded him and tugged at his tail and his ears and his legs and all other available parts of his body.

At last, with wearied muscles, the robbers gave him up as hopeless; and after a brief discussion they decided that the retreat must not be longer delayed by a donkey that was as good as dead and no more use than a stone. So they divided his load between me and the horse, and drawing a sword they sliced both his ham strings. Then, lugging him a little aside from the road, they flung his yet-breathing body over a deep precipice.

Reviewing the fate of my fellow campaigner-in-misery, I concluded that I had better henceforth drop all guile and deception, and show myself to my masters as an honest and deserving ass. For I overheard them conversing, and learned that we should very soon reach our halting-place and that this would mean repose and journey's-end, since it was their lair and headquarters that we approached. And finally, after passing up a gentle gradient, we arrived at our destination. All the booty was unloaded and stowed away inside; and lightened of my oppressive pack I indulged in a refreshing dust-wallow in lieu of a bath.

At this juncture I cannot avoid digressing into a description of the locality and of the cave which the robbers inhabited. Thus I shall test out my natural faculty and at the same time give you the opportunity of discovering whether I was in mind and understanding the ass that I seemed.

First, there was a rugged mountain darkly clustered with wild thickets, and very high. Its shelving sides, encompassed with boulders so steep and broken as to be unscalable, were traversed in every direction by pitted and deeply scored gullies which, blocked up by brambles, made the place a natural fortress. From the topmost crag a spring gushed out in a great hub-bubbling spate, and hurtled its silvery headlong stream down the slope. Lower, it forked off into various rivulets, and inundated the valley with standing arrays of water, and enclosed the mountain-base as if with a landlocked sea or a dammed river.

Above the cave, on the open space of rock, there was reared a steep tower and sheepcote. This was built massively of thick hurdles with extended flanks suitable for sheep-folding. Before the entrance there ran a scanty hedge-track instead of portico; and you might safely (I fear) call this the robbers' reception-room. There were no other buildings to be seen save a small but haphazardly thatched hut, in which sentinels, chosen by lot from the band (as I afterwards learned), kept watch at night.

Tying us with a stout halter to the opening, they crept one after the other into the cave, squeezing through the narrow passage. Inside, they roared insultingly at an old crone who though hobbling bent with age seemed to be the sole housekeeper of this crowd of young fellows.

'Hey now,' they complained, 'you creaking old corpse, hey now! You're too dirty to be alive, and there's not enough go in you to fall dead. What's your game, squatting here lazy at home? Why isn't there something at this late hour to refresh us after all our trouble and danger? You do nothing day and night but guzzle wine down into that rampaging belly of yours.'

'Oh, no, no,' quavered the crone with squeaks of terror, 'my brave masters, my good young masters, Oh, no, there is more than enough stew ready. You can smell how beautifully it's cooked. And there's a baker's-shopful of bread, and wine poured out brim-high in well-rinsed cups, and water standing hot for your usual splash of a bath.'

At her words they at once undressed themselves and nakedly took their ease before the glow of a huge fire, sluicing themselves over with warm water and rubbing in the oil. Then they stretched their limbs round a table garnished profusely with good food.

No sooner had they reclined than in trooped an even larger band of young men whom it did not need a second glance to identify as robbers. For they too were conveying plunder; gold and silver coins, goblets, and silken garments embroidered with threads of gold. These men revived themselves with a bath like the others, and then reposed on the couches with their associates. Waiters, selected by lot, handed round the dishes; and the company ate and boozed confusedly, with the broiled meat in a pile, the loaves in droves like sheep, and the lines of winecups several deep.

The jokes were horse-play; the songs were uproar; the wit was smut. The scene was that of the half-brute revelling Lapiths and Centaurs – till at last the most stalwart member of the party rose as spokesman:

'We have gutted the house of Milo at Hypata,' he said. 'A fine day's work. Besides the heap of good luck that our manly onset has brought away, here we are back at barracks without a single casualty – not to mention the reinforcements eights hoofs strong. But you that went on a roving commission among the towns of Boeotia have returned with numbers sadly reduced and Lamachus your doughty leader lost – a man whose life was worth far more in my opinion than all the booty you collected. However, there's no doubt that it was his own fearless heart that did for him, and the name of such a hero will go down to history with that of the kings and the captains of battle. But as for the rest of you, you're a pack of fine frugal robbers to be sure, peddling timorously in cheap-jack thefts, sharking about baths, and snooping into the huts of old women.'

Here one of the second band interposed. 'So you're so badly educated that you don't know what everybody else knows: that the bigger the house, the easier the burglary. The point is that it's no matter how many servants there are in a large household; for every one of them in the panic thinks more of his own skin than his master's goods. But people who lead a solitary existence, watching every penny, fight to the bitter end and their last drop of blood to protect even a trifle; and if they've put a tidy sum together, they'll go to any pains to keep it safe. Just listen to this story and you'll agree with me.'

The Tale of the Robber

WE had scarcely entered the seven-gated city of Thebes before we instituted careful inquiries into the status of various citizens: the first step of an efficient robber. Thus we learned of one Chryseros, a banker, who had large funds at his disposal, but who went to any extreme to conceal the extent of his riches through fear of being called on to undertake some civic offices as income tax. He lived alone in a lonely spot, satisfied with a small but heavily fortified house, roosting ragged and dirty above his golden eggs.

We consequently decided to make our first inroad upon this miser; for in our contempt of a single brace of fists we relied casually on finding the crib easy to crack. So we lost no time. By dusk we were prowling round his door, which we thought it best not to unhinge or force open, let alone smash down, lest the screech of the panels should rouse the neighbourhood and ruin us. Then that indomitable captain of ours, Lamachus, trusting in his own world-famous hardihood, softly pushed his hand through the hole used for inserting the key, and tried to shoot the bolt.

93

But Chryseros, that lowest of two-legged hounds, was on the watch, aware of all that was preparing. With a light step and not a breath of noise, he stole up and suddenly with one violent swipe hammered a big nail through our leader's hand, pinning him to the door panel. Then leaving him nailed there like a poor wretch on the cross, Chryseros scurried aloft to the roof of his hovel and began shouting in a stentorian voice, summoning the neighbours, urging each one by name, and howling that the cause was theirs as well as his since his house had burst into flame. So everybody whose property was in the danger-zone ran out to help, flurried with the scare.

We were in a damned dilemma. We must either be mobbed or desert a comrade. Thus, with Lamachus's consent, we had recourse to a desperate solution, the only one that we could propound. For we cut off our organizer's arm near the shoulder-joint. With a single blow we clove clean through the bone and gristle; and abandoning the arm we halted and bound up the wound with strips of cloth so that we shouldn't be betrayed by the blood-trail. Then we carried off what was left of Lamachus at our best speed.

The increasing outcry drove us on; and between our fear for our beloved captain and the dread of some sudden onslaught we lost our nerve and ran. But Lamachus found it as deadly to hasten as to stand and wait. So that glorious hero, with his unquenchable spirit, gave a long speech imploring us again and again by the sword-hand of Mars and the truth of our Oaths to rescue a good comrade from crucifixion and captivity at a stroke.

'For how,' said he, 'can a conscientious robber survive the loss of his right-hand that did all the robbing and throat-slitting? He'd be happy to ask for a confederate hand to ease him of life. '

And when he couldn't with all his eloquence persuade any of us to such an abominable deed, he drew his sword with his left-hand; and after kissing the blade repeatedly he thrust it with determined force deep into his breast. In honour of our noble captain's courage we wrapped the maimed corpse in a linen vestment, and then committed it to the lair of the sea. And now our Lamachus lies with the whole ocean for his burial-shroud.

Thus he found an end worthy the heroism of his life; and

94

Alcimus as well, scrupulous plotter as he was, could not get away any better from the snares that Fate was weaving. He broke into the cottage of a snoring old woman, and climbed straight into the upper bedroom. Most negligently he omitted the duty of strangling the hag, and went on instead with dropping down her belongings, one by one, out of the above-window, so that we could make off with them.

When he had busily stripped the room of everything else, he grudged the old girl even the mattress on which she snoozed. So he rolled her out of it, and was jerking at the coverlet to throw it out as well, when the wicked old thing fell on her knees before him.

'Why in heaven's name, my son,' she cried, 'are you giving away the poverty-stricken rickety furniture of a miserable old woman to her rich neighbours that this window over-looks?'

Alcimus hearkened to her crafty remark and thought that she was speaking the truth. Afraid that the objects which he had thrown out or was in the act of throwing might fall, not into his friends' hands, but through some mistake into another person's backyard, he leaned out of the window. For he safely meant to take a good look round the premises and to cast a business-eye over the allegedly rich next-door house.

As he stretched out with more zeal than prudence, the aged piece of wickedness came up behind him; and choosing the moment when he was most off his balance, straining for-ward for a good view, she gave him a push. It was a slight push, but sudden and unexpected, and it toppled him out head-first.

He fell a great distance, and he fell on a very large stone that happened to lie below. So he splintered and tore the cage of his ribs; he spewed out rivulets of blood; and after gurgling up his story he departed this life on which he was crucified. We buried him like his leader, and sent him in the wake of Lamachus, a worthy follower.

Bereaved thus of two of our right-hand men, we dropped all our Theban projects and moved on to the next city, Plataea. There we found everyone chattering about a certain Demochares who was sponsoring a Gladiator-Show. For, being a man with the highest connexions and cele-

95

brated for his wealth and liberality, he furnished amusements for the populace as splendidly as accorded with his position. Who so talented as to possess the fund of eloquence needed to recapitulate in adequate phrase the inexhaustible details of his profuse display?

There were gladiators (the very best names); hunters well known for their agility; and criminals who had forfeited all claim on society and who were being fattened to feast the wild beasts. There were stages built up with stakes, towers of joisted beams like movable houses frescoed richly on the outside, luxurious receptacles for the animals destined to be slain. And as for the animals, they were all kinds imaginable; for he had taken no end of trouble in importing from abroad the noble creatures whose bellies were to sepulchre the condemned men.

But apart from all the other ruinous items he had concentrated the resources of his estate on collecting a bevy of enormous bears. Besides those snared by his own huntsmen and those bought at heavy expense, others had been donated by his zealous friends; and the whole set were being reared with unstinted care and cost. These blazoned and magnificent preparations for the pleasures of the public did not, however, evade the evil eye of Fate. For the bears, pining away in their protracted captivity, weakened by the broiling summer heat, and deteriorating in their narrowed quarters, were afflicted by a sudden plague; and their numbers dwindled considerably.

Everywhere in the streets you could see the hulks of expiring bears strewn about like wrecked ships; and as a result of this the dirty mob (forced by rude poverty and pinched bellies to gulp down any offal that came their way as long as it cost nothing) stole out and served themselves with fresh steaks.

Considering this state of things, Babulus and I had a clever idea. We carried one of these bears, the brawniest we could find, into our lodgings as if we meant to cook it. There we stripped the hide from the flesh, taking particular care to keep the claws in place, and leaving the head of the beast attached entire to the neck. We then patiently scraped the hide, sprinkled it all over with sifted ashes, and spread it to dry in the sun. And while the sun of heaven was sucking out the oils, we stuffed ourselves mightily with the sub-

96

stantial meat and made those of the band who were with us take the following oath: That one of our number who was accounted the stoutest in body and mind, and who voluntarily offered himself, should be sewn up in the skin and pretend to be a bear and that after he had been conducted back to Demochares' house, he should slip out when everything seemed opportunely quiet at night, and make it easy for us to win entrance.

The plan was so astute that several of our valiant society were encouraged to volunteer. But Thrasyleon was elected by general agreement as most suited for carrying out the risky enterprise. Therefore, as the pelt had now become pliable and tender, he drew it about himself with a serene smile; and we fitted the edges together with close stitches, and took the further precaution of concealing the seams beneath the shaggy masses of hair. Thrasyleon's head we thrust into the hollow behind the jaws where the beast's gullet had been excavated, while we left small punctures about the nostrils and eyes as breathing-holes. Lastly, we shut our dauntless comrade (now a wild beast) in a cage which we bought fairly cheap and into which he nimbly lurched without a second's hesitation.

The preliminaries thus concluded, we set about putting the masquerade into action. We ferreted out that there was a certain Nicanor, a Thracian by birth, who cultivated the friendship of Demochares; and we forged a letter in which Nicanor was supposed to declare that like a good friend he was seizing this graceful opportunity of dispatching the first-fruits of his hunting. And then, as dusk was deepening, we presented to Demochares under cover of the friendly darkness the forged letter and the cage that held Thrasyleon.

Demochares admired the dimensions of our bear and expressed his obligation for this timely gift from his dear friend. He then ordered ten goldpieces to be counted out from his coffers to remunerate the men who brought so welcome an object.

Meanwhile, with the usual excitement that any novelty or queer sight provokes in the minds of men, a gaping crowd jostled around the cage; but our Thrasyleon prevented any ill-effects from their prying curiosity by making wild rushes at the bars from time to time. Everyone agreed in pronouncing Demochares a fortunate and favoured man, since after such losses in his menagerie he had discovered some way or other of re-stocking and beating his bad luck; and Demochares gave instructions for the brute to be removed at once to the outhouses with the utmost care.

Here I spoke up. 'Oh master,' I cried, 'have a heart. Would you put this animal, baked with the sun and wearied with the jolting on the road, out there among all the other bears – and they, so I hear, not properly recovered? Wouldn't it be better to leave him in some open space near your house, where the breeze can reach him? Beside a cooling lake, if you've got one? Don't you know that this type of animal always couches under the shadow of trees, or in dewy nooks, or near to refreshing spring water?'

Demochares was perturbed at my advice when he recalled how many bears he had lost; so there was no difficulty in obtaining his permission to deposit the cage wherever we thought best.

'What's more,' said I, 'here we are, ready to keep a look-out all night on the cage and to give the beast his food and drink, sharp to the right moment. For a tired beast he is, what with the heat and the worry of the journey.'

'We have no need of your attendance on that score,' replied Demochares. 'The whole household is now well broken-in as far as feeding bears is concerned.'

So there was nothing for it but to say good-bye. Passing out of the city gate we sighted a monument some distance from the road in an out-of-the-way recess. There we forced open the lids of some coffins, which were already loose with decay and age, and which now held nothing of their tenants but a little ash and dust. These we were reserving as lockers for the expected plunder.

Then lingering (as our profession enjoins) for that hour of moonless night when the human soul sinks most heavily under the clogging rush of early slumber, armed with swords we drew up our ranks before Demochares' gates, in redemption of our pledge to sack the house. Thrasyleon seized the same robbers' moment of darkness to creep stealthily out; and he stabbed every one of the guards that lay asleep beside the cage. Then he cut the porter's throat; and taking out the key he opened the folding-doors. We bustled in, and he showed us the way to the strongroom in the bowels of the house, where during the evening he had shrewdly noted them bestowing a great pile of silver plate.

The combined weight of our shoulders soon burst the door down; and I told each man of the storming-party to cumber himself with as much gold and silver as his back accepted, to deposit it in the trusteeship of the dead (who alone never default), and then to scamper back for more. Meanwhile I, for the common good, would stay on my own at the threshold and keep a studious watch till their return. The spectacle of the bear padding about the corridors of the house was calculated to scare back any of the domestics who chanced to be roused. For what man, however brave and high-spirited, would not be startled into flight by the apparition of such a huge beast, particularly in the dead of night? Who would not ram home the bolts and remain shut in his room, sweating with terror?

But all these well-laid plans were sent awry by an unfortunate accident. While I was anxiously awaiting the return of our friends, one of the servant lads was disturbed by the pad-pad, as the gods would have it. He crept quietly out and saw the bear running loose and wandering all over the house.

Preserving a steadfast silence, the boy retraced his steps and reported to the others what he had seen. No time was lost, the whole household streamed out, filling the house. Torches, lanterns, wax-tapers, tallow-candles, and all the other gadgets for giving light, routed the darkness. And not a single man there but swung some weapon or other – club, spear, naked sword – and with these they blocked up the entries. Then they shouted-on some hunting-dogs, long-eared and shag-coated, to get the wild beast at bay.

As the tumult continued to swell, I came out of the house as quickly and obscurely as I could; and planting myself behind the gate, I beheld Thrasyleon putting up a marvellous fight against the dogs. For now that he had death clear in sight, never for a moment forgetting himself and our tradition and the call of glory – he refused to surrender – even there in the jaws of hell's dogs. In fact, he kept up a grim mime in the role that he'd adopted. Now retreating, now pouncing forwards, he swerved and twisted so fiercely that at last he broke through the lines.

But though he got free as far as the public road, he could

not escape with his life. All the mongrels from the neighbouring alley (and a savage swarming flock they were) joined forces with the hunting-dogs which had come bounding out of the house in pursuit. A shocking and tragic sight it was that I then saw: our Thrasyleon surrounded and over-run by a howling mob of dogs, and striped all over with their fang-marks.

This horrible scene was too much to bear. I mingled with the rabble that gathered around and choosing the only possible way of covertly assisting my brave comrade, I tried to divert the leaders of this chase.

'What a great shame,' I cried, 'what a foolish act, to destroy such a fine specimen! What a waste of money!'

But no words that I could devise were of any avail to the ill-starred chap. A tall man came charging fearlessly out of the house, and drove a spear straight into the guts of the bear. Another did the same; and then several of them, throwing off their fears, came up to close quarters and vied in stabbing him. As for Thrasyleon the honour and flower of our brotherhood, though his spirit that deserved never to die was finally sent flying, yet he stuck to his game. Not a human cry, not a word of pain, did he utter to break his oath. Mangled with the bites, gored with the steel, he acted his suffering part without one break in his courage; and every noise he made was a growl or a wild beast's bellow.

And so profound was the impression of terror and doubt that he left on the crowd, not one of them all dared to put even a finger on the beast that lay dead – not till broad daylight, when a butcher, a trifle more courageous than the rest, approached shyly and cautiously; and cutting open the belly he stripped the mighty robber of his bearskin.

Thus we lost Thrasyleon; and Thrasyleon gained a niche in the annals of fame.

We ourselves hastily redeemed our booty from the safe-deposit of the incorruptible dead, and proceeded at tiptop speed to evacuate the Plataean territory. And as we went we could not help repeating to ourselves that it's no wonder you can't find fidelity anywhere among the living since in revulsion from our dirty tricks it has now emigrated to the shades of death. So what between the swag we carried and the rough roads we travelled, we arrived home with three of our comrades reported as gone. The stuff that we requisitioned you see for yourselves.

. . . . .

At the conclusion of this narrative they all made libation of pure wine in golden cups to the memory of the deceased comrades; and then, after having sung some hymns that flattered god Mars, they rested awhile. Meanwhile the old woman poured us out some fresh barley in such lavish measure that my horse, champing amid this unchallenged plenty, must have thought that he was at a Priests' Supper.[1]

But although I had constantly dined on barley, I was used to having it finely ground and carefully boiled in broth. So, poking round, I nosed out the corner in which the hunks of bread left by the whole band were thrown together. There I gave my jaws some steady practice, aching as they were from a day-long fast and dry with cobwebs of disuse.

When the night was advanced, up jumped the robbers broad-awake, struck camp, and variously weaponed (some taking swords, others disguising themselves as ghosts) sallied out intent on business. But no drowsiness however leaden could stop me from masticating away with unslackened energy; and whereas before, when I was Lucius, I could leave the dinner-table satisfied with a loaf or two, yet now my belly was so bottomless that I had almost chewed through three basketfuls, and daylight had dropped in on me, and I was still frantically at work. At length, bridled by an asinine shamefacedness, I quitted my food with the utmost reluctance and ambled off to drink from a nearby streamlet.

A few moments later the robbers came straggling home, disconcerted and anxious, with no plunder of any kind – not even a raggletaggle cloak. All the force of their swords, all the knavery of their fingers, and all the derring-do of their confederacy, had caught nothing except a lonely girl – a lady by her figure and the cut of her dress – belonging

[1] 'Priests' Supper': The Salii (priests of Mars at Rome) were noted for their good living. See later phrases in the book.

to one of the best families roundabout – by God, a girl not beyond the love of an ass (such an ass as I was, anyway) as they bore her into the cave lamenting and tearing out patches of her hair and her clothes.

They stood her up and addressed her in words intended to comfort, 'Now my girl, you're perfectly safe. Nobody'll touch you. Have patience, and consider yourself as nothing but a valuable investment; for we've only taken to this game through being hard-up. There's not a doubt your parents will ransom you, miserly as they are, since it's only a flea-bite out of their money-bags that we're asking in return for their own flesh and blood.'

With suchlike blarney they tried to soothe the grieving girl in vain. What did they expect? She wept, and would not cease weeping, her head bent between her knees. So they summoned the old woman, and gave her instructions to sit at the prisoner's side and distract her with agreeable chat, while they themselves departed on their daily trails.

But no gossip that the old trot wheezed out could divert the wench from her continuous tears. Indeed, the latter merely moaned louder; and such a succession of sobs heaved up her sides that even I could not refrain from weeping.

'Oh to think of it,' she cried, 'here am I, ravished from such a house and home, such kind servants, such respectable parents; here am I, now nothing but a plaything, a piece of stolen property, shut up like a slave in a stone cell, deprived of every little comfort to which I was born and bred, at the mercy of such a mob of robbers and horrid prize-fighters! How can I leave weeping? How can I manage to keep living at all?'

Thus she moaned until worn out by her anguish of mind, throat-strain, and exhaustion of nerves, she let slumber close her glazed eyes. But she had not dozed for more than a few minutes when suddenly she started out of her sleep in a fit of dementia. She began to inflict far more grievous damage on herself, beating her breasts with fists of madness and pummelling her lovely face.

The old woman hobbled up and made some scared inquiries into the cause of this fresh outburst. With a deep groan the girl replied, 'Now I'm ended, now I'm ruined, now I give up every scrap of hope. There's nothing for it but a sword, or a halter, or a precipice. Nothing.'

The old woman began to chafe at this; and with a nasty scowl she told the girl to speak out and say what was ailing her, and why after going quietly to sleep she was scratching the same old sore of lamentations.

'I suppose,' she said, 'you've hatched some plan to do my young fellows out of their hard-earned ransom-money. Well, get on with your tricks. I don't give a damn for your tears. Tears are nothing in a robber's busy life. So stop, or I'll have you burned alive-O.'

Dismayed by this threat, the girl kissed the old woman's hand. 'Please don't, my dear mother,' she begged. 'Have enough of the milk of humanity to bear awhile with my wretched lot. I'm sure that there's a sense of pity still warm in you. You've seen so much of life, you've grown grey and holy. Listen to the tale of my misfortunes.

'There was a fine-looking young man, sprung from one of the most distinguished families; and everybody in the town felt personally interested in his career. He was my first cousin, only three years my elder, and we'd been reared together from babes. We grew up inseparable, sharing the same roof, and more the same room, the same bed. Betrothed we were by every pledge that mutual affection can devise. Our vows were exchanged; all nuptial preludes were completed; our parents had agreed; the marriage was registered. The young man, attended by a crowd of relatives and acquaintances, was offering up victims in the temples and public sanctuaries. The whole house was wreathed with bay, glowing with torches, echoing with hymeneal songs. My poor mother, supporting me on her bosom, was helping me on with my charming wedding-dress and stopping every moment to press upon me the honey of her kisses as she whispered heartfelt prayers for the fruitfulness of my womb.

'All of a sudden there clattered upon me a whole horde of robbers like gladiators in the ring, jumping about like a battle and flashing their naked furious swords about. They made no effort to stab people or snatch things. Instead, they lunged towards our bedroom in a thick column. In they came. Not a servant resisted them or put up even a bodkin in our defence. And me half dead with horror, me swooning with fear, they tore from the breasts of my mother. So our marriage was broken-up and spoiled,

103

like the marriage of the daughter of Attis[1] or that of Protesilaus.

'And now I've had a most gruesome dream that's brought all my misery back, that's made it a hundred times worse. For I saw myself dragged violently out of the house, out of the marriage-suite, out of the bedroom, out of the very bed – out into the trackless deserts where I called on the name of my luckless husband. And he, as soon as he found himself widowed of my embraces, came following me, still dripping with unguents – following me as I fled on feet not my own.

'And while he was crying out distractedly that his beautiful wife was stolen, and clamouring for people to help him, one of the robbers was so enraged at this persistent pursuit that he snatched a stone lying at his feet, and threw it at my poor young husband and killed him. It was this ghastly sight that terrified me awake out of my dreadful dream.'

The old woman echoed back the girl's sighs. 'Cheer up, my young lady,' she said. 'Don't get the wind up because of the meaningless skurry of a dream. For besides that the images of a daydream are said to be mere phantasy, you often find that the visions of the nights go by contraries in what they express. For instance, weeping or being beaten or (sometimes) having your throat slit means that you're coming into money or meeting with a windfall – while on the other hand laughter and a good bellyful of honey-cakes, or finding yourself a bride all of a lovely sudden, portends that you're going to be sad of heart or sick of body or afflicted in some way or other. But I'll do my best to take your mind off your troubles with some pretty fablings and old-wives' tales.'

With that she began her story.

---

[1] 'Attis': Hippodameia was Attis' daughter; at her marriage with Pirithous occurred the quarrel of the Centaurs and Lapithae. The reference to Protesilaus is vague. He was separated from his loving wife Laodameia shortly after their marriage and died at Troy.

The Tale of the Old Woman

ONCE upon a time there lived in a certain city a king and queen, and they had three daughters remarkably beautiful. But though the two elder girls were as comely as you could wish, yet it didn't strike you dumb with despair to have a look at them – while as for the youngest girl, all man's praising words were too poor to touch (let alone becomingly adorn) a beauty so glorious, so victorious.

Citizens in crowds, and droves of pilgrims, were attracted by the fame of the extraordinary spectacle. They pressed about her, and stood moonstruck with wonder at her unapproachable loveliness. They raised their right hands to their lips, laying thumb and forefinger together and throwing her a kiss of reverence as though it were the goddess Venus herself that they adored. Already the word had gone abroad through the nearby cities and bordering countries that a goddess had been brought forth by the deep-blue womb of ocean, and nourished by the froth of the curling waves; and that she now dwelt among mortals, allowing them to gaze promiscuously on her divinity – or that, at the very least, Venus had had a Second Birth (this time from earth, not water): a Venus endowed with the flower of virginity, and germinated from a distillation of the stars.

Every day the tale drifted farther. Soon the neighbouring islands, most of the mainland, scores of provinces, were echoing with the news. Many were the hurrying men that made long journeys by land and over the deep seas, only to gaze upon this splendid product of the age. No one set sail for Paphos; no one set sail for Cnidos – no, not even for Cythera – to come into the presence of Venus. Her sacred rites were forgotten; her shrines were falling into ruin; her cushions were trampled on; her ceremonies were neglected; her images were ungarlanded; and the old ashes lay dirtying the desolate altar.

A young girl had supplanted her, and the divinity of the mighty goddess was worshipped in the shrine of a human face. In her morning walks the virgin was propitiated by the victims and food-offerings due to the missing Venus. When she strolled down the street, the people rushed out and presented her with votive tablets; or they strewed her way with flowers.

This intemperate attribution of divine rights and qualities to a mortal girl deeply incensed the actual Venus. Transported with indignation, and shaking her head in a towering rage, she uttered the following soliloquy:

'I the primal Mother of all living, I the elemental Source of energy, I the fostering Venus of the girdled earth – I am degraded to sharing my empire and honour with a mere wench. My name, engraved on the heavens, is defiled by the excrement of earth. I must forsooth be vaguely content with the remnants of another's worship and with the duties paid to a deputy. A girl that will one day die borrows the power of my name. It meant nothing then that shepherd Paris, whose good taste and integrity Love himself admitted, set me above the other great goddesses as the Queen of Beauty. But this giglot whoever she may be shall not smugly usurp my dignities. I shall take measures that she may soon be sorry for her charlatan charms.'

So anon she summoned her son, that winged lad, the naughty child who has been so spoilt that he despises all social restraint. Armed with flames and arrows he flits in the night from house to house. He severs the marriage-tie on all sides; and unchastised he perpetrates endless mischief; and he does everything save what he ought to do. This lad, prone enough to harm on his own lewd initiative, Venus whetted-on with her words. She brought him to the city of our tale and pointed out Psyche – for that was the name given to the girl. Moaning and incoherent with wrath, Venus related the story of her rival's beauty and insolence.

'I beseech you,' she said, 'by the tie of mother-love, by the sweet wounds of your arrowhead, by the honeyed warmth of your torch, provide your parent with her revenge, her full revenge. Exact heavy retribution for these contumelious charms. And, above everything else, do your best to give her the fate that I ordain. Let the virgin be gripped with most passionate love for the basest of mankind – one that Fortune has stripped of his rank and estate, and almost of his skin – one so vile that his wretchedness has no parallel anywhere.'

Thus she spoke. Whereupon with loose-lipped kisses she long and closely farewelled the lad, and then sought the margin of the tide-swept shore. She trod the spray-tips of the tossing waters with her rosy feet; and lo, the sea fell calm over all its glossy surface. At once, as if by pre-arranged signal, her marine retinue appeared. The daughters of Nereus rose, chanting in chorus, and with them Portunus[1] shaggy with his sea blue beard, Salacia[2] with her bosom full of fishes, dwarf Palaemon driving a dolphin-chaise, and troops of Tritons bounding out of every wave. One Triton gently wound his tuneful conch; another held a silken ombrelle to shade her from the sun's fierce heat; another floated ahead, holding a mirror up before his mistress's face; and others swam yoked to her car. This was the company attending Venus on her progress to the palace of Oceanus.

Meanwhile Psyche, for all her manifest beauty, reaped no benefit from her pre-eminence. She was gazed at by all, praised and mazed; but no man, king or prince or even commoner, raised any pretensions to her hand in marriage. They admired her as a sample of divinity, but only as men admire an exquisitely finished statue. Long before, the two elder sisters, whose ordinary beauty had made no noise among distant populations, had been wooed by kings of good standing; and now they were happily married. But Psyche, lonely lass, sat sad at home, mourning her forlorn fate, weak in body and sick at heart; and she hated the beauty that gave pleasure to all the world save herself.

Accordingly the sorrowing father of this ill-fated girl suspected the wrath of the gods; and dreading some visitation from heaven, he consulted the ancient oracle of the Milesian God.[3] With prayers and sacrifices he besought the powerful deity to bestow a marriage-bed and a husband on this slighted maid.

Apollo, though a Grecian and Ionic, yet (for love of the composer of this Milesian Tale) gave a Latin response which translates as follows:

> *King, stand the girl upon some mountain-top*
> *adorned in fullest mourning for the dead.*
> *No mortal husband, King, shall make her crop –*

[1] 'Portunus': Harbour-god, also called Palaemon.
[2] 'Salacia': Sea-goddess with name derived from *salum* the 'salt sea'.
[3] 'Milesian God': Apollo.

it is a raging serpent she must wed,
which, flying high, works universal Doom,
debilitating all with Flame and Sword.
Jove quails, the Gods all dread him – the Abhorred!
Streams quake before him, and the Stygian Gloom.

When the announcement of the holy oracle was delivered,
the king, formerly so pleased with life, dragged himself
sadly home and unfolded to his wife the injunctions of this
melancholy response. They all lamented, wept, groaned,
for several days. But at last arrived the dread hour when
the shocking oracle must be consummated. The procession
was formed for the fatal wedding of the unfortunate girl.
The torches burned dully, choked with ash and soot; and
the tunes of the marriage-flute were replaced by plaintive
Lydian melodies. The gay hymeneal-songs quavered away
into doleful howls; and the bride wiped her tears with the
nuptial veil itself.

The entire city turned out to show its mourning respect
for the afflicted family. A day of public lamentation was
at once sympathetically ordered. But the necessity of obeying the dictates of heaven demanded that the sad-faced
Psyche should be surrendered to her fate. The death-
marriage was sorrowfully solemnized; and the funeral of the
living bride moved on, attended by the whole populace.
Thus the weeping Psyche was present, not at her wedding,
but at her funeral; and while the anguished parents,
horrified unendurably, strove to delay the ghastly procession, the girl herself exhorted them to submit.

'Why rack your old and harrowed limbs for ever on a
cross of misery?' she cried. 'Why waste your breath, dearer
to me than my own, in this endless moaning? Why do you
disfigure with ineffectual tears those faces that I honour
so truly? Why do you destroy the light of my life in those
sad eyes of yours? Why do you tear your grey hair? Why
do you beat your breasts, hallowed with the milk of love?
Are these torments to be the glorious guerdon that you
win through my surpassing beauty?

'Too late you realize that the deadly shaft of envy has
cruelly smitten you. When the tribes and the nations were
hymning me with divine honours, when all their voices
chimed in titling me the second Venus, that was the hour

for grief and tears, that was the hour when you should have given me up for lost. Now I feel, now I realize, that Venus is my murderess, and none other. Lead forward, and stand me up on the rock to which the response devoted me. Why should I lag? Why should I shrink aside from the coming of Him that has been born to destroy the world?'

The virgin said no more. She took her place in the flocking procession and strode onwards resolutely. At length they arrived at the appointed crag on a precipitate mountain-top; and there they deposited the girl and left her. The nuptial torches, with which they had lighted their way, now spluttered out in the tears of the onlookers, and were dropped. With heads drooping, the procession turned back. As for the poor parents, demoralized by their loss, they barred themselves up in their darkened palace and abandoned their lives to an everlasting gloom.

But as Psyche lay trembling apprehensively and weeping on the top-shelf of the crag, a gentle breath of fondling Zephyrus fluttered and tweaked her dresses, and puffed them up. Gradually raised on the palm of a tranquil wind, she was smoothly wafted down the steep and rocky slope, and laid softly on the lap of the valley, on flower-sprinkled turf.

BOOK THE FIFTH

PSYCHE, pleasantly reposing in a tender verdant nook on a couch of dewy grasses, felt all her agitated limbs relax; and she drifted into a sweet sleep, from which she awoke fully refreshed. Her mind was now at peace. She saw a grove composed of tall and thick-boughed trees. She saw a fountain flashing with waters like glass in the middlemost of the grove.

Near to the plashing foot of the fountain there stood a palace built not by human hands but by divine power. You had but to give one glance into the hall to know that you stood before the gorgeous pleasure-house of a god. The lofty ceilings, delicately fretted out of citronwood and ivory, were upheld by pillars of gold. The walls were completely crusted with silver modelling, while shapes of wild beasts and of other animals flanked the entrance. A marvellous man it was (a demigod, a very god at least) that deftly savaged silver to such forms.

The pavement itself was a mosaic of gems splintered and fitted together so as to weld their colours and to represent various objects. O madly happy, more than happy, must be that man who can trample on jewels and carcanets! All the other parts of this extensive mansion were equally splendid beyond estimation. The walls, inlaid with ingots of gold, lighted the rooms with their own warm glow, so that even if the sun withdrew the house would still exude illumination – so effulgent were the rooms, the porticoes, the doors. The furniture too was constructed on the same lordly scale; and the place might easily have been reckoned a castle of heavenly masonwork, used by Jove during his visits to mankind.

Invited by this delightful outlook, Psyche approached nearer; and timidly affecting courage, she crossed the threshold. The lovely vista lured her on; and she wandered through the premises, wondering at all she saw. Farther in, she found magnificent storerooms crammed with every luxury. No wish but found its fulfilment there.

But more wonderful even than these vast riches was the total absence of all closures, all bars, all janitors. The treasure of a world lay before her, unforbidden.

While she was gazing round in rapture, a bodiless voice addressed her. 'Why, lady,' it asked, 'do you stand astonished at this fine show? All that you see is yours. Hie therefore to the bedroom, and rest your wearied body on the couch; and when you so desire, arise and bathe yourself. We whose voices you hear are your handmaidens. It is our duty to obey all your wishes; and when we have attended to your bodily comforts, a banquet fit for a queen will be served.

Psyche felt herself happy and safe in these counsels of divine providence. She hearkened to the aerial Voices, and soothed away all her tiredness – first in sleep, and then in the bath. The moment this was done, she saw near by a half-moon dais with a raised seat and all the materials for a restorative meal. Joyously she seated herself.

Immediately cups of nectarous wine and relays of dishes garnished with every conceivable dainty were set before her by some spiritual agency; for not a servant appeared. And though she could see no human being, yet she heard people speaking around her; and these Voices were her only servants.

After she had sumptuously dined, One entered unseen and sang; and Another played on a lyre, and both lyre and lyrist were unseen. And then a rich harmony, like the sound of many interwoven Voices, was borne upon her ears; and though she could still see no human form, she seemed to stand in the midst of a mighty choir.

When these diversions were over, Psyche yielded to the suggestions of the dusk and retired to bed; and when the veils of night were drawn, an insinuating murmur floated into her ears. Then, afraid for her maidenhead in that lonely place, she quailed and was all the more shaken because she did not know what threatened.

But as she shuddered the anonymous bridegroom drew near, and climbed into bed, and made Psyche his bride, and departed hastily before sunrise. At once the waiting-voices entered the bedroom and solicitously tended the young bride with her ruptured virginity.

Thus her life went on, day after day; and habit brought its trails of pleasure, and the sound of the unknown Voices was the solace of her solitude. But meanwhile her parents were muddying the dregs of their existence with grief and lamentation; and the story, spreading far and wide, was carried at last to the ears of her elder sisters, who forthwith left their homes in mourning and hurried back to console their parents.

On the night of their arrival Psyche's husband remarked – for she could feel and hear him, she could do all but see him – 'Psyche, my precious, my darling wife, termagant Fortune has an ugly trick ready for you, which needs (I think) the shrewdest counterblast on our part. Your sisters, dismayed by the report of your death, are endeavouring to trace you. They will climb up yonder crag. If then you should chance to hear their outcry, make no answer, do not even look their way. If you act otherwise, you will bring on me a heavy misfortune and on yourself utter destruction.'

Psyche promised, assuring him that she would be an obedient wife. But when he and the night drained away together, the poor girl spent the whole next day in weeping and moaning, exclaiming that she was now hopelessly lost; for not only was she confined in a heavenly dungeon, deprived of all human intercourse, but she was not allowed to relieve the minds of her sorrowing sisters or even to look at them from a distance. Without indulging in food, bath, or any other amusement, but copiously weeping, she lay down to rest. A little later, her husband (appearing at her side somewhat earlier than usual) embraced her as she wept, and thus expostulated:

'O Psyche, my love, is this what you promised me? What am I your husband to expect of you now? What am I to hope for? Daylong and nightlong you grieve, and you lie within my embrace as on a cross of torment. So be it. Do as you desire, and follow the destructive bias of your whims. When repentance comes, you will remember my warning – too late.'

At this she begged and swore that she would kill herself, till she extorted from her husband the licence that she desired, to see her sisters, soothe their grief, and put her head together with theirs. At last the young beseeching bride gained her point, with a further concession: that she would give her sisters as much gold and jewels as she wished.

But one condition he emphasized so repeatedly as to scare her: never to let any guile of the sisters lure her into inquiries concerning her husband's identity – or by her sacrilegious curiosity she would cast herself down from her exalted height of Fortune and never again enjoy his embraces.

She thanked her husband gratefully. 'O no,' she said, restored to cheerfulness, 'I'd rather die a hundred times than lose your darling caresses. I love you, desperately love you, whoever you are. I cherish you like my own soul. I would not exchange you for Love himself. But all the same I think you ought to grant my prayer. Bid Zephyrus this coachman of yours to fetch my sisters down – as I was fetched.'

And she kissed him persuasively, and murmured endearments, and twined him with her arms and legs, and said in a wheedling whisper, 'O my honey, O my husband, O you sweetsweet soul of your Psyche.'

Unable to resist her coaxing compulsion, her husband felt his will reluctantly drown beneath her kisses. He promised that she should have all her wishes; and then at the first smudge of light he vanished from the arms of his wife.

The sisters had inquired the locality of the crag where Psyche had been left. They hurriedly climbed the slope; and standing on the rock they wept and beat their breasts till the boulders and scarps resounded with their inconsolable screams. They called on their hapless sister by name till the piercing echoes of their grief reached all the way down the valley. Psyche in her agitation ran wildly out of the palace.

'Hallo there!' she called back. 'Why are you making yourselves so miserable, and all for nothing? Here is the person you mourn. Cease this wailing. Dry those tears that have wetted your cheeks for so long. In a moment you can hold in your arms the sister that you're lamenting.'

Then she summoned Zephyrus and informed him of her husband's permission. Obeying her commands, in a jiffy he brought the sisters gliding unharmed down to Psyche upon the downiest blast. In a tangle of embraces, a flurry of kisses, the girls turned one to the other until the tears, sealed for a space, burst forth again – this time from excess of joy.

'Now come inside,' said Psyche. 'Come into our house and learn to smile again. You must cheer up with your Psyche now.'

With this prologue she showed them all the resources of her house of gold, and introduced them to the household of attendant Voices. She gave them a tiptop entertainment – first, all the luxuries of the bath; then, the spirit-served delicacies of her table – till, at length satiated by the inexhaustible supply of god-sent riches, the elder sisters began to nourish a jealous hatred in the depths of their hearts. One of them was particularly tireless in interrogating Psyche minutely as to who was the master of this divine residence, what kind of man he was, and how he shaped as a husband.

Psyche however managed to follow out her husband's instructions and let nothing slip to betray her secret. But making the best of the situation she told them that he was a young man, extremely handsome, with cheeks just shaded by the downiest of beardlets – and that most of his time was employed in country-sports and mountain-hunting. Then, to save herself from any contradictory phrases that would expose the truth, she loaded her sisters with gold and jewelled necklaces; and calling Zephyrus she bade him convey them back to the summit.

When these orders had been obeyed, the excellent sisters returned home, burning with a rancorous jealousy that swelled at every step. Soon they were chattering with mutual indignation. One said to the other:

'So now you see how daft and cruel and unjust is Fortune! Did it overjoy you to find that we sisters, though we have the same parentage, have very different lots? Here are we, the elders by birth, delivered as bondsmaids to foreign husbands, packed far away from homeland and parents, like exiles. That's our life. And here is the youngest daughter, the end-product of our mother's decrepit womb, owning all that wealth and a god for a husband – and she doesn't even know how to make a proper use of her good fortune. You saw, sister, what a mass of necklaces lie about the house, and what value they are – what glistening stuff, what sparkling gems, what parquets of gold, she treads carelessly underfoot. If in addition to this she has the fine-looking husband that she describes, then there is no woman happier in the whole world. Perhaps when he is in the clutch of long habit and the ties of their affection are strengthened, this god of a husband will make her a goddess too.

'By Hercules, that's what he's done. That's the explanation of her airs and graces. Think of her. Think of her condescending pride. The woman breathes the goddess already, she with her attendant Voices and her ladyship over the very winds. But I (poor nothing) am fettered to a husband older than my father, a man who's balder than a pumpkin and as passionate as a peascod, a man who (to make matters worse) locks and bars up the whole house, the suspicious fool!'

'And I,' answered the other, 'I have to lie down tamely under a husband who's tortured and twisted with gout, and who consequently cultivates my venus-plot very sparsely. I spend most of the time in chafing his crippled chalky fingers and scalding my dainty white hands with stinking fomentations, filthy napkins, and horrid poultices. My role is not wife but nurse-of-all-works. You, sister, seem to tolerate your position with quite a deal of patience – I might say, low-spiritedness – for I believe in saying what I think. For my part I won't endure for another moment the good fortune that has dropped into the lap of one who doesn't deserve it. Recollect also how overbearingly, how sneeringly she behaved towards us; and how her puffed-up attitude peeped out of every boast that she couldn't control as she showed us round; and how she bundled on us against her will a few oddments of her huge wealth; and how then, bored with our company, she gave orders for us to be swept-up and blurted and whizzed away. I'm not a woman, I can't squeeze out another breath, unless I bring down this fine erection of her fortunes; and if these insults rankle in you too, as they certainly ought, then let us concert some workable plan. First of all, let us agree not to show these things we're carrying to anyone––not even our parents. In short, we must not admit that we know she's alive and well. It is quite enough to have had the vexation of seeing what we have seen, without scattering abroad the news of her glory among the family and the whole city. For there's no glory when nobody knows how rich she is. We'll teach her that we're not her slaves but her elder sisters. So for the present let's return to our husbands and our poor mediocre houses; and then after thoroughly digesting the situation let's return equipped to lessen her pride.'

The two wicked sisters agreed on this wicked plan. They hid all the priceless gifts; they dishevelled their hair; they beat their faces (which deserved the blows); they redoubled their feigned lamentations. Then, having depressed their parents and reopened the sores of the old people's grief, they set off for their homes to finalize the schemes of harming (or rather murdering) their innocent sister.

Meanwhile Psyche's unknown husband once more warned her during his bedtime colloquies. 'Do you see what great danger threatens you? On the horizon Fortune launches the stormcloud. Unless you take the most active measures, it will soon be thundering upon you. These vicious wolf-bitches are straining every sinew to catch you in an impious snare. Their aim is to persuade you to look upon my face – which as I have admonished you, if you once see, you will never see again.

'If then these bloodsucking harlots return daggered with their venomous thoughts – for they will return, I know – hold no communication with them. If you find that beyond you through your natural candour and your gentle inexperience, at least hear no inquiries that they make about your husband, and answer nothing. For before long our family is to be increased; and you, child as you are, yet bear a child in your womb. If you keep your peace concerning our secret, that child will be divine. If you profane our secret, it will be mortal.'

Psyche glowed with happiness at the news. She abandoned herself to the comforting hope of divine offspring. She foretasted joyfully the glory of this future pledge and the dignity of a mother's name.

She counted the marching days, the lapsing months; and in her novitiate of gestation she wondered how her precious womb could swell so richly from so tiny a prickling. But those pestilent and repulsive Furies, breathing their viperous virulence and hurrying with damned zeal, set out once more; and once more Psyche was warned by her fleeting husband:

'The day of judgement comes, the awful danger. The malices of your sex, your own blood in hatred, have risen against you. Camp is struck; the battle-line is drawn up; the charge is sounded. Your wicked sisters have unsheathed the sword; the blade is at your throat. Alas my sweetheart Psyche, what agonies hem us in. Have mercy on yourself and on me; and by your inviolable silence save your home, your husband, yourself, and our baby from the dreadful ruin that menaces us. Refuse to see or hear these vile women who cannot claim the name of sister after this murderous hate, this severance of all the ties of blood. Leave them to stand like Sirens on that crag, making the rocks re-echo with their ominous voices.'

Psyche replied with hesitant tears and sobs, 'Already, I should have considered, I have provided you with clear proof that I was trustworthy and able to control my tongue; and you will be just as pleased at the firmness of mind that I'll show now. All you have to do is to tell Zephyrus to obey orders as before. You ought at least to let me see my sisters to compensate for not seeing your sacrosanct lineaments. By these aromatic tresses curling about your face, by these apple-cheeks tenderly like my own, by that breast pleasant with an indescribable warmth, by my hope of seeing your face at least mirrored in my unborn babe's! say yes to the loving prayers of your worried suppliant. Breathe into your devoted Psyche a new soul of joy. Never any more shall I beg to see your face. Henceforth the deep dark night will mean nothing to me. I clasp you, my only light.'

Beguiled by her words and her yielding embraces, the husband wiped away her tears with his own hair, and promised that she should have her wish. Then he vanished the moment light was born.

But the brace of sisters, sworn in conspiracy, did not even visit their parents. They went straight from shipboard to the crag, made with haste. They did not even dawdle for the arrival of the carrier-wind, but leaped into the valley-depth with uncontrollable foolhardiness. Zephyrus however was mindful of the royal command. He reluctantly received them on the bosom of his soughing blast and bore them to the ground. With quickening steps the pair restlessly dashed into the house; and hiding behind the name of sisters they embraced their quarry. Then, strewing a smile upon the pit of their hoarded guile, they flattered her.

'Psyche, you're not as slim as you used to be. Soon you'll be a mother. Oh, you can't think what a joy for us all you're carrying in your reticule. The whole house will simply be wild with delight. Oh, how happy we will be to amuse your golden baby. For if he only matches his parents in beauty – and so he must – then he'll be a pure love.'

Thus with a prattle that sounded like affection they won Psyche over. She at once made them seat themselves to recover from the fatigues of travel. She had them laved in warm flowing baths and entertained them at a choice repast where most-tasty dishes and concoctions marvellously came and went. She ordered the harp to twang, and it rippled sweetly – the flute to play, and its notes issued forth – the choir to sing, and they sang. The music ravished the souls of the hearers with its delicious cadences; but not a performer was to be seen.

But not all the honeyed song with its tempering sweetness mitigated one whit the wickedness of the scheming women. They guided the conversation towards the hidden snare and made deftly oblique inquiries as to the husband, what kind of a man he was, and where he was born, and what was his family.

Psyche in extreme artfulness forgot her former account and produced a fresh fiction. She said that her husband was a merchant from the adjoining province, a man of tremendous wealth, now middle-aged with a sprinkle of grey in his hair. Then again she abruptly changed the subject, loaded her sisters with presents, and sent them back on their wind-carriage. But while they were returning home, borne aloft on the tranquil breath of Zephyrus, they conferred as follows:

'What are we to say, sister, of the lurid lies of that idiot? One moment her husband is a young fellow that trims a beard of the softest down. The next moment he's a middle-aged man with hair showing silvery. Who can this be that in so brief a space suddenly becomes changed into an old man? There's only one explanation, my sister; and that is that this worthless woman is telling us a string of lies, or that she doesn't know herself what her husband looks like. But whichever supposition is true, she must as soon as possible have all these riches whipped away from her. And yet if she has never seen his face, it must be a god that she has married and a god that she is bearing us under her belt. If that's so, and if she does become the mother of a divine babe (which heaven forbid), I'll string myself up on the spot in a noose. Therefore let us go meanwhile to see our parents, and develop some scheme on the lines we have laid down in our discussion.'

Thus inflamed, the sisters made a disdainful call on their parents, and tossed feverishly awake all night. Then, desperate in the morning, they rushed back to the crag, and by the usual vehicle of wind descended in frenzy. They squeezed out some tears from under their lids, and guilefully said to Psyche:

'Here you sit smiling when it's only blissful ignorance that stops you from seeing the terrible danger you're in. But we, who watch over your affairs so vigorously, are nailed on a cross of painful apprehension. We have discovered for an absolute fact something that in true sympathy with all sorrow and misfortune we cannot keep to ourselves any longer. We've discovered that it's a monstrous, twining, twisted, coiling, venomous, swollen-throated, ravenously gaping-jawed Serpent that reposes with you secretly in the night. Don't you recall the Pythian Responses that announced you the destined bride of a bloodthirsty beast? Besides, many of the country-folk who go hunting in these regions, and scores of the neighbours, saw him gliding home in the evening from his pasturage and swimming across the shoals of the river hard by.

'Everybody is saying that he won't long keep on pampering you with enticing complaisances in the way of food. But as soon as your womb is fully rounded with pregnancy he will gobble you up as an appetizing morsel in a prime state. So it's up to you to decide whether you want to listen to us, your sisters, who are thinking only of your best advantages – whether you want to escape death and to come to live with us, safe from all attacks; or whether you want to be engulfed in the bowels of a cruel beast.

'But if you're so keen on your rural solitude full of nothing but Voices – so attached to the filthy and dangerous embraces of clandestine lust, and the caresses of a poisonous serpent – at least we have discharged our duty like loving sisters.'

Psyche (poor girl) so sincere herself and so tender-hearted was stiff with horror at this dreadful disclosure. Whirled out of all her senses, she took no heed of her husband's admonitions and of her own promises. She felt herself swept before an avalanche of anguish. Trembling, with all the blood shocked out of her face, she managed at last in a strangled voice to falter out a few words:

'O my dearest sisters, you're still as loving as ever. You've acted as you ought, as your sisterly duty dictated. I'm sure that all you've been told seems to me genuine. For I've never seen my husband's face, and I don't know where he comes from. I only hear him whispering at night. I have to accept a husband of unknown standing, a shape that flees the light. So I agree that you must have hit the truth. He is some monster. He spends his time in frightening me from looking at him, and in threatening me with some great evil for being curious about his face. So if you can bring a ray of hope to your poor misguided sister, don't lose a moment. For if you neglect that, you'll undo all the good which your care has done me so far.'

The wicked women, having thus won the approaches to their sister's defenceless heart, emerged from their ambushes and frankly assaulted the simple girl's panic-stricken meditations with the drawn sword of craft.

Accordingly the first answered. 'Since the bond of blood obliges us to consider no personal danger when your life is at stake, we will show you the only road which leads to safety. This plan is the result of our long, long thought. On the side of the bed where you usually lie, hide a very sharp razor, whetted on the palm of your hand to the finest edge. And hide a lamp, trimmed and full of oil, a lamp that burns with a steady flame, behind some of the bedroom-hangings. Make all these arrangements with the utmost precaution. When the Thing has slid into the chamber and climbed up on the bed, wait until he's stretched out and begun to breathe heavily inside the coils of sleep. Then slip out of the sheets and tiptoe on bare feet slowly along the floor.

Rescue the lamp from its shroud, and by the light's direction find the moment for this glorious deed. Boldly lift up your right-hand. Slash the blade down with all your strength, and sever the head of the baneful Serpent at the nape of the neck. And don't think we'll be far. We shall be anxiously standing-by for the signal that your safety is secured. Then together we'll remove all this property; and and we'll soon see you married to a human being like yourself.'

With all these arguments they poured flame into the vitals of their sister; and when they saw that she was fully kindled, they at once abandoned her. Afraid to be caught within the area of the approaching crisis, they were carried to the crag by the usual sudden blast; and hastening with brisk terror to the quay, they sailed away.

But Psyche, left alone (if a girl tormented by wild Furies can be considered alone), flooded and ebbed with sorrows like a stormy sea. She began to prepare for the ugly deed with assured intention and obdurate heart; but almost immediately she hesitated irresolute, distracted with wavering impulses and decisions. She hurried, then lagged. She was bold, then timid. She was doubtful, then furious. And (strangest of all) in the same person she hated the beast but loved the bridegroom. Yet as evening drew on the night, she made a last demented effort and prepared the scene for her wicked deed.

Night came; and her husband came; and after some amorous skirmishes he fell into a heavy sleep. Then drooping in body and mind, yet fed with unusual strength by the cruelty of fate, she brought forth the lamp and seized the knife, boldly shedding her sex.

But as soon as she raised the lamp and unbared the mystery of her bed, she saw the sweetest and gentlest of all wild creatures: Cupid himself, a beautiful god beautifully lying on the couch. At sight of him the flame burned cheerfully higher, and the razor dulled its sacrilegious edge.

But as for Psyche, she was terrified at the sight. She lost all self-control; and swooning, pallid, trembling, she dropped on her knees and sought to hide the knife – deep in her own bosom. And so she would have done, had it not been that the blade, shrinking from such an atrocity, fell to the floor out of her heedless hands.

And then, for all her faintness and fear, she felt her flagging spirits revive as she gazed at the beauty of the god's face. She saw the gay lovelocks of his golden head, drenched with ambrosia – the curls gracefully drifting over his milky breast and ruddied cheeks, some in front and some behind – while the very lamp-flame guttered before the flashing splendour.

On the shoulders of the flying god there bloomed dewy plumes of gleaming whiteness; and though the wings themselves were laid at rest, yet the tender down that fringed the feathers frisked in a continuous running flutter. The rest of his body was so smoothly warmly rounded that Venus could look on it and feel no pang at having borne such a child. At the foot of the couch lay his bow, his quiver, and his arrows: the gracious weapons of the mighty god.

While Psyche stood spellbound with insatiable delight and worship, impelled by wonder she began to handle her husband's weapons. She drew one of the arrows out of the quiver and tested its sharpness, on the tip of her thumb. But pressing unduly hard (for her hand still trembled) she pricked the skin and evoked some tiny drops of rose-red blood. Then, burning more and more with desire for Cupid, she laid herself broadly upon him; and opening her mouth with forward kisses she applied herself eagerly to the embrace, fearing only that he would wake too soon.

But while she stirred above him in the extremity of agonized joy, the lamp (actuated either by treachery, or by base envy, or by a desire to touch so lovely a body – to kiss it in a lamp's way) spewed a drop of glowing oil from the point of its flame upon the god's right shoulder.

O bold and reckless lamp! base officer of love! to burn the very god of Flame – you that some lover, inspired by the need to possess the beloved even at night, first devised.

The god, thus burnt, leaped out of bed; and spying the scattered evidences of Psyche's forfeited truth, he made to fly mutely out of the clasp of his unfortunate wife. But Psyche, as he rose into the air, caught hold of his right leg with both hands and clung there, a wailing drag upon his upward flight. Into the cloudy zones they soared, until her muscles gave way and she dropped to the earth.

The god her lover did not desert her as she lay upon the

ground. He alighted upon a nearby cypress and gravely admonished her from its swaying top:

'O simple-hearted Psyche! Putting aside the commands of my mother Venus who had bidden me infatuate you with some base wretch and degrade you to his bed, I chose rather to fly to you myself as a lover. I acted rashly, well I know. I the world-famous archer stabbed myself with my own arrowhead. I took you for my wife – only to have you think me a wild bear and raise the blade to sever my head . . . which bears those very eyes that loved you so fondly.

'This it was I bade you always to beware. This it was against which my loving-heart forewarned you. But as for those fine advisers of yours, they shall pay heavily for their pernicious interference. My flight is penalty enough for you.'

As he ended, he spread his wings and soared out of sight. But Psyche lay prostrate on the ground and strained her eyes after her winging, vanishing husband, harassing her mind with most piteous outcries; and when his wings with sweeping strokes had rapt him out of her life into the vast distance, she crawled to a nearby river and threw herself from the bank into the waters. But the gentle stream, in horror and in reverent fear of the god who can heat even the dank water-deeps, took Psyche on the soft curl of a wave and laid her safe on the thick green turf of the bank

It chanced that at this moment Pan the country-god was seated on the river-lip, embracing Echo, goddess of the mountainside. He was teaching her to sing all kinds of tunes. Near by, she-goats gambolled along the winding pasture of the banks, cropping the weedy tresses of the river. The goatfoot god, aware of Psyche's sad fate, compassionately called the sick and stricken girl to his side, and comforted her with friendly words:

'Pretty maiden, I am a country-fellow, a shepherd, but my mind is stored with much odd knowledge as the result of long experience. If I may hazard a guess (which among wise men goes by the title of a divination) I judge by these halting and stumbling steps, and by the extreme paleness of your face, and by the incessant sighs you heave, and by the sad look in your eyes, that you are madly in love.

'Hearken then to me. Seek no longer to lose your life by

dashing yourself to pieces or by any other such recourse of despair. Lay grief aside. Cease your sorrow. Woo Cupid with adoring prayers. For he is the mightiest of the gods, a wanton lad and spoilt. Press him with grateful offers of compliance.'

Thus spoke the shepherd-god; and Psyche, making no reply beyond an obeisance to his divinity, wandered on. And when she had dragged herself a little farther, she came at the dusk of day by some unmapped by-path to the gates of the very city over which the husband of one of her sisters was king. Discovering this, Psyche asked that her sister should be informed who had arrived. She was then quickly ushered in; and after an exchange of embraces and compliments, the sister inquired the causes of her visit. Psyche answered:

'I suppose you remember the advice you gave when you persuaded me that it was a beast lying with me under pretence of marriage, and that I ought to kill him with a sharp blade before he gulped poor me down into his greedy maw. Well, I followed out your suggestions until I got as far as holding up the lamp over his face to assist me. But what I saw was the most wonderful heavenly sight: the very son of goddess Venus, Cupid himself, I tell you, stretched in quiet sleep. I was wonderstruck before such a happiness and distraught with my excess of joy; and while I stood there not knowing what to do in my glory, by my cruel bad-luck a burning drop of oil spirited out of the lamp on to his shoulder. He was startled out of his sleep by the pain and opened his eyes to find me armed with flame and steel.

' "In punishment for your shocking conduct," he said, "get out of my bed immediately. Take away all your belongings, and I'll marry your sister instead" – and then he mentioned you by name. "I'll marry her straightway with full marriage-ceremony."

'And then he told Zephyrus to puff me away, past the precincts of the palace.'

No sooner had Psyche finished speaking than the other, pricked-on by ravening rash lust and rankling jealousy, rushed out to tell her husband a story fabricated on the spur of the moment – something about a rumour of her parent's death – and then taking ship she proceeded with all speed to the crag as of old.

Although the wind was blowing from the wrong quarter, yet in her flustering hopes she screamed. 'Receive me, Cupid, a wife that's worthy of you. And you, Zephyrus, buoy up your mistress.'

Then she leaped out into the air, and fell headlong; and not even as a corpse was she able to find the landing that she desired – for her limbs were torn to pieces by the jutting rocks, and strewn down the face of the cliff, as she deserved; and her entrails provided nourishment for the birds and beasts that laired in the cliff; and thus she perished.

Nor was the punishment of the other sister long in fulfilment. For Psyche's wandering trail led her to another city, where that other sister dwelt. Psyche gave her the same misunderstanding; and the woman, lured by the hope of supplanting her sister, dashed off to the crag and fell into the same death.

Meanwhile Psyche travelled through many peoples, resolute in quest of Cupid; and Cupid, wounded by the lampspilth, lay moaning in his mother's bedroom. Then a white seagull, the bird that skims across the waves of the sea with its wings, dived down into the bosom of the waters. There, accosting Venus as she washed and swam, the bird informed her that her son was confined to bed, complaining of a severe burn; that his cure was doubted; and that gossip and insult of all kinds were being bandied about among mankind, involving the reputation of the whole Venus-family. 'The lad has been whoring in the mountains,' people were saying, 'while Venus has given herself up to aquatic sports – and in consequence there is no Joy, no Grace, no Elegance anywhere nothing but the Rude, the Rustic, and the Uncouth – no Marriage-bond, no Social Intercourse, no Love of Children; nothing but an utter Lack of Order, and an unpleasant Horror of anything so low as Nuptials.'

Thus did the meddlesome chatterbox of a bird whisper into the ear of Venus, tearing Cupid's reputation to tatters. And Venus in a pet instantly exclaimed:

'So this fine son of mine has already set up a mistress, has he! Come now, you're the only true loving servant I have, what is the name of the wench that seduced my ingenuous-hearted son who's not yet in man's clothes? Is she one of the tribe of Nymphs, or of the company of the Hours, or of the choir of the Muses, or of my own train of Graces?'

The garrulous bird needed no second bidding. 'I don't know, mistress,' he said, 'I'm not sure. I think the girl that he's so badly smitten with, is named . . . let me see . . . if my memory doesn't deceive me, her name's Psyche.'

'Psyche!' Venus cried in a fury of indignation. 'Surely he hasn't picked out Psyche, the pretender to my throne of beauty, the rival of my renown! And, insult added to injury, he has taken me as a bawd, for it was my finger that pointed the way to the trollop.'

With this complaint she rose up out of the sea, and hurried to her Golden Chamber, where she found her sick son, just as she had been told. Before she was through the door, she began yelling at him. 'Fine goings-on! so perfectly in accord with our position in the scheme of things and your good name! First of all, you trample on the express orders of your mother – your queen I should say. Next, you refuse to stretch my enemy on the cross of dirty embraces. More, at your age you, a mere boy, entangle yourself in a low lewd schoolboy affair – just to annoy me with a woman I hate for daughter-in-law. But no doubt you presume, you jokester, you profligate, you disgusting fellow, that you are my only high-born son, and that I'm past the age of bearing another. Well, I wish you to know that I do intend to have one, at once, a far better son than you've ever been. No, to make you feel your disgrace more keenly, I'll adopt one of the sons of my slave-girls; and I'll hand him your wings and flame and bow and arrows and every bit of your equipment, which you know I didn't give you to use like this. For there's not a single strap of it that was supplied at your father's expense.

'But from earliest childhood you've been naughtily inclined. You have ungovernable hands, and often have so far lacked respect for your elders as to beat them. And your mother herself, me, me I repeat, you daily expose before the world, you parricide. And often you've struck me and despised me as if I were a widow. You don't even fear your stepfather, brave and redoubtable warrior as he is. Not a bit of it. You're for ever making him pledge wenches and make a fool of himself, all to torture me.

'However, I'll see that you're sorry for your games. You'll

learn what a sour and bitter thing marriage is. But now that you've made a laughing-stock of me, what am I to do? Whither shall I wander? What snare will hold this slippery young scoundrel? Shall I seek help from mine enemy Sobriety whom I have so often offended for the sake of this wilful boy?

'No, I shrink from any contact with so coarse and unfashionable a woman. Yet the comfort of revenge is not to be spurned, whatever the instrument. I must consult with her forthwith. She is the one. She will castigate this good-for-nought soundly. She shall empty his quiver and blunt his arrows, unstring his bow and quench his torch. She will purge his body with the strongest medicines; and I shall believe that I have atonement for my injury when I have shorn those golden locks which my hands have so often dressed – when I have clipped those wings which I have dyed in my bosom's fount of nectar.'

With these words she flung herself in rage out of the room, peevish with true venereal-bile. But she had hardly left ere she met Ceres and Juno, who perceiving her flushed countenance asked why she spoiled the charm of her sparkling eyes with such a sullen frown.

'Glad we've met,' replied Venus. 'I want you to help me to carry into action the purpose of my outraged breast. Make inquiry, I beg, with all your resources for that runagate vagabond Psyche. For the notorious scandal about my family must be known to you, as well as the villainy of the son that I disown.'

The two goddesses, aware of all that had happened, did their best to soften the anger of Venus.

'What is there so terrible,' they asked, 'in your son's conduct that you should combat his pleasures so obstinately, and be so eager to destroy the girl he loves? Is it really such a crime to flash a smile at a pretty girl? Haven't you noticed that he's a male, and a young man at that? At least you must know how many years old he is – or does he bear his years so charmingly that you want to think of him as a child for ever, Can it be that you (his mother and more, a woman-of-the-world) insist on scrutinizing all your handsome son's little pleasures, taxing him with his wild oats, scolding him for his love-affairs, and reproving his responses to the very arts and lewderies you inspire? What god, what

127

man, who will not revolt when he finds that you, who scatter the seeds of desire on every side, would repress the loves of your own household and close the door of the workshop where female frailties are compounded?'

Thus did they through fear of his arrows espouse the cause of absentee Cupid, and graciously stand bail for him. But Venus, indignant that her injuries should be treated with levity, turned her back and in all haste set off again towards the open sea.

BOOK THE SIXTH

MEANWHILE Psyche was wandering to and fro, day and night, searching restlessly for the track of her husband – all the more eager because, though she had provoked his wrath, and though he might still be unrelenting before the blandishments of a wife, yet he might be won by her offer to be his slave. At length she saw a temple on the summit of a tall mountain.

'How do I know,' she cried, 'that this may not be the mansion of my lord?'

Straightway she began to climb the steep slopes up which despite all her tiredness she struggled strenuously, goaded by hope and dedicated love. Under this stimulation she reached the lofty ridges and at last entered the divine residence. There she saw blades of wheat, some sheaved, others twisted into garlands; and she saw ears of barley. And there were scythes, and all the apparatus of harvestwork – lying haphazardly about as when they have been dropped from the lax hands of reapers in the sweltering heat. Psyche set to work sorting out and ordering all these objects in their proper places; for she reflected that it was wrong of her to show lack of reverence for the shrine and ceremonies of any god, and that the best course lay in courting the benevolent compassion of them all.

While she was diligently engaged in these chores, she attracted the notice of Ceres Lady of Bounty, who called out from far away:

'O Psyche, sad one, are you there? Venus wanders in bitter quest over all the world, seeking fiercely for your trail. Her heart cries out for dreadful vengeance. She is gathering together all her divine energies to surround you with terror. Can you then pause to take my affairs under your wing or to consider anything but your own safety?'

Psyche cast herself before the goddess, wetting the holy feet with tears and sweeping the ground with her tresses.

Amid a thicket of supplications she asked for the favour of Ceres:

'By your right hand of Plenty, I implore you. By your joyous Ceremonies of Harvest; by your Mystery enclosed in Osier-baskets; by the winged Gig of your familiar Dragons; by the Furrows of the Sicilian Glebe, the Rape of the Chariot, the Earth that yields not up its own, the Descent into the Night of the Nuptials of Prosperine, and the Ascent into the Light of the Maiden's Restoration; by all the other Symbols which the Sanctuary of Eleusis in Attica preserves in Silences – stand-by your suppliant Psyche in the hour of her deep need. Permit me, at least for a few days, to shelter myself among the layers of wheat until the passage of time mitigates the raging rancour of the mighty goddess, or until an interval of rest refreshes the body that daily stress has now exhausted.'

'Your tears and prayers,' answered Ceres, 'move me to pity; and I wish to succour you. But I cannot afford to put myself into the bad grace of a person so near-akin, to whom I am bound by a long-standing Treaty, and who is, moreover, a very worthy lady. Therefore, begone from these precincts forthwith, and take it as an extreme favour that I do not hold you here a prisoner.'

Repulsed when hope had beaten high, Psyche felt more miserable than ever. She stumbled back down the hill; and going on her way she shortly caught a glimpse of an ingeniously designed temple glimmering in a shadowy grove. Eager to neglect no chance of aid however vague, she decided to make a bid for the unknown god's patronage; and approaching the sacred doors, she beheld costly offerings, and vestments embroidered with letters-of-gold hung on the boughs of trees and the doorposts. These recorded gratefully the name and kindness of the goddess to whom they were dedicated.

Psyche knelt and clasped the yet-warm altar with arms of entreaty. Brushing away her tears, she besought the goddess:

'Sister and Wife of potent Jove! whether you linger in the ancient shrine of Samos which exults in your birth, your baby-cries, your sucking-days; or whether you are standing in the happy abode of lofty Carthage, where you are worshipped as a Virgin driving through the heavens in a lion-chariot; or whether you are ruling over the renowned walls of the Argives beside the banks of Inachus, where you are glorified as the Bride of the Thunderer and Queen of the Gods – you whom all the East venerates as Zygia,[1] and whom the whole West calls on as Lucina – be you Juno the Saviour and save me hard-beset. Free me from the fear of imminent evil, for I am at the end of my tether, and I know that you are ever ready to be a prop to pregnant women in danger of their lives.'

As Psyche kneeled in prayer, Juno appeared before her in all the queenly dignity of her god-head. 'By my holy Faith,' she said, 'I would that I could lend an ear to your request. But propriety will not permit me to run counter to the wishes of Venus, my daughter-in-law, whom I have always cherished as my own child. Besides, I must not forget the Laws which forbid the entertainment of fugitive slaves against the inclination of their owners.'

Terrified by this second wrack of her fortune, and no longer able to continue the search for her flyaway husband, Psyche abandoned all hope of safety. Thus she communed with her own thoughts:

'What support can I expect to find, what remedy for my anguish, when even goddesses, no matter how sympathetic, must deny me their good-word? Whither shall I turn, when there are snares on every side? What roof may shelter me, what darkness hide me, from the inescapable eyes of mighty Venus?

'There is nothing for it then, Psyche, but to bid your heart be manly, renounce boldly all shiverings of hope, deliver yourself a hostage to your mistress's wrath, and humbly (if not too late) wear down her cruelty. Who knows, moreover, whether you may not find in his mother's house one whom you have sought so long?'

Thus she prepared herself for a doubtful submission, which seemed to mean certain destruction; and she sought in her mind for the words with which to preface her surrender. Venus, dropping all earthly methods of inquiry, returned to heaven. She ordered out the chariot, which Vulcan goldsmith had finished-off for herself with the most delicate and painstaking workmanship, and had presented to her on the threshold of their marriage. The golden

[1] 'Zygia': Juno as presider over marriage (*zygos*: yoke).

chariot was adorned with exquisite carvings – so that half
its value may be said to have been in the empty spaces left
by the diminishing file. Four white-bright doves, out of
the flocks that nested about the chambers of their lady,
stepped forwards and bended their rainbowed throats with
happy preenings to take the jewelled yoke. Then, as soon
as Venus was seated, they flew merrily away. The coach of
the goddess was followed by irrepressibly chirruping
sparrows, who wantoned as they went, while other sweet-
voiced birds announced the approach of the goddess with
cheering honey-trills of song. The clouds dispersed. Heaven
lay bare to its daughter; and the upper-air gladdened to up-
bear her deity. Nor were the tuneful retinue of great Venus
fluttered by fear of encountering eagles or greedy hawks.

She drove direct to the lordly citadel of Jove, and with a
haughty air expressed herself as in urgent need of the
services of the crier-god Mercury; nor did the sky-blue brow
of Jove refuse its nod. Exultant Venus, companioned by
Mercury, precipitately descended from heaven, and thus
earnestly addressed him:

'Brother of Arcady, you know well that your sister Venus
never did anything without the presence of Mercury; and
you must have heard how long I have been vainly searching
for my absconded slave-girl. The only resource left is to
have you make public proclamation after her, with due
offerings of reward. Then get to work at once. Do as I bid.
Broadcast a full description with all details, so that no one
can plead ignorance as an excuse for the crime of naughtily
sheltering her.'

So saying, she handed him a booklet containing Psyche's
name and other particulars and thereupon departed home.
Mercury obediently set to work. He travelled across the
face of the earth, dutifully performing the required offices
of crier. He announced:

'Ho, if anyone can produce in person, or give information as to the place of concealment of a certain runagate
princess, a slave-girl of Venus, Psyche by name, let him hie
to Mercury the crier at the rear of the Murtian[1] Sanctuary,

[1] 'Murtian': The temple of Venus Murtia (or guardian of the
Myrtle) which was built on the Aventine Mount at Rome. (A double
entendre perhaps is intended as the myrtle-leaf was an emblem of the
female genitals).

and receive by way of reward seven times a Kiss of Bliss and once a Kiss honeyed-beyond-measure by the interjection of her alluring tongue.'

After this specifying proclamation, all mankind were converted into rivals zealously competing for the coveted prize. Psyche consequently banished all remaining hesitations; and she was nearing the gates of her lady's dominion, when she was met by one of Venus's best servants, Mistress Habit by name. At once Habit bawled out at the top of her voice:

'So here you are, you wicked wench! You know who's mistress now, eh? Or do you pretend, to add to the rest of all your harlotries, that you don't know what a world of trouble we've been taking to sniff you out? I'm glad you've fallen in my hands and not another's; for you've strayed into the very jaws of hell, and you'll find that what's coming to you (you rebel) has a very nasty edge to it.'

With that she grabbed Psyche by the hair and dragged the unresisting girl along to Venus. As soon as the mistress recognized the maltreated prisoner, she burst into a loud laugh – the laugh of a person in a rage – and tossed her head and scratched behind her right ear.[1]

'At last,' she said, 'you've condescended to call on your mother-in-law. Or perhaps you meant to visit your husband, who lies at death's door because of your doings? Make yourself at ease. I'll receive you as a good mother should. Where,' she called, 'are those servants of mine, Care and Sorrowing?'

The pair entered, and Psyche was handed over to their ministrations. They followed out their mistress's instructions, scourging and tormenting the poor girl; and when she had been racked on the cross of pain, they brought her back for Venus to gloat upon.

Again Venus laughed harshly. 'Look at her,' she said. 'The whore-fruit that swells her belly quite stirs my pity, since there lodges the glorious scion that is to make me a doting grandmother. Of course I shall be happy to be made a grandmother in the very flower of my age; and the son of a cheap slave-girl will be the grandson of Venus. And yet I'm talking nonsense in calling him my grandchild; for

[1] 'Scratched behind her right ear': The throne of Nemesis was behind the right ear (Pliny).

133

unequal marriages, consummated in a country-hole without witnesses or the father's consent, cannot possibly be considered binding in law. The child therefore will be born a bastard – that is, if I allow you to bring the brat to birth at all.'

After this denunciation she leaped upon Psyche, tore her clothes into shreds, tugged out her hair, shook her by the head, and beat her black and blue. Then taking wheat, barley, mullet, poppyseed, pease, lentils, and beans, and mixing them into a single confused hillock, she said:

'To my eyes you're such an ugly slut that the only way you're ever likely to get a lover is by working your fingers off for him. Separate this promiscuous mass of seeds. Sort out each grain; and collect them all in their original heaps. See to it that you obtain my approval by having the task finished when I return at dusk.'

Committing the huge heap of seeds to Psyche's care, she departed for a marriage-banquet. But Psyche did not lift a hand towards the hopelessly confused mound. She sat staring in silent stupefaction at the impossible task. Just then an ant (tiny toiler of the fields), realizing what a monstrous labour had been set the girl, felt himself revolted with pity for the mighty godling's mate and with anger at the mother-in-law's cruelty. Dashing busily about, he summoned the whole tribe of ants that were at work in the nearby meadows, invoking them thus:

'Have pity, O ye nimble-footed swarms born from Great Mother Earth. Have pity and come promptly on all feet to the succour of the wife of Love, a sweet-faced girl in danger of her life.'

Then quickly more and more of the six-footed people flurried and scurried in waves of haste, sorting the mass, carting it grain by grain away – until at last when every grain was separated into its right heap they hurriedly vanished. When night came, Venus returned from the nuptial feast, warm with wine and redolent of balsam, her whole body twined with glowing rose-wreaths. As soon as she saw the incredible task duly done, 'Slut,' she said, 'this is no work of your hands. He did it all, the lad you seduced to the hurt of both of you.' Then casting her a crust of brown bread, she retired to sleep.

Meanwhile Cupid was shut in his bedroom, in solitary

confinement, partly to prevent him from chafing his wound by some act of wanton self-indulgence, partly to keep him apart from his beloved. The lovers, thus divided though beneath the same roof, passed a long and bitter night. But the moment that Aurora came riding up, Venus called Psyche and spoke as follows:

'Do you see that strip of woodland growing along the banks of the river, where the greenery bends down over the spring hard by? Shining sheep wander there, with thick fleeces the colours of gold, pasturing without a shepherd. I bid you to go thither and bring me speedily back, by whatever means you like, some of the wool of their fleeces.'

Psyche went out willingly, not to perform the set task but to find release from her miseries by jumping off a rock into the river. But when she came to the river, a green-growing reed (foster nurse of flowing music), divinely inspired by a soft breath of articulate sweetness, thus murmured a prophecy:

'Poor Psyche, so tired, so sorrowful, pollute not my holy waters with your lamentable death; nor seek yet to approach the dangerous wild-sheep that fill these banks with terror. While burning in the rays of the sun, they borrow his heat; they range in formidable frenzy; and with buttings of their sharpened horns and rocklike heads, or (as oft happens) with their poisonous bites, they worry men to death. Then wait till the sun of noon has slackened the reins of his heat – till the spirit of the river breathes out a lulling influence, and beasts sleep. Lie hidden meanwhile under the shade of that lofty plane-tree which drinks from the same breast of waters as myself. As soon as the sheep have ceased from wandering in madness and lie down to rest, then shake the branches of the neighbouring trees and you will find the woolly gold is sticking richly to the lower twigs.'

Thus the single-hearted reed humanely showed the wretched Psyche how to save her life. Psyche carefully went ahead with the instructions, and found that they paid her well. The theft was easy and she returned to Venus with a bosomful of the downy burning gold. But even then, after the success of this perilous second task, she was unable to earn her mistress's regard. Smiling bitterly with knitted brows, Venus said to her:

'I am not deceived. This deed is also bastardly mothered. Next time I shall test you properly, to see if you are really imbued with such resolution, my stout-heart, and with such singular providence. Do you see the top of yonder high and precipitous mountain? From that crest there gush the dusky waters of a black springhead, which are damned-up in the valley below; and thence they seep through to the Stygian Marshes, and feed the hoarse torrent of Cocytus. Out of the depths of that loftily bubbling spring fetch me this phial full of icy water.'

With these words she gave her a bottle of cut crystal, adding even more savage threats than previously. Psyche began the climb towards the summit of the mountain with anxious care; for she thought that there at last she would find the conclusion of her miseries. But as soon as she reached the skirts of the described ridge, she saw the deadly difficulty of the enterprise. For a tall boulder, huge in bulk, rugged and affording no foothold, vomited from the midst of its stone-jaws the ugly jets of spring water which, falling straight out of a cavernous hole that sloped downward, ran into a deep, narrow, covered water-course and were thus carried underground into the valley below. On both sides along the cracked crags there crawled with long out-stretched necks a brood of fierce dragons, keeping unflagging watch with indefatigable eyes – the relentless glare beating on lidless sockets. And the voices of the water muttered unceasingly to themselves as they foamed onward:

'Hurry away.'
'Beware, come not nigh.'
'Why, oh, why. Take care.'
'Back I say.'
'You will die.'

Psyche stood chilled to stone before the improbability of the task. Her body stayed there upright; but all her faculties departed and left her so empty of will, so crushed under the sense of doom, that she was deprived even of the power to weep – that last solace of the despairing. But the agony of the innocent soul is apparent to the mastering eyes of Providence. For the royal bird of high Jove (swooping eagle) suddenly appeared, coming with wide-spread wings, mindful of his ancient obligations to Cupid – by whose agency he had rapt-up the Phyrgian lad to be Jove's cup-bearer.

Therefore, bringing timely aid, the eagle transferred his allegiance to the perplexed wife of the god, and left the trails of Jove high in the heavens. Flapping about the girl's face, he thus addressed her:

'Ah, simple one, unlearned in the world's ways, how can you hope ever to dip a finger or snatch one drop of this holy and no-less murdering stream? Have you never heard that these Stygian waters are dreaded by all the gods, including Jove himself; and that as you mortals swear by the Power of the Gods, so the gods swear by the Majesty of Styx? But give me that phial.'

Without another word he tore the bottle from her and gripped it in his claws. Then he soared up with wide, strong, sweeping wing-strokes, dodging the rows of ravenous teeth and the three-forked jetting tongues of the dragons. He steered his veering course to left and right until he reached the crest and filled the phial from the quarrelling waters that told him to begone or it would be the worse for him. But he pretended that Venus herself had dispatched him for the draught; and by this stratagem he managed to approach near enough for success.

Psyche joyously received the full bottle, and returned quickly to Venus; but even now she could not appease the wrath of the offended goddess. For, menacing her with heavier and more vicious shames, the latter finally said with an implacable smile:

'You seem to me a witch as subtly witted as you are black-hearted, or how did you dispose so nimbly of my commands? But there is one task more, my puppet. Take this box,' she went on, handing it over, 'and go instantly to the depths of hell and the ghastly home of death. Then present the box to Proserpine and say: Venus's compliments, and would you please send back a scrap of your beauty, at least enough to eke out a winter's day; for Venus regrets that through her devotion to her son's sick-bed, she has wasted and fretted all her own. But don't linger on the way, for I must prink myself with this borrowed beauty before I go to the Theatre of the Gods.'

Now Psyche saw that she was trembling on the brink and that she was frankly designated for immediate destruction;

137

for Venus had dropped her mask and bidden the girl take herself off on a message to Tartarus and the Shades. So she thought that the quickest way to obey would be to go to the top of a high tower and jump; for this seemed to her the straight road down, the easiest road by far, to hell.

But when she got there, the tower suddenly spoke to her. 'Why, poor girl,' it said, 'do you seek death by dashing yourself to pieces? Why do you thoughtlessly collapse under the final danger that you are called on to face? Once your spirit is driven out of your body, you'll be packed off to the depth of Tartarus quick enough; but you won't be able to return on any pretext. Hearken to me. Lacedaemon, a noble city of Achaia, is not far hence. Seek out Taenarus, which is hidden deviously near by. There you will find the ventilation-hole of hell; and through the yawning door leads down an untrodden track. Cross that threshold, and hold on straight along that passage, and you will come to the kingdom of death. But beware of pressing forward unprovisioned into those caverns of darkness. You must take in each hand a sop of barley-bread soaked in honey-wine, and in your mouth two bits of money. When you have travelled a fair part of your hellish journey, you will encounter a lame ass laden with wood, and an ass-driver lame as well. The man will ask you to pick up some of the chips that have dropped out of the load. Do not stop; do not answer; pass quickly. Then go directly on till you come to the Dead River, where Charon, after extorting his due price, ferries the incoming traffic across to the Farther Shore in his patched skiff. Greed, you see, flourishes among the dead. Neither Charon nor the great god Dis, his father, does anything unfee'd. The poor man on his deathbed must not forget his viaticum; and if he should have no money in his fist, men refuse to let him breathe his last. Therefore, to this foul old man give one of the coins you carry for your fare; but make him take it with his own fingers from your mouth. While you are crossing the unrippled stream, a dead man floating on the surface will raise his rotted hands and beg you to lift him into the boat. Resist the impulse of unlawful pity, I warn you. When you have crossed the river and gone a little farther inland, you will see some old women at work weaving, and they will beg you to lend a hand. But it would be wrong for you to meddle. All these efforts to delay you are traps set by Venus; and there will be others as well, to trick you into mislaying one of the sops. But you must realize that such a loss would be irreparable. For without a second barley-cake you would be cut off forever from the light. A colossal dog, sprouting three large fiercely ravening heads, snaps and barks thunderously at the dead, whom he may scare but cannot injure. Unwearyingly before the threshold and dark Palace of Proserpine he stands, guard of the Plutonian Void. Appease this dog with one of your sops, and pass safely on. Then you will find yourself in the very presence of Proserpine, who will receive you with all kindly courtesy. She will bid you seat yourself on cushions and eat of a luxurious meal. But you must sit on the ground and ask for a scrap of brown bread. Then explain your message; and after taking what she gives you, return, diverting the fanged dog with the remaining sop. Give the greedy ferryman the coin that you have reserved. He will row you back, and you can retrace your steps till you come to the Choir of the Stars of Heaven. But I give you one especially strong warning. Do not open or peep into the box you carry, and repress all curiosity as to the Imprisoned Treasure of Divine Beauty.'

Thus that discerning Tower offered Psyche its vaticinatory services. Psyche went straightway to Taenarus, correctly equipped herself with coins and sops, and ran down the infernal passage. She passed the stumbling ass without a word, paid the river-fare to the ferryman, ignored the prayers of the buoyant corpse, scorned the deceitful request of the spinsters, bribed the raging dog with the sop of bread, and entered the mansion of Proserpine. She refused the seat of ease and the morsel of luxury. Sitting humbly at the queen's feet and gnawing only a slice of wholemeal bread, she performed the embassy of Venus. The box was at once secretly filled, closed, and handed to her. She then cheated with the second sop the howling dog, paid the sculler with the other coin, and emerged from hell, brimming over with new life.

She gazed once more upon the sun and worshipped the tide of Light. Then, despite her anxiety to complete her errand, she felt a rash curiosity mount to her head. 'Here now,' she murmured, 'what a foolish carrier of divine beauty am I, who do not cull the tiniest little smudge for myself, so that I may please my beautiful lover.'

With this intention she opened the box. But it held no Recipe of Beauty. In it lurked Sleep of the Innermost Darkness, the night of Styx, which freed from its cell rushed upon her and penetrated her whole body with a heavy cloud of unconsciousness and enfolded her where she lay. For she collapsed doubled-up on the ground; and there she lay without the slightest stir, a corpse asleep.

But Cupid's wound had now healed into a scar; and he himself could not bear his long separation from Psyche. So he slipped out through the high window of his chamber, where he was enclosed. His wings, strengthened by their rest, bore him even swiftlier than before, as he hastened to find his Psyche. Delicately purging her of the Sleep, which he put back in its original lair the box, he roused Psyche with a charming prick of his Arrow.

'Look now,' he said. 'Again you have ruined yourself, unhappy one, by your uncontrollable curiosity. Now go ahead and complete the business with which my mother entrusted you. I shall see to the rest.'

With these words her lover rose airily on his wings, while Psyche lost no time in carrying Proserpine's present to Venus. But Cupid, wasted and lean-jawed with excess of love, had recourse again to his tricks. On wings of haste he climbed the peak of heaven; and kneeling before great Jove, he pleaded his cause.

Jove stroked the cheeks of Cupid, and taking the lad's hand kissed it. 'Although, my son and master,' he said, 'you never pay me the respect which the Parliament of Gods voted me – although, on the contrary, you assault with swarming blows this breast of mine, in which repose the laws of the Elements and the motions of the Stars – although you defile my life with continual episodes of earthly lust, to the subversion of the Laws, the Julian Edict against adultery, and the Social Order – though you injure my name and fame with the blots of fornication, transforming my serene majesty into snakes, flames, wild beasts, birds, and cattle – yet, remembering by reputation for moderate action, remembering that you have been nursed in these very hands, I shall grant your prayer. At the same time you are aware that you had been strengthening your position

. . . So, if there is any young girl on earth at the moment showing a particular aptitude in charms, you ought to make her mine in recompense for my present services.'

Having thus spoken, he bade Mercury summon forthwith an Assembly of the Gods and announce that if any member of the Heavenly Host stayed away he (or she) should be fined ten thousand pieces of money. This threat soon packed the Celestial Theatre; and taking his seat on the exalted throne lofty Jupiter made the following speech:

'Conscript Gods, enrolled in the scroll of the Muses, this youth whom I have reared with my own hands is thoroughly well known to you all. I have deemed it advisable to restrain the heated impulses of his young blood by some means or other. No further reasons need be adduced beyond the daily scandal that he creates with adulteries and all manner of profligacy. All occasion for this must be removed, and his youthful sportiveness must be hampered with nuptial fetters. He has chosen a girl and seduced her. Let him take her and possess her. Let him hold her in his arms and never depart from the delight of that embrace.'

Then turning to Venus he continued: 'And you, my daughter, dry your tears; and do not fear that the family-tree and your rank will suffer from this wedding with a mortal. For I shall legislate that the marriage is not a misalliance but perfectly in accord with usage and the civil code.'

He then instructed Mercury to snatch Psyche up and bring her to heaven; and on her arrival he handed her a cup of ambrosia. 'Drink this, Psyche,' he said, 'and become immortal. Cupid will never swerve from your embrace, and you will live in an eternally celebrated wedlock.'

So it was done; and a glorious marriage-banquet was served. The bridegroom reclined in the seat of honour, holding Psyche to his breast; and Jupiter was seated similarly with Juno; and so on with all the other gods in their right precedence.

Then Jupiter was presented with a bowl of nectar (the wine of the gods) by his special cupbearer the country-lad, while Liber filled for the rest. Vulcan cooked the dinner; the Hours emblazoned everything with roses and other flowers; the Graces scattered balsam; the Muses sang in harmony; Apollo chanted to his lyre; and beautiful Venus danced, her gestures chiming with the music. The arrangement of the concert was as follows: the Choir, Muses; Flautist, Satyrus; piper, Paniscus.[1] Thus at last Psyche was properly married to Cupid; and in due time she bore him a daughter, whom we call Joy.

．　　．　　．　　．　　．

Such was the tale told by the crazy drunken old woman to the captive young girl. I stood not far off, grieving by Hercules! that I had no tablet and pen to note down so pretty a nonsense. But now the robbers returned with their spoils, having involved themselves with some combat or other. Nevertheless a section, composed of the more ardent spirits, proposed that they should leave the wounded at home to be tended while they dashed back to rescue the remaining plunder which (they said) had been stowed in some cave. So, having gobbled down a meal, they cudgelled me and the horse out and drove us along the road, intending to load us with the abandoned goods. They led us on till near evening when wearied-out with the ups-and-downs and windings to-and-fro we arrived at a certain cave. There, after hardly giving us time to get our wind, they beat us quickly home again, heaped with the spoils.

So hurried and apprehensive were they in this retreat that they drove me by their swipes against a stone which lay in the road, and I fell down. Then they beat me thick and fast to make me rise, which I did as well as I could, being now damaged in my off-leg and near-hoof.

'How long,' cried one, 'are we to waste food on this back-number of an ass that's now gone lame as well?'

'He's brought us bad luck,' said another. 'He's accursed, and ever since we had him we've got nothing to show but hard-knocks and the best men dead.'

'You're right,' said a third. 'As soon as he's brought home this load that he's trying to shake off, I mean to chuck him over a cliff to make a first-class supper for vultures.'

While these fellows so meek and mild were arguing over modes of slaughtering me, we arrived home again; for fear

[1] 'Paniscus': One of the wood-satyrs.

had clapped wings to my hoofs. They at once busied themselves unloading us, forgetting all about our stabling-needs
or even my destruction; and collecting the wounded comrades who had stayed behind, they bustled off once more –
to make up for time lost (they said) by my slowness. Meanwhile a very serious doubt was cropping the herbage of my
mind as I considered the threats of death. For I said to
myself:

'Why do you stand still, Lucius? Why wait to be no
more? Death stares you cruelly in the face; the robbers are
determined, and the means lie ready to hand. You see the
nearby cliff and those jagged rocks sticking out of the sides,
which will rip you up and make mincemeat of you before
you reach the bottom. For this far-famed Magic, which has
bestowed the looks and the daily toil of an ass upon you,
forgot to drape you in the ass's thick hide. Your skin is as
tender as the skin of a horse-leech. Come on, be a man at
last. Run away and save yourself while you can. Here's a
fine chance of escape, while the robbers are away. Are you
scared of a half-defunct old woman whom you can finish-off
with one kick of your lame hoof? But then whither across
the earth shall I flee, and who will give me friendly shelter?
Yet these are futile and asinine divagations; for where is
the traveller who would not gladly seat himself on a saddle-
beast roaming riderless?

So I gave a sharp tug, broke the thong that fastened me
to the entrance, and clattered off as fast as my four hoofs
would carry me. But I was unable to escape the kite's-eyes of
the wide-awake old woman. When she saw me free, she
gave chase with a boldness beyond her sex and years; and
grabbing the end of the thong, she pulled hard on it and
tried to lead me back. I, however, thinking of nothing but
the thieves' ruthless design, put aside all feelings for her
age and felled her to the earth with a back-kick. But even
when tumbling over she still hung tenaciously to the thong,
so that in my gallop I dragged her for some distance along
the ground. All this while she went on screeching in ear-
cracking tones for the help of some stronger hand. But her
volley of howls was quite ineffectual, since there was nobody
to come to her aid except the captive girl; and she attracted
by the noise, ran out of the cave and turned her eyes, by
Hercules! on a scene of striking originality. For she saw

a grey-haired Dirce[1] swinging, not from a bull, but from an ass.

Losing no time, the girl with manly resolution gave a very pretty performance of her own. She jerked the thong out of the old woman's grasp, coaxed me sweetly to halt for a moment, vaulted lightly upon my back, and urged me on once more to the gallop. Stimulated by my own natural wish to escape, by the ambition of liberating the maiden, and by the encouragement of the smacks with which she constantly admonished me, I made the ground ring with my four feet as loudly as any courser of them all. I also did my best to bray back answers to the girl's charming chidings. Sometimes, moreover, I twisted my neck round, under pretence of scratching my back, and kissed her dainty feet.

At length she fetched up a deep sigh and turned her beseeching face towards heaven. 'You Gods on high,' she cried, 'deliver me from these terrific snares; and you hard-hearted Fortune, cease your hate. Content yourself with the crosses I have borne. And you, the engine of my life and liberty, O bear me homeward safe. Restore me to my parents and my beautiful lover; and you will find what thanks will be yours, what honour you will earn, what food I shall shower upon you. First, I shall finely comb your mane and adorn it with my maiden necklets. Next, I shall elegantly part and curl the rough and matted bristles of your tail till they are soft enough to dress; and then I shall lead you out for the overjoyed people to cheer you; and daily I shall pamper you as my saviour, feeding you with soft kernels and mellow fruits from my apron of silk.

'But these delicacies, and a life of ease, and no worries whatsoever, will not be all. You shall be enshrined in glory. I shall perpetuate the memory of my present calamity and of divine providence by dedicating in the vestibule of my house a tablet carved with the Story of our Flight. There the eyes will see it, and the ears will hear it, told for all time in learned narratives, simple as it is, under the title: The Royal Virgin Fleeing Captivity on Ass-back. You will

[1] 'Dirce': The wife of Lycus king of Thebes whom he married after divorcing Antiope. Zethus and Amphion tied her to the horns of a bull.

be enlisted among the miracles of antiquity. Your deed will make all believe that Phrixus truly swam across the sea on a ram, that Arion piloted a dolphin, and that Europa straddled a bullock. And indeed, if Jove once loved through an ox's throat, why should not the face of a man or the lineaments of a god be obscured under the hide of an ass?'

While the girl repeated these prayers and promises interspersed with frequent sighs, we arrived at the meeting-point of three roads. She plucked at the halter and tried hard to turn me up the road on the right, which led to her parents' house. But I, who knew that the robbers had gone that way to reclaim the rest of their plunder, strenuously resisted and thus mutely (in my mind) expostulated:

'What are you doing, you miserable girl? What is your aim? Why this hurry to die? What are you trying to make my feet do? You're merely seeking your own death, not to mention mine.'

While we were tugging in different directions and squabbling over the path like men in a legal tussle over the ownership of a piece of earth, the robbers laden with their booty appeared, recognizing us at a distance on account of the clear moonlight. They greeted us with malicious laughter; and one of the band thus saluted us:

'Whither away at such a gallant trot? Aren't you afraid of the Shades and Ghosts that haunt the dead of night? And you, most honourable wench, can it be your parents that you've slipped out to visit on the sly? Come, we'll offer ourselves as an escort for your unchaperoned virginity, and show you the shortest cut home.'

Then another of them seized my halter and turned me round, whacking me well and hard with a knobbly stick that he carried. But I, objecting to hasten back to a sudden death, recalled my hurt hoof and began to bob my head and hobble.

'What's this?' said the man who had turned me round. 'At your old trick of stumbling and staggering! These tumbledown legs of yours were able to gallop but they can't walk. Yet a while back you were leaving Pegasus at the post, for all his wings.'

While my pleasant friend cracked these jokes, emphasizing their points with his cudgel, we arrived at the outer breastwork of the den; and there we found the old woman with a rope round her neck, hanging from the branch of a tall cypress. The thieves cut her down, and at once dragged her by her own rope to the cliff-edge, over which they tossed her. Then, putting the girl in chains, they wolfishly attacked the dinner which the hapless old woman had prepared for them – so that she still served them, dead as she was.

While they were gluttonously engulfing the food, they opened the discussion how best to punish us and revenge themselves. As usual in a disorderly assembly, the opinions varied greatly and included burning the girl alive, leaving her for beasts to devour, nailing her on a cross, flaying and racking her. But one and all agreed on the death-sentence. At last, a man with a conciliatory tone of voice obtained a moment's silence and addressed the meeting:

'It is not consonant with the Constitution of our Band, nor with the merciful attitude of the individual members, for you to impose a penalty greater than the crime; or to use wild beasts, crosses, flames, or instruments of torture; or to precipitate anyone unprepared into the darkness of death. But if you hearken to my advice, you will grant the girl her life – yes, the life that she deserves. You have not, of course, forgotten what you have already decreed as the fate of this ass: a lazy beast and a gormandizer, now convicted of pretending to be lame and of aiding and abetting the runaway virgin. I vote therefore that his throat be slit tomorrow. Then, after his guts are scooped out, let the virgin be stitched up in the belly of the ass that has preferred her company to ours. Let only the girl's head project, while the rest of her body is imprisoned in this beastly embrace. Then let the ass with the virgin in his belly be exposed on some cliff-edge to the full force of the furying sun.

'The pair of them will thus suffer all the penalties that you have righteously ordained. For the ass will be killed, as he has long deserved. And the girl will endure the bites of creatures of prey, since her limbs will be gnawed by worms; the fierce heat of fire, since the broiling sun will scorch the ass's belly and the anguish of the cross, since dogs and vultures will tear out her entrails. Count up her other pangs and torments as well – she will be the living inmate of the stomach of a dead beast; her nostrils will

146

be nauseated with the foul stench; she will waste with a hunger that nothing can end but death; and she will strive in vain to free her hands and escape by suicide.'

The thieves voted for this proposal whole-heartedly, without a dissentient voice. When my long ears gathered their decision, what remained for me to do but mourn for tomorrow's dead donkey?

BOOK THE SEVENTH

As soon as darkness went scurrying from the creamy approach of day, and the clear chariot of the sun had charmed the earth with colour, one of the robbers entered the cave – or so I judged the man, noting the exchange of salutations. This man sat down gasping near the door; and after he had recovered his breath he made the following announcement to the band:

'As to the house of Milo at Hypata which we lately ransacked, we may now drop all apprehension and feel easy. For after you had forcibly removed everything you could find, and retreated to the camp here, I mingled with the eddies of townfolk; and looking grieved and indignant I watched what steps were being taken to investigate the burglary – and whether, and how far, they would go about arresting the robbers – so that I might recount it all to you, according to instructions.

'Well, one Lucius, whoever he is, was set down by unanimous uproar as the obvious contriver of the affair – and this not from mere guesswork but on circumstantial evidence. For this Lucius a short while before had palmed himself off by forged letters of introduction as a respectable man, and so far crawled into Milo's favour that he was received into the house on the footing of an old friend. After staying there several days he cajoled the housemaid with his lying love-talk into letting him have the free run of the place, every bolt and bar of it; and sure enough he kept spying into the parts where the valuables were stored. It was adduced as not the least proof of his complicity that he disappeared on the night of the robbery, at the very same moment in fact, and hasn't been heard of since. He had his flight all ready prepared too, so as to baffle pursuit and cover up his tracks; for his white horse was waiting in the stable, and it disappeared along with him.

'Moreover, his servant was found skulking in the house; and being accused as accessory to his master's felony and flight, he was committed to jail by order of the magistrates and put to the question several times on the following day. But though tortured till at death's door he didn't confess anything. However, a detachment of men were sent to Lucius' homeland to bring him to trial if possible.'

While this account was being given, my withers were wrung. I compared my former fortune with my present dilemma, and that happy Lucius with the benighted ass; and it occurred to me that not without due cause did the antique philosophers insist on describing Fortune as stone-blind, with eyes unsocketed. For she invariably confers her riches on the base and undeserving, and never once favours a mortal whom she could respect. Always she attaches herself to men whom if she could see she would forsake instantly. And what is more intolerable, she forces on us labels that not only fail to adumbrate our character, but even completely falsify it, so that the wicked preen in the reputation of virtue and the innocent meet with cruel detraction. Here am I (I mused) who have felt her heaviest hand in this brute-guising, this assumption of the most degraded of quadrupeds – I whose sad lot would make hardened sinners weep for pity – I am slandered as guilty of burglary in the house of my esteemed host! Burglary do I say? Parricide would be nearer the mark; and yet I am prevented from rebutting the charge, from uttering even one word of self-defence.

However, when I heard the accusation made in my presence, I was afraid that my silence might be misconstrued as bad-conscience; and unable to wait one more agonized moment I did my best to shout, 'He has lied!'

The first syllables indeed I bellowed out again and again; but I found myself powerless to complete the sentence. I still stuck over the opening and kept braying 'Hee haw—' no matter how tautly I vibrated my pendulous lips.

But why do I complain at such length of Fortune's spite, since she did not shrink from making me fellow-slave and yoke-mate with my own underling of a nag?

While these thoughts were stormily crossing my mind, I was recalled to a more important consideration: that I was destined, by the decree of the robbers, to be sacrificed as a victim to the departing-spirit of the girl. I cast continual glances at my belly, feeling as if I was already pregnant with the poor wench.

The robber who had come in with the news of my false accusation drew out a thousand gold pieces which he had concealed in the seams of his cloak – rifled (he said) from various travellers and now conscientiously contributed to the common treasury. Then he made anxious inquiry as to the condition of his comrades. When he was informed that the pick of the band had perished in the course of a series of unslackening exploits, he gave it as his opinion that for a while the highways should be left in peace and that attention should be paid rather to filling the gaps in the ranks by a Recruiting Campaign. This new blood would restore the association to its original fighting-strength. Pressure could be put on the laggards, while the hope of high remuneration could be held out to the more likely lads; and not a few would gladly renounce a low and servile lot in life to attach themselves to a group organized on such an imperialist basis. He himself (he continued) had done a little private recruiting already. Encountering a fellow young in years, stalwart in build, and handy in a scrimmage, he had finally persuaded this new acquaintance to use his sinews, rusting with disuse, to better advantage; to make his strong limbs profitable before it was too late; and to extend his brawny hand, not to beg alms, but to demand gold.

The whole company applauded this speech; and they passed a resolution to accept the new man as a thoroughly satisfactory recruit and to canvass the countryside for further additions to their depleted ranks. The newcomer left the cave and returned in a few minutes, ushering-in a sturdy young fellow who came fully up to specifications; for there was no other man present worthy of comparison with him. Besides his mighty thews he was a whole head taller than all the others; and yet the down was only beginning to spread across his cheeks. He was poorly clad with patched odds and ends of cloth strung anyhow together, through which his broad breast and brawny belly seemed bursting.

Such was the man that strode in. 'Hallo,' he said, 'vassals of the warrior-god Mars and henceforward my trusty fellow-campaigners. Welcome merrily a merry lad – a dare-devil that takes a stab in the body as cheerfully as a gold-coin in his hand, and laughs at bugbear death. Don't think that I'm a beggarly crawling fellow; and don't estimate my merits from my rags. Once I was captain of a valiant band that devastated Macedonia from one end to the other. I am that famous freebooter Haemus the Thracian, whose name is enough to overawe a whole province. Theron was my father, who in his time was also a robber of renown. I was nourished on human blood and reared among the choicest groups of the profession, the heir and rival of my father's power. But I lost in a short time the whole of that numerous and valiant band and all its magazines. For I made an attack, frowned-at by Mars, upon a high functionary of Caesar's who had fallen on evil days. But I'd better start at the beginning or I'll muddle the tale.'

The Tale of the New Recruit

THERE was an officer who held a prominent position in Caesar's court, and who was well regarded by Caesar himself. But a cabal of envious malignants succeeded in chasing him into exile. His wife Plotina, a woman of rare devotion and honour, who had yielded her tenth tribute to his marriage-bed and the establishment of a family, cast aside with contempt all the charms and comforts of town-life. She became the companion of his flight and the sharer of his misfortune. She cropped her hair and dressed herself to look like a man; and she wound around her body strings of jewels and belts sewn with gold pieces. Then she passed intrepidly through the companies of soldiers that guarded her husband with naked blades, partook of all his perils, kept unceasing watch over his safety, and endured incessant hardships with the spirit of a man.

After they had concluded the worst of their land-troubles and sea-terrors, they were moving towards Zacynthus,[1] which a disastrous chance had selected as their temporary residence. But when they had got as far as the coast of Actium, where we on our return from Macedonia were

[1] 'Zacynthus': The island of Zante.

roving at the time, they knocked-up a seaside cottage that they could see from their ship and there they lodged for the night, to escape the tossing of the waves. We broke-in and burgled everything; but we were in a tight corner before we were out again. For the lady overheard the first creak of the gate; and running into the bedroom she disturbed the whole house with her busy outcry. She called on the soldiers and her servants, each man by name; and she shouted to the neighbours for rescue. Luckily every man was in such a funk that he ducked away to save his own skin, and so we managed to get out again unharmed.

But this estimable woman (for we must give honour where it's due), this paragon of a true wife – a favourite for her unaffected goodness – besought the protection of Caesar's godhead, and obtained a speedy pardon for her husband and a full requittal for the assault. Caesar expressed a dislike for the existence of Haemus' Band of Robbers; and the band disappeared in no time. So much can the mere nod of a great prince effect. The Society was hunted out by the imperial army, cornered, and cut to pieces; and I was all but swallowed up in the massacre. This is how I slipped through. I draped myself in a loose-cut woman's robe, one with drooping folds; I stuck on my head a kind of woman's turban; I changed my shoes for the white sort that women wear; and thus blurred and disguised as one of the worser sex, I mounted on an ass carrying barley-sheaves and rode clear through the lines of the enemy.

They all agreed in thinking me a female ass-driver and let us pass unchallenged; for in those days my hairless cheeks were as softly rosy as a young boy's. Yet I have not degenerated from my father's fame and my own consciousness of worth, though I shall not deny that I felt a tremor when I found myself surrounded by martial blades. Taking full advantage of my disguised sex, I burgled villas and strongholds singlehanded, and amassed this trifle of pocket-money.

Ripping open the seams of his rags he poured out two thousand gold pieces before them all. 'There,' said he, 'my mite – or shall I call it my entrance fee, throwing myself into the bargain? That is, if you'll agree to elect me as your true and tried lieutenant. Say yes, and before you know where you are I'll coat your cave with gold for you.'

Without a flicker of hesitation the robbers as one man voted him their captain. They also produced a shabby-splendid garment, which he donned after throwing off his gold-dusty rags. In this new guise he saluted each man in turn. Then, after he had been placed at the head of the table, his captaincy was inaugurated by a supper and some heavy drinking.

The conversation soon turned on the subject of the virgin's escape, my part in her flight, and our horrible death-penalties. The new recruit asked where the Virgin was; and when they showed him where she lay shackled, he cast his eyes over the company with a sniff of scorn.

'I'm not so stupid, or at least not so rash,' he said, 'as to oppose your verdict. But I should have a reproachful con-science if I didn't speak straight from the shoulder in all matters touching your profit. Allow me to have my say then; for I'm thinking only of your good – and if you object to my proposal, you are free to come back to your donkey-tricks. It's my motto that the Robber who takes a right view of his Duties makes Cash his paramount consideration, and certainly not Revenge which is often as dangerous to the doer as to the sufferer. If therefore you throw a wench away on an ass, you will gratify your wrath; but wrath has no market-value. I suggest that the girl be conveyed to some city and put up for sale. A young pretty thing like her would be a goldmine, sold retail. I've known bawds in my time, one of whom would be likely I think to offer a big figure for such a wench, with the intention of laying her out in a suitable high-class brothel where she wouldn't slip away in such a hurry. And if you're still thinking of revenge, what do you want better than to shut her up in a bawdy-house? So there you have my opinion as to the most expedient plan – though of course you must judge for yourselves.'

Thus the pleader for the robber's revenue championed our cause, constituting himself the glorious Saviour of the Virgin and the Ass. The others held a long deliberation, during which every wavering opinion drove nails into my entrails and stretched me spiritually on a cross. At last, however, they all came round to the new recruit's advice.

and at once unfettered the girl. But as for her, the instant that she beheld the young man and heard him mention bawds and brothels, her breasts heaved with anticipatory pleasure. A feeling of disgust for womankind crept over me when I saw this wench, who had feigned such love for her young wooer and such anguish for her broken nuptials, was now exhibiting unabashed eagerness to enter a foul and filthy brothel. The profession and character of the whole of womankind trembled in the balance; and the decision depended on the judgement of an ass.

But the young man once more took the floor. 'Come on,' he said, 'let us supplicate Mars to lend us a hand in selling this girl and finding volunteers. I notice, however, that there is no beast for sacrifice and not enough wine for a rousing good booze-up. So choose me and ten others for company; and we'll be off post-haste to the next town and come back with food and drink fit for a priest.'

So he went out with a detachment of ten; and the rest made a blazing fire and set up an altar of green turf to the god Mars. The foragers soon returned, carrying some skins plump with wine and herding a lot of cattle. They picked out a large ram heavy with the shag of years, and sacrificed him to Mars, swordsman and friend. Then a first-rate dinner was got ready.

'You must count me in as your active ringleader,' said the newcomer, 'not only when on filibustering raids but also in your festive moods.'

Setting-to with remarkable dexterity he soon had completed the domestic preparations. He swept, tidied, cooked, seasoned, and served like a professional; but above everything else he plied each man with deep draughts of wine without a moment's pause. Sometimes, under pretence of fetching a needed article, he came hovering round the girl, gaily bestowing upon her scraps of smuggled food and wine-cups which he had previously sipped; and she showed no loss of appetite, ate and drank – and when coaxed for a kiss promptly kissed him and waited for more.

I was vastly annoyed at the sight. 'Alas,' I mused, 'have you forgotten your marriage and the love of your lover, you slut of a virgin? Do you prefer this bloody man of violence, this stranger, to the young man (not of my acquaintance) to whom you are betrothed at home? Does not your conscience

154

prick you that you trample on all true-love and play the whore among these spears and swordblades? What if the other robbers got wind of these pranks Then you'd bring a donkey's-death upon yourself and kill me in the process. The fact is that you are having your sport at the risk of my skin.'

While I was thus falsely accusing the maid in my own mind with all the rhetoric of rage, I caught the hint from some remarks (vague in themselves but clear enough to an intelligent ass) that this was not Haemus the famous pillager, but Tlepolemus the girl's bridegroom. For after an exchange of whispers he began to speak more openly. No more regarding my presence than if I had actually departed this life, he exclaimed, 'Cheer up, Charite, my sweetheart! not much longer now, and all your foes will be the prisoners.'

Then I noted that, while he was very abstemious himself, he became more hearty and pressing in the potations that he poured for the others. He was now providing wine without water, a little warmed; the robbers were drowsing and toppling with the fumes of their intoxication; and by Hercules! I got the notion that he had dropped some sleeping-drug into their tankards. At last, when they were one and all sprawled like corpses in their coffins of drunken sleep, Tlepolemus at his leisure bound and knotted each man; then he heaped the whole mob together as securely as he could; and placing the girl on my back, he set his course for home.

As we neared the city, all the inhabitants poured out to see the fulfilment of their prayers. Parents, relations, retainers, slaves, house-servants, came jostling along, laughing, flooded with delight. Then there was something worth seeing indeed: a Procession of people of every age and sex, and (novel and memorable turn) a Virgin riding in triumph on an Ass. For myself, I surrendered to the spirit of the day, and chose to respond actively rather than to seem unaware of my own share in the glory. So I pricked up my ears; I expanded my nostrils; I brayed full blast – or, more adequately, I trumpeted with a noise like the noise of thunderclouds.

When we reached the girl's home, she was welcomed into her chamber by the cherishing parents, while I was led straight back to the cave by Tlepolemus at the head of an army of townsfolk and beasts of burden. And gladly enough I went; for, curious in all concerns, I was particularly interested in watching the capture of the robbers. We found them still fast-fettered with wine even more than with the ropes; and after the lair had been ransacked and demolished, we were laden with the gold and silver – while the invaders rolled some of the robbers, bound as they were, over the nearby precipice, and beheaded others with their own swords.

Then we returned to the city, exultant and merry at this complete vengeance. The robbers' hoard was turned over to the public exchequer, and the rescued girl was formally espoused to Tlepolemus. My mistress paid me the most tireless attentions, nicknaming me her saviour and ordering my manger to be heaped on her marriage-day with barley and enough hay to glut a Bactrian camel. But what dire and deserved execrations did I hurl at Fotis for having turned me into an ass instead of a dog when I saw the tykes crammed to bursting with the scraps and snappets of the bountiful feast.

After the marriage-night (first venus-lesson, which can be repeated but not matched) the new bride never left off telling her parents and her husband what gratitude she owed me, till they promised to load me only with marks of their esteem. Holding a family consultation, they discussed with their most intimate friends the problem of a suitable reward. Someone suggested that I should be stabled indoors, to lead a life of leisure and to grow fat on the best barley, beans, and vetches. But this was opposed by another speaker who said that liberty should be the first thought and that it would be best to let me run free in the meadows among the herds of horses, tupping at my pleasure and begetting numbers of baby-mules for the owners of the mares.

The keeper of the stables was accordingly summoned; and I was delivered over to him, after he had been exhaustively told how to treat me. A happy ass it was, an ecstatic ass, that trotted at his side. For now I was to know nothing more of baggage and pack; and once I was free, I was sure to find some roses among all the flowers that would arrive with Spring. And then the further thought occurred to me that since they had favoured me with such grateful signs of recognition while an ass, how much more startling would be the benefits conferred on me when I regained my human shape.

But when the chief herdsman had taken me some distance outside the city, I found myself very far from the fine living and easy ways that I had expected. For his wife, a miserly bad-hearted woman, at once yoked me to the mill, whacked me with a green switch, and wrung her daily bread out of my sore carcass. Moreover, not satisfied with making me the drudge of her own flour, she ground corn for her neighbours and prostituted my weary round-and-round for money. Then after all my heavy toil she denied me even the food that had been ordered for me. For she sold my barley (banged and ground in the mill of my own labour) to the farmers of the vicinity; and I, dragging all day at the fatiguing machine, was given nothing but some dirty clotted bran full of grit, late in the evening.

Crushed as I was by these miseries, cruel Fortune had new crosses in store – in order, I suppose, that I might boast of having done my duty loyally whether roaming or homing (to use the words of the song). For the stableman, following out his mistress's instructions late in the day, turned me in for a period among the herds of horses. A free ass at last, I kicked up my heels and sidled with obvious capers in the direction of the mares, looking them over and selecting the most eligible concubines.

But my gay hopes were soon succeeded by the terrors of death. For the stallions – stall-fed and filled with the juicy meadow-grass to make them mad for the mares – were naturally wild creatures more than a match for any ass, and they were in addition snortingly suspicious of me as an intruder liable to bastardize the stock. So, in contempt of all the laws of Hospitable Jove, they rampageously pursued me as an abominable rival.

One of them with broad beetling chest and towering head flicked at me with his forefeet like a pugilist. Another, turning his back of solid brawn, let fly with his hind legs. Another, with a vicious neigh, threw back his ears, bared his snickering, gleaming teeth, and chewed me all over.

It was like what I had read in the Tale of the Thracian King who used to toss his unfortunate guests to be mangled and devoured by wild horses. For so mean with his barley was that powerful tyrant that he cheaply alleviated the hunger of his ravenous horses by throwing them a human carcass or two. In the same way I was so harried by the horses pawing and charging at me that I wished I was once more trudging in the mill-round. But Fortune, insatiable in imposing crosses on me, had thought out another plague.

I was employed in carrying timber from the mountain; and a boy was placed over me, the most villainous boy ever born. I did not object merely to stumbling up and down the steep slopes for miles, or to wearing away my hooves by striking them on sharp flints. No, it was the incessant whack-whack of the lad's cudgel aching into the very marrow of my bones that was the worst. By dint of always aiming his blows at the same spot on my off-haunch, he managed to break the skin and dig a large ulcerated hole. It was a trench, or rather a window, in my flesh and although it oozed with blood, he still beat me there. Further, he laid such trusses of wood on my back that you would have thought it was an elephant's cargo, not an ass's. Then, as often as this ungainly pile sagged over on to one side, he never removed some of the faggots (those that had caused the trouble) and thereby eased me a little of my oppression. Instead of equalizing the distribution, he brought the balance back by adding stones to the lighter side; and after all that, unsatisfied with these injuries and the cruelty of excessive loads, he would himself jump upon my back, when our track led us across a river, to keep his hide-boots dry – as if he were merely adding a flea's weight to the bulk of my burden.

If I chanced to slip and fall over in the sliddering silt and mire of the river bank through the timber overbalancing, did that wonder of all ass-drivers give me a helping-hand as he should have done? Did he pull at my bridle, lift me up by the tail, or at least remove a portion of the wood till I could struggle up? Not he. However tired I was, he gave me no assistance; but beginning from the head (indeed, from the tips of my ears), he made the hair fly from my whole body, belabouring me with a big stick, till his blows served as poultices to cure me of lying down.

Another torment he devised for me as follows: He

gathered a posy of thorns, selecting those with sharp and venomous prickles; then he twisted and knotted them into a bundle which he tied under my tail as a pendulous cross for me to bear – for at every step the spindles were pulled against me, prickling and scoring me with their spikes. I was thus in a sad choice of evils. When I hurried along to escape his merciless cudgel, I was stabbed even more fiendishly by the thorns; and if I halted a moment to ease the pain, he beat me until I moved on again.

In fact, this villainous lad seemed to think of nothing else but ways of driving me to desperation; and this he confessed in the threats of sudden death which he levelled against me. One day, at last, an episode occurred which goaded his frightful malice into even greater outrage. He had been peculiarly overbearing and provoking, and I had lifted up my strong hind legs to kick; and for this he retaliated brutally. He led me along the highway with a heavy load of tow and flax stoutly roped together; and he dropped into the midst of the load a burning-coal which he stole from a neighbouring village.

The coal glowed awhile among the fibrous stuff; then gathering strength it burst into flame, and what seemed my funeral pyre enveloped me. I could see no possible escape, no hope of life whatsoever; and such a blaze allowed me no standing-still, no time for deliberation. But Fortune had a smile left for me when in utter calamity; perhaps she merely wished to preserve me for further mishaps, but at least she rescued me for the moment from a murderous intention. For my eye was caught by a pool of muddy water near at hand, the remnant of yesterday's rain. Into this pool I gave one wild leap, immersed myself, and extinguished the flame in one sizzle. Then, freed by the same roll from my load and from the horror of death, I climbed out.

The insuppressible rascal of a lad actually put the blame of this heartless act upon my suffering shoulders. He swore to all the farmhands that while passing near the villagers' fires I had purposely stumbled to burn off my load; and he added with a jeer, 'How long are we to waste food on this flaming ass?'

A few days later, he tried even worse tricks. He sold the timber at a neighbouring cottage; and leading me home with nothing on my back, he declared that he was unequal to such an unmanageable beast and that he henceforth refused the thankless job.

'Look at him,' he grumbled. 'Did you ever see such a lazy, lousy brute? Rightly is he called an ass. His other vices were bad enough, but his latest game is one too much for me. As soon as he spies a traveller (whether it's a good-looking married woman, or a ripe girl, or a little pretty boy), he shakes off his load, sometimes snapping his girths, and he runs at whoever-it-is like mad. With that face of his, he yet tries to make love to humans. He knocks them down, and strides over them, and goes-on in all kinds of ways that he oughtn't to know anything about, and tries to straddle the victim of his beastly pleasures. Yes, he purses up that slobbery mouth of his and munches the girl under pretence of kissing her. There's no end of quarrels and uproars on account of these games of his, and soon it'll become a police matter. Only this morning he saw a decent young woman; so off in all directions he flings the faggots that he's carrying, and charges at her full tilt. Then he shoves her over into the muddy ground, the playful sweetheart that he is, and tries to pretend that he's her husband before all the world. If the woman hadn't had such a good pair of lungs, and if some travellers hadn't been near enough to hear her protest and to come and drag her out from under his hoofs, she would have died with the shock and the crucifixion of this animal's assault; and then all of us would have paid for it with our lives.'

With lying stories of this nature, during which my moral suffering was intensified by my dumbness, he incited the shepherds earnestly to destroy me. At last one of the listeners said, 'Why don't we immolate this common cuckolder and universal paramour as his dirty deeds deserve? Here now, boy. Cut off his head; throw his guts to the dogs; and keep the rest of his flesh to feed the labourers. Then we'll rub his hide with ashes, dry it, and carry it to our masters. We can easily concoct a tale about a wolf killing him.'

The brat, my accuser, made no bones about it, but set about putting the shepherd's proposal into action. Glorying in my discomfiture and calling to mind my effort to kick (which I grieved had been so unsuccessful) he began sharpening his blade on a whetstone. But one of the bumpkins interposed.

'It's a shame,' he said, 'to slaughter so sturdy an ass, just because he's rank full of rut, when all you have to do is to slash off the wherewithal of his prankish behaviour. After that he won't be getting up to any more bedtime nonsense, and you won't be feeling any more worry. What's more, he'll get stouter and better-covered. For I've known many slow-disposed asses, as well as mettlesome horses that were so raging for the mares that they were too nervy and ferocious to handle; but after being gelded they grew so placid and flaccid that they were not only fitted for carrying loads but broken into any odd job. So if you all agree with what I say, I'll bring the tools from home after I've been to the next market – which will only mean a very short delay. For I'll come straight back to geld this wild young spark of his troublesome appendage and make him as gentle as a lamb.'

Delivered once more from the shadow of death by this proposal, but reserved for a terrible fate, I moaned and lamented as if I were losing all my body instead of a mere excrescence upon it. I meditated suicide by fasting or jumping over a cliff; such a course would mean death, but a sound death. While, however, I was hesitating over my choice of exits, the lad who was my evil spirit led me out next morning as usual up the mountain-track. He tied me to the low-hanging branch of a large ilex-tree; and wandering a little farther on, he began to cut down a load of faggots with his axe – when ho! I saw a grisly bear poke its huge head out of a nearby cave and come creeping towards us.

Aghast at the sudden apparition, I recoiled with the full weight of my body upon my haunches, leaving my head still straining strangled aloft in the halter. The strap broke; and I went helterskelter down the mountain (not merely on all fours, but by a propulsion of the entire frame) till I landed on the plain below, still running hell-for-leather from the terrifying bear and the boy worse than any bear.

A man who was passing noticed me straying all on my own. He rounded me up and climbed on my back; then, thumping me with a staff that he was carrying, he made me turn into a side-lane which I did not know. I submitted to his guidance willingly, thinking that I would thus escape the horrid excision with which I was threatened. The blows

I did not greatly heed, since I was well used to that sort of violent treatment. But Fortune, inveterate in her opposition, with sad haste spoiled my fine chances and tumbled me into a new mess.

Some of the herdsmen had gone out over the whole countryside in search of a lost cow; and a party of them ran up against us. They instantly recognized the halter as their master's property, and went to lead me away. But my rider with a brave show of impudence resisted and called upon gods and men to witness:

'What does this assault mean? Why do you lay hands on me?'

'What's all this gab about uncivil behaviour?' answered the herdsmen. 'This is our ass you're kidnapping. Tell us where you've hidden the body of the lad that drove him, you murderer!'

Whereupon they knocked the fellow to the ground, and kicked him, and banged him, and bruised him – while he all the while kept swearing that he had seen no one with the ass but had found it astray without a driver, and that he had taken charge of it to claim a reward from the owner for restoring it safe and sound.

'Ah, I would to heaven,' he exclaimed, 'that I'd never set eyes on the ass, or that he could speak with a human tongue and tell you how innocent I am. Then you'd be sorry for what you've done.'

But he protested to deaf ears; for the aggrieved herdsmen hauled him along with a rope round his neck to the thickets on the mountainside, where the lad was in the habit of cutting wood. The lad was nowhere to be seen; but bits of identifiable flesh were strewn all over the ground. I knew very well that bear-fangs had done the deadly work; and so, by Hercules! I would have spoken up if the faculty of speech had not deserted me. All that I could do was to gaze in silent glee at the spectacle of my revenge.

After they had with great difficulty searched out and fitted together the scattered fragments of the corpse, they buried the result; and then they led away my Bellerophon[1] as a flagrant sneakthief and bloody assassin to a temporary prison in the village. There they kept him overnight for

[1] 'My Bellerophon': The rider of Pegasus. Lucius is flattering himself.

162

early delivery to the Law, to make him pay (they said) the penalty. In the meantime, while the parents were moaning over the dead lad, who should appear but the rustic who had now come according to his word to operate upon me!

'It's not his fault for once,' said a man, 'this misfortune. But tomorrow you can cut anything you like out of the vile ass – his head if you like – and there'll be help enough.'

Thus I was reprieved for another day; and how gratefully I thanked the lad who, kindly at least in death, had obtained me another day's respite. I was, however, given no time to enjoy a little peaceful gratitude. For the mother, bewailing her young son's early death, rushed into my stable, wrapped in black and flooding with tears, strewing ashes on her grey hair (which she tore out in handfuls) and passionately beating her breasts.

'Is it right that this ass should take life so easy with his head stuck in a manger, gorging away, for ever swelling out his greedy bottomless guts, and not care one flick of his ears for my rent heart or the ghastly fate of his demised master! Ho, so he blinks scornfully at weak old limbs, does he! He thinks to get off scot-free after such a terrible crime! Perhaps he thinks that he'll convince me he's innocent; for the worse the villainy, the more those that did it think they'll escape, despite their bad conscience. Now gods' faith! you vile quadruped, even if you could filch the use of speech for a while, do you think you could persuade even a drivelling idiot that you had nothing to do with this atrocity, when you could have given a good kick or bite on my poor boy's side! You could often lift your hoofs against him; why weren't you so quick about it when you had a chance to save his life! You should have dashed away with him on your back, and snatched him from the bloodstained hands of this slaughtering robber. Above all, you ought not to have fled alone after throwing and deserting your master, your comrade, that fed you. Don't you know that those who refuse to help people in danger of their lives are punished as offenders against all the decencies of society! But you shan't grin over my losses a moment longer. I'll let you feel that true grief is strength enough for any sinews.'

After this denunciation, she slipped off her girdle and tied all my feet together as fast as she could, so that I should not get in any kick of vengeance. Then catching up a large

163

stake that was used to bar the stable-door, she went on swiping me with it till, overpowered with its weight, she let it drop from her nerveless fingers. Complaining of the too-speedy tiredness of her arms, she ran out to the hearth and returned with a live coal which she shoved between my hind legs – until, invoking my sole remaining line of defence, I filthied her face and eyes with a squirt of liquid ordure. Blinded and stinking, she fled; and I was saved. Otherwise I should have been the Meleager of asses, destroyed by the brand of a deranged Althea.[1]

[1] 'Althea': Meleager's mother who burned the brand which represented her son's life because he killed her brothers.

BOOK THE EIGHTH

THAT night at cockcrow there arrived from the adjacent city a young fellow whom I thought I recognized as one of the household of Charite – the maiden that had been my suffering mate among the robbers. Taking a fireside seat (while his fellow-servants grouped around) he declared the following strange and heinous details of her death and of her whole house's ruination:

'You grooms and shepherds, cowherds too! our Charite is no more. Sadly and calamitously, but not alone, she has gone down to death. However, if you are to grasp the tale, I must go back to the first cause of these events which deserve to be consecrated in the form of an Authentic Narrative by men more qualified than myself, men to whom Fortune has bequeathed the gift of composition.'

The Death of Charite and Tlepolemus

THERE was a young man living in the next city, born of noble parentage, prominent in society, heavily endowed with money, but addicted to tavern-highlife, whores, and daylight-drinking. Thus he fell into low company in the thieves' underworld; and his hands were dyed with human blood. His name was Thrasyllus. As soon as Charite had ripened for the marriage-harvest, this man thrust himself into the front rank of her wooers, and pressed his suit with avid ardour. But though he was easily the most brilliant match among her admirers, and though he sought to bribe her parents with lavish gifts, he was rejected on account of the bad odour following his name; and he thus suffered the shame of being repulsed.

So when the hand of my master's daughter was given to the worthy Tlepolemus, then this Thrasyllus (nursing fixedly the blasted babe of his passion, and feeding passion on the indignation felt at his repudiated offer) sought occasion for a deed of blood. At last, grasping the forelock of the seasonable moment, he girded himself for the execution of his brooded project. On the day when the girl was freed from the threatening blades of the brigands by the astuteness and courage of her lover, Thrasyllus elbowed into the congratulatory throng. His exultation overtopped that of the others so pointedly, and he expressed such interest in the present happiness as he hoped offspring of the newly wedded pair, that he was received into our house as one of the most distinguished guests – a position warranted by the exclusiveness of his family tree.

He now assumed the cloak of tenderest friendship, to hide his criminal designs; and by assiduous cultivation of the young couple, by continual converse and appearance at their dinner-table, he became an indispensable favourite; and he himself drifted unawares into an inextricable obsession for lust.

Natural enough; for the fire of cruel love begins as a spark charming us with faint glow. But when it has been fed with the fuel of familiarity, it soon blazes out and wraps the man in total flame.

Thrasyllus long pondered how he might discover a fit covert for clandestine confabulation with the wife. But he realized more and more that all adulterous avenues to her embrace were closed by the unceasing thicket of observers; that the well-knit bond of a fresh and enlarging affection could never be dissevered; and that the girl, even if she wished to succumb (which was impossible), would ruin everything by her infinite ignorance of all cuckolding technique. Yet he felt himself driven with disastrous energy to conceive her as what she wasn't in order to keep hope alive for what he could never get. Matters once considered arduous seem easy enough when love is daily chafed. Mark then, sirs, I beg you, and diligently note the deed in which the spasms of his inordinate desire culminated.

One day Tlepolemus, joined by Thrasyllus, went out to scour for wild beasts – if roebucks may be dignified by that term; for Charite used to beseech her husband never to run after animals weaponed with tooth or horn. Well, the beaters located the lairs; snares were spread round the leafy shaded hillock; and the word was given to turn in the high-pedigreed hunting-dogs that they might rouse the quarry from their couches under the criss-crossing branches. At once, obedient to their expert training, the dogs scattered to block every exit, taking up the scent in silence. Then at a suddenly exchanged signal they one and all gave tongue and made the forest ring with the hoarse harmony of their barks.

But it was no roebuck, no timid deer, no hind (mildest of wild things), that appeared. It was a giant boar, the like of which was never seen. His scaly skin was knotted with brawn; the bristles rose along his stiffening spine; the foam was dripping from his clashing teeth; his eyes were maddened with a red-shot glare; he launched himself, a thunderbolt with grumbling jaws. The more venturesome of the dogs that went worrying him, he ripped up with his tusks and hurled out of the way; then, smashing through the net (which was cobweb to his first plunge), he crashed away.

We were all overwhelmed with panic, being accustomed to go hunting without risk to ourselves. Defenceless, without proper weapons, we obscured ourselves as effectively as we could behind bushes and tree trunks. But Thrasyllus, grasping this chance to work his treachery, insidiously invoked Tlepolemus:

'Why do we stand here nerveless with surprise, as low-spirited with fruitless fear as our slaves, flitter-brained as scared wenches, while such a splendid prey slips through our fingers? Why not mount and run him down? Here, a javelin for you – a lance for me!'

Wasting no more breath, they leaped on horseback and chased at full gallop after the beast, which, confident in its deep-rooted strength, swung round to meet them. Glowing amid the conflagration of its own fury, it gnashed its teeth and stood snarling as it decided which man to attack first. Tlepolemus flung his javelin and left it quivering in the beast's back; but Thrasyllus, disregarding the boar, charged at the horse that Tlepolemus was riding, and slashed its hamstrings with his lance.

The steed, sliding down into a puddle of his own blood, toppled over backwards and (trusty though he was) rolled his master in the mire. In a flash the raging boar rushed upon Tlepolemus as he struggled to rise; and Thrasyllus was so far from feeling remorseful for the evil already perpetrated, or even satiated by the cruel plight in which he saw his friend, that he raised his lance and (while Tlepolemus was seeking to defend his bloodstreaming body and piteously crying for help) he thrust him through the right thigh. He did this the more boldly as he calculated that the wound would be identical with the fang-marks. Then he pierced the boar again and again, and easily slew it.

When the young husband was thus disposed of, Thrasyllus called us out from our hiding-places; and we ran up howling for our dead master. The murderer, with his life's-aim attained and his deadly enemy laid low, was bursting with joy; but he screwed his emotions away, gloomed his face over, and looked the picture of misery. He dolorously embraced the body of his victim and counterfeited dutifully all the pageant of mourning – save that the tears refused to trickle. Thus, pitching his show of grief in the key of our true sobs, he blamed the beast and not his own hand for the day's event.

Hardly had this villainy been performed when a rumour of Tlepolemus' death was loosed. Aimed directly at the bereaved house, it lost no time in piercing the ears of the poor widow. The moment she heard the news (the last she will ever hear), in a transport of hysteria she ran out, maenadizing in uncontrollable suffering, through the crowded city streets and the green fields, screaming with shrill madness upon her husband's fate. Grieving, the citizens gathered in her train; all whom she met, infected by her sorrow, came trooping after; the whole city poured out to see her frenzy.

At last she came to where her husband lay. She swooned, throwing herself across the body, and all but sent her soul to join the man to whom she was devoted. With difficulty her friends unclasped her. Spared, she respired and despaired.

The body was borne to its tomb – the citizens turning out in mass to accompany the funeral procession. Thrasyllus was to be seen inexhaustibly bellowing and beating his bosom, and even shedding the tears which his first efforts at grief had failed to produce, but which now bubbled out from excessive joy. He huddled his true emotions away behind a torrent of affectionate words. He called on the deceased as his dear friend, his boyhood chum, his comrade, his brother – and then broke down, trying to utter his name. He lost no opportunity of taking hold of Charite's hand as she sought to beat her breasts; of comforting her outbursts; of hushing her laments; of blunting the prick of her affliction with sympathizing phrases; of twining a garland of solace with instances of life's variable fortunes; of officiously laying his consolatory hands upon her, while thus discharging the offices of humanity; and of fostering his own dirty desires by these thefts of pleasure.

As soon as every funeral respect had been paid to the dead, the young widow was restless to join her husband; and at once she reviewed all the possible means. She settled on one that was gentle and effortless, that needed no crude blows, that was like ebbing into peaceful sleep. She refused to eat; she neglected herself altogether; and shortly she would have faded out of the living light into the ultimate darkness. But Thrasyllus intervened with tireless urgency. He never ceased from his own persuasions; and moreover he impressed the aid of her friends and relatives, and finally her parents, till at length the girl was won over to freshen her broken body (pallid and unclean from her vigil) with bathing and then with food.

She did so unwillingly, yielding to the reverence that she felt for her parents, and to the religious obligation involved. With no smiling face, but with a more resigned expression, she went about the common duties of the living, as she was bidden. But deep in her breast, deep in the recess of her being, she pastured regret and pang upon her life. All day, all night, she pined in hopeless longing; and she paid divine honours with regular ritual to some images of the dead man which she had had carved with the insignia of Bacchus. Thus she crucified herself daily on her very solace.

Meanwhile, Thrasyllus (the rash silly scoundrel) acted up to his name. He could not wait till tears had drained her grief, till the agitated waters of her mind were stilled, till misery had tired itself out by its own superflux. No! he did not shrink from raising the subject of remarriage while she was yet bewailing her lost husband, yet rending her dresses, yet tearing her hair; and by his foul imprudence he unbared the secret guarded in his heart, his unspeakable treachery.

Charite felt such horror and hatred at this loathly

exposure that she fell in dead-swoon as if knocked to earth by some thunderblast, some malignant star-breath, some god-darted lightning-stroke. Her soul was clouded out. Coming to herself after a space, she sobbed wildly as she recalled her scene with villain Thrasyllus. Then constraining her feelings she asked for time in which to come to a deliberate decision.

During this respite the ghost of miserably murdered Tlepolemus lifted his wan and bloodstreaked face upon her chaste dreams, and addressed her thus:

'Sweet wife of mine – a name that no other man may ever use to you – even if memory is perishing from your heart, even if the chance of my bitter death has snapped the bond of our love, contract a happier marriage with what man you will. Only, deliver yourself not into the sacrilegious hands of Thrasyllus. Hold no conference with him. Recline not at table with him. Lie not down in bed with him. Shun the bloody hand of my butcher. Begin not a new life with the stain of parricide.[1] These wounds from which your tears have laved the blood were not all wounds from the fangs of a boar. The lance of bad Thrasyllus has parted us.' And then he related all the circumstances, and described the murder in detail.

When Charite had first laid her head upon the pillow, the tears were oozing from her sleeping eyes and wetting her cheeks; but now, twitched out of her slipping sleep as if by a tug of the rack, she reassumed her unquenchable lamentations. She tore her nightdress and bruised her comely arms with relentless knuckles.

But she revealed the secret of the night to no one. She concealed what she had learned of the crime, and quietly determined to punish the abhorrent murderer and to release herself from a life grown intolerable. Again the abominated but pushing suitor accosted her closed ears and molested her with his self-betraying marriage proposals. This time she gently evaded them; and masking her purpose with admirable craft she thus answered his importunate supplications and wheedling prayers:

'As yet the sweet face of your brother, my dearest husband, rises before my eyes. As yet the cinnamon-scent

[1] 'Parricide': A term used very loosely in Latin idiom, so as to cover almost any treason.

of his ambrosial body pervades my nostrils. As yet the beautiful Tlepolemus lives in my breast. You will therefore act most advisedly for the best if you allow a harrowed woman the necessary time for correct mourning. Leave me till a year has cleared away the residue of widowing months. I ask this for your own obvious good as well as for the sake of my reputation, since by an over-early marriage we might easily arouse an understandable resentment in my husband's embittered ghost and thereby endanger your life.'

But Thrasyllus was unmollified; he was hardly even cheered by the advanced promise; and he persisted in insinuating his wickedly whispering tongue into her wounded ear – until, simulating surrender, Charite answered, 'One very serious concession at least, Thrasyllus, you must grant, I entreat you; and that is that we may be bedded in the most stringent secrecy. No member of the household must guess at what we're doing till the year is fully passed.'

Thrasyllus was quite overcome by this pretended compliance. He jumped at the idea of privately possessing the girl, and looked longingly for night and its veil of darkness, setting one image of lust above the whole world else.

'But take every precaution,' said Charite. 'Come properly muffled. Bring no one whatsoever with you. At the first watch, approach my door without speaking. Whistle once, only once; and then wait for my nurse. She will be sitting ready behind the panels, and she will open the door for you. Step in, and let her lead you without any knowing light to my bedroom.'

This tomblike setting for their nuptials had no terrors for Thrasyllus. He suspected nothing; and seething with impatience he had no complaint except that day would never go and dusk would never come. When at last the sun gave way to night, clad as Charite had commanded he was admitted by the nurse vigilant in his deception, and high with hope he stole into the bedroom. There, the old woman, fawning on him by her mistress's instructions, produced in the darkness cups and a flagon filled with drugged wine. She conveyed to him Charite's apologies for being detained awhile at her father's sick-bed, and handed him the wine which he swigged with unsuspicious thirst until he nodded

171

fast asleep. As soon as he was stretched helpless, Charite was summoned. She rushed with manly courage and impetuous rage to where the cut-throat lay, and stood quivering above him.

'Here he is,' she cried, 'the faithful comrade of my spouse! Here he is, the marvellous hunting-man! Here he is, the loving swain! This is the hand that shed my blood. This is the beast that harboured treacherous complots against my life. Those are the eyes that I have evilly charmed – the eyes that now foreshow their coming punishment. For they are darkened, and henceforth will be dark for ever. Sleep sound. Dream happily. I shall not hurt you with a sword or spear. Heaven forbid that I should make you my husband's equal, even in death. Your eyes shall perish in your living head; and you shall see now only in dreams. I will make you think your enemy's death more blessed than your own life. Nevermore shall you behold the light. You shall need a hand to lead you. You shall not embrace Charite. You shall not enjoy your hoped marriage. You shall neither rest in the cradle of death nor exult in the joys of life. But you shall wander like a vague ghost between light and darkness. Long shall you seek the hand that pricked out your eyes; but you shall not know against whom you raise your moan, and such ignorance is the worst of all miseries. But I shall make libation of the blood of these light-holes at the sepulchre of my Tlepolemus. I shall offer up your eyes to his holy spirit.

'But why do I unthriftily let one moment pass when I might be torturing you as you deserve, when you perhaps are dreaming that you embrace me your damnation? Wake from the darkness of sleep to a black hell. Lift up your sight-less face. Look upon vengeance. Comprehend your wretched-ness. Reckon up your loss. Thus have your eyes attracted a chaste woman. Thus have the nuptial torches lighted up your bed. You shall have the Furies as girls of the chamber; and your companions shall be blindness and the perpetual pricks of conscience.'

Raving thus fatefully, Charite drew out a sharp pin from her hair and stabbed out both his eyes beyond all cure. Then leaving him to blink awake blinded and agonized out of his drunken stupor, she snatched up the naked sword which Tlepolemus was wont to wear. Out she rushed demented through the streets, straight for her husband's tomb. Whatever her purpose, it was clearly desperate.

At once we and everyone else deserted our houses and anxiously pursued. Each man shouted out for someone to wrench the blade from her frenzied hands. But Charite, taking her stand by the sarcophagus of Tlepolemus, waved us away with the gleaming weapon; and when she perceived that all about her were dissolved in sighs and sobs, she spoke as follows:

'Away with all these distressing tears! Away with these moans that jar upon my courage! I have taken vengeance upon the bloody sticker of my husband. I have punished the man who would have plundered me by marriage. It is now the time for me to make with this swordpoint a passage to my Tlepolemus.'

Thereupon she narrated coherently the story that her husband had unfolded in the dream, and the trickery that she had used to inveigle Thrasyllus. Then she drove the sword deep beneath her right breast; and stammering a few broken words she yielded up her manful ghost. The friends of the unfortunate woman at once washed her body scrupulously; and laying it by Tlepolemus' side they reunited her for ever with her beloved husband.

When Thrasyllus was informed of her death, he thought that he could never invent a suicide proportionate to the sufferings which he had caused. A sword-stroke seemed a poor expiation for such guilt. Therefore he had himself carried to the sep'ulchre – where, crying out repeatedly, 'Harken, you wronged spirits, of my own free will I come a sacrifice,' he ordered the doors to shut upon him. Thus he suffered a self-inflicted death, dying of starvation.

. . . . .

Such was the tale which the man with many deep suspirations and tearful pauses told the heavily sorrowing rustics. The latter, fearing what innovations might result from the change of masters and sincerely commiserating the evils come upon their old house, made up their minds to flit. The head of the stables, into whose charge I had been given with such auspicious recommendation, rifled everything of value that was stored in the cottage; and loading me and the other beasts with the collection, he deserted his home of many a long day. We (the animals) carried the women and children; we carried the pullets, geese, kids, and whelps; in short, whatever could not keep our pace was lent our legs for the journey. But ponderous as my share of the plunder was, I jogged on without any show of protest, so glad was I to leave the detestable gelder far behind.

Having crossed a steep and forested mountain ridge, we descended to the meadows on the other side; and just as dusk was drifting across the roads, we arrived at a bustling and populous township. The inhabitants here insisted that we must not venture farther that evening, or even next morning. Packs of wolves, they said, were prowling every-where, ravaging everything. Surprisingly big and strong, fearless in their ferocious tactics, the beasts had over-run the whole district, infested all the tracks, and waylaid travellers like footpads. Indeed, driven by intense hunger, they had even stormed outlying farms, and the farmers felt themselves no safer than their defenceless cattle. The roads along which we meant to travel (our informants went on) were littered with half-gnawed human corpses and whitened with bones from which the flesh was torn; we ought there-fore to use all caution in our programme and to make it a first point to travel only when light was broad, the day advancing, and the sun at full-strength – avoiding all possible ambush-lairs (for light puts reins on the wandering fury of wild beasts), and proceeding in compact formation with no stragglers. Thus we might pass safely through the dangerous country.

But our scoundrelly runaway drivers were dazed into rashness by their hurried desire to escape at all costs the dreaded hue-and-cry. So they paid no heed to these sensible warnings; and without waiting for dawn they loaded and forced us to take the road shortly after midnight. Fearful of the danger which I had heard predicted, I immediately took good care to shove my way into the middle of the huddling herd of beasts, intending to hide myself and to protect my rump from any marauding fangs; and everyone there looked on in wonder to see me out-trotting the fleetest of the horses.

But this speed was an indication not of natural nimble-ness but of terror; and so the thought came to me that that horse of renown Pegasus flew out of fear more than any-thing else, and that he had been worthily fabled as Winged because he skipped and bounded almost sky-high in his dread of being nipped by the flame-toothed Chimaera.

Meanwhile the herdsmen who drove us began arming themselves as if for battle. Some men took lances; others took spears, or darts, or clubs; and several picked up stones, which the rugged road supplied in plenty. Others again bore sharpened stakes; and many of the party were brand-ishing lighted torches to scare the beasts. There was nothing lacking but a trumpet to complete the picture of battle-array. But after thoroughly frightening ourselves with these unneeded preparations, we dashed ourselves into a far worse trouble. For whether dislodged by the uproar of such a mass of men and the terrifying blaze of the firebrands, or whether called away on other business, the wolves took no notice of us and we never sighted even a single cub in the far distance. But the labourers on a farm which we chanced to pass judged us to be robbers in a gang. Falling into a panic as to our intentions, they loosed against us an army of huge hurtling mastiffs, mad as wolves or bears and trained ferociously to protect their master's property. These brutes they urged on with all the hollos and whistles intelligible to dogs, until the whole kennel rushed at us – their savage tempers exasperated by the din of their owners.

The dogs encompassed and leaped at us from every side, lacerated cattle and men indiscriminately, and mauled several of us that they dragged down. By Hercules! it was a remarkable if wretched spectacle: the yapping host of insensate dogs, tearing at the fugitives, snapping at those who stood their ground, mounting upon those that were down, and biting their way through our whole band!

Bad enough; but a worse attack succeeded. From the roofs and from the top of an overlooking hill the peasants showered brick-bats upon us. We were unable to decide which murder to guard against: the dogs below, or the stones above.

One of the missiles landed on the head of the woman who was squatting on my back. Hurt with the impact, she began to weep and scream for her husband the herdsman to come and save her. This man, bellowing out upon the

175

gods as he wiped the blood from her brow, at last obtained a hearing.

'Why do you assault and bully us poor hardworking travellers so cruelly?' he cried. 'What gain do you expect to squeeze out of us? What have we done to bring you upon us? You don't live in the holes of wild beast or the dens of savages – then how can you get any satisfaction out of seeing human blood shed?'

At these words the hail of stones ceased to rattle; the cloudburst of mad dogs ebbed from our shins; and one of the peasants shouted to us from the top of a cypress tree, 'We're not going a-robbing either, and we don't want to touch a thing that's yours. We're only slaughtering to stop you from getting in first. So now that's understood you can go your way in peace and quiet.'

We resumed the journey, our appearance now well variegated by our wounds – some of us being cut with the stones, some scored with the teeth, but all damaged somewhere. Forging ahead a little farther, we came on a grove environed with tall trees and pleasantly set amid lush meadows. Here our leaders thought that it would be as well to pause awhile, refresh themselves, and dress the various wounds that irked their bodies. First they lay panting on the grass till their fatigue had a chance to mend; and then they busied themselves in applying different remedies to their hurts. They washed away the caking blood in running spring water; they held vinegar-steeped sponges to their bruises; they tied up their cuts with bandages – each man doing his best to ease himself in his own way.

Meanwhile an old man was spied on some rising ground; and the goats browsing about him plainly announced him a goatherd. One of our people called out to him, inquiring if he had any milk for sale, whether new-drawn or freshly made into cheeses. The goatherd shook his head. 'How is it,' he answered, 'that you're thinking of food or drink or any such eating matter? Don't you know what sort of a spot you're in?'

With these words he turned and drove his flock quickly in the opposite direction. His speech and hurried departure struck our herders with no trifling dismay; and while they were timidly discussing how they could learn the nature of their camping-place, and wondering whom to ask, another old man appeared. This was a big man but bowed with years. He leaned upon his staff and shuffled his weary feet along, weeping thickly. When he saw our company, he fell on his knees, lugubriously turning from one man to another and thus beseeching them:

'By your fortunes, by your guardian-selves,[1] as you hope to reach my distant age still hale and happy, assist a despairing old man. Save my little boy from death, and restore him to my grey hairs. My grandson, the sweet companion of my wayfaring, tried to catch a sparrow chirping on a hedge. He fell into a ditch below. Hidden it was by low shrubbery; and there he lies in peril of his life. I know he lives because I heard him crying to his granddad, crying for help. But I am old and weak, as you behold – too weak to rescue him. O sirs, you that still boast youth and strength, you can easily aid a poor unhappy old man and his child for him, the only child, the last hope of his blood.'

As the old man made his request and tore his whitening hair, we were all stirred to pity; and one of our men (the youngest, bravest, and most sinewy of them all, the only man moreover come without a scratch out of our late skirmish) leaped to his feet and asked where it was the boy had tumbled in. The old man pointed out some ragged bushes a short way farther on, and solicitously led the youth towards them.

In the meanwhile, after the cattle had attended to chewing the grass and the men to renewing their energy, the baggage was re-attached and all were ready to start. The leaders whistled and bawled to the young man who had gone off; and then perturbed at his non-appearance they sent a messenger to inform the lagging comrade that the time was come to move. But in a few moments this second man came running back to us, trembling and ghastly pale, with strange news of the absentee's fate. He had seen the fellow stretched flat upon the ground with a large portion of his body already gulped down the jaws of a monstrous dragon that coiled over him – while the hapless old man had altogether disappeared.

These tidings at once reminded them all of the goat-

---

[1] 'Guardian-selves': The genii or protecting spirits. Every man possessed one. The oath of the soldiers (Book IX) is sworn on the Emperor's Genius.

herd's exclamations, which were now clearly seen as a warning against this bloodthirsty neighbour. In abject flight the company scampered from the pestilent vicinity, thrashing us on before them with merciless sticks. Completing a brisk and lengthy lap of our journey, we arrived at a village where we rested for the night; and there I heard a notable anecdote which I shall now relate:

The Tale of the Bailiff

T H E R E was once a servant who was entrusted by his master with full control of the estate, and who acted as bailiff for the extensive farming-property where we were putting-up This man had married one of his fellow-servants; but he fell into guilty intercourse with a free-woman of the outer world. Griped with rage at discovery of this peccadillo, his wife burned all his account books and everything that she could collect out of his storeroom. Then, not satisfied with this retaliation upon her erring bedmate, she turned her wrath back upon her own bowels, twisted a rope round her neck, tied it to a baby which she had borne her husband, and jumped into a deep well, baby and all.

The master was extremely annoyed at her death, and ordered the arrest of a servant who had provoked his wife to such unseemly conduct. Then he had the man stripped, smeared all over with honey, and bound fast to a fig-tree, where a countless horde of ants (hurrying trickles of quick-life) had built their nests in the rotten trunk.

As soon as the ants smelt the honey sweating out of the man's body, they swarmed upon him; and with tiny multitudinous nips they shred by shred pincered out all his flesh and entrails. The man hung on this cross of slow torture till he was picked quite clean; and the skeleton can be seen to this very day strung up on the tree of death, dry white bones.

.   .   .   .   .

Quitting this ill-omened house where the farm-hands were still upset by this episode, we continued our march. Travelling all day across a plain we came tired-out on a proud and well-populated city. Here our men determined to set up their permanent hearth and home – partly because they could find no more dependable place in which to hide from any belated pursuers, partly because they knew the district to be plentifully blessed with provisions. They gave me and the other beasts three days in which to get fit and make ourselves more saleable; and then they led us out to the market. The crier roared out the price of each of us; and all the horses and the other asses were quickly purchased by well-to-do gentlemen. Me, however, the buyers either disregarded or regarded insultingly.

After a while I lost my patience at their way of poking me about and looking at my teeth to compute my age; and at last, when one man with a particularly offensive hand refused to leave off jabbing his dirty fingers into my gums, I snapped at him and nearly maimed him for life. This earned me the name of being a vicious brute, and further deterred the buyers.

Then the crier, lifting up his raucous voice till his throat almost split, pelted me in my misfortune with rotten jokes:

'Why do we stand here trying to sell this caricature of an ass, that's as old as the hills? His hooves are out-of-date, and his carcass is scraggy. He's idle except when backsliding, and his sole use in the world is to have sieves made out of hide. Let's make a free present of him to any man that won't grudge him a handful of hay.'

In this manner the crier had all the market-folk rolling with laughter; but my cruel Fortune (which, far as I had fled, I had been unable to out-distance – which, deeply as I had paid, I had been unable to placate) once more squinted her blind eyes upon me and selected a buyer – yes, somebody bought me – the man most likely to give me a worse time. A eunuch bought me, wicked old eunuch, bald on the top and grizzled-curly over the ears, one of the lowest of the low among the charlatans that turn the Syrian Goddess into a beggar-wench, huckstering her about the highways and the towns, and jingling on cymbals and castanets. This man, taking a fancy to buy me, asked the crier what was the country of my origin.

'Cappadocian,'[1] answered the crier, 'and strong as they make 'em.

[1] 'Cappadocian': Cappadocia had no particular breed of ass but produced a large percentage of the slaves sent to Rome. Cf. *The Satyricon*.

The eunuch next inquired my age.

The crier cracked another joke. 'The astrologer who calculated his nativity,' he said, 'told me five years; but probably the ass can best inform you out of his own mouth what is the registered number. For I certainly wouldn't like to bring the law down upon me for selling you a true-born Roman citizen as a slave. But if you take the risk and buy him, you'll have a good honest servant ready to do your pleasure at home or abroad.'

This odious buyer then went on with question after question till he came anxiously to the subject of my disposition.

'Gentle?' exclaimed the crier. 'He'll do anything you ask of him. Why, that's not an ass you're looking at; it's a lamb. He's not a biter, nor is he a kicker. He's such a model of an ass that you'd think he was a godfearing man hiding under an ass's skin. Prove it for yourself. Just put your face between his hind legs, and you'll see in a twinkle how patient he is.'

Thus the crier exerted his wit on the old gipsy, who, seeing through the mockery, exploded in rage. 'Here you deaf and dumb fossil!' he shrilled. 'You cracked crier! may the all-potent and all-procreant Syrian Goddess, and holy Sabazius, and Bellona, and the Idaean Mother, and Our Lady Venus with her dear Adonis, strike you blind for the scurrilous scoffs you've been slinging at me all this while! Do you think, you lout, that I'd put the Goddess on the back of a buck-jumping beast? That I'd let him give the Divine Image a spill? That I'd let him send me running about with my hair loose in the wind to find a doctor for my Goddess sprawling in the mud?'

When I heard this speech I considered going mad and curveting into the air as a sample of my intractable spirit and a warning against the purchase. But the man, keen to own me, planked down the money (seventeen pence), which my master promptly snatched up, as overjoyed as I was worried. Philebus (so my new owner was named) took immediate possession. He caught hold of the straw-bridle round my neck and led his new serving-beast straight towards home.

As soon as he reached the threshold, he cried out, 'Girlies, troop up and spy the darling slavelet I've bought you.'

The girls, however, turned out to be a band of eunuchs, who at once began squeaking for delight in their splintering harsh womanish voices, thinking that it was really a man brought home trussed to do them good service. When they saw their mistake (not a stag[1] as proxy for a virgin, but an ass for a man) they turned up their noses and sneered at their chief, saying that this wasn't a servant for them but a husband for himself. 'But mind,' they ended, 'don't keep the pretty chickabud all to yourself. Don't forget that your dovie-wovies want a look-in sometimes.'

Thus prattling, they took and fastened me to a manger. There was also among them a portly young fellow, well-versed on the flute, bought at market out of their collection-box. When they went out to carry the Syrian Goddess in processional, he walked in front, blowing tunes; and when they came indoors, he acted as rooster for the set of hens. My arrival was witnessed by this man with an expression of pleasure. He heaped the manger high with fodder and rapturously welcomed me. 'You come in good time to take over the wear-and-tear of my job. Long life and good service to you, my ass! and what a chance to get my breath back for myself!'

These remarks made me brood over the troubles in store for me; but next day the priesthood went out in a body, gowned in all the colours under the sun and hideously bedizened. Their faces were ruddied with cosmetics and their eyes ringed darkly; they wore little turbans; their linen was saffron-hued; and they were surpliced with silk. Some had donned white tunics covered with purple stripes pointing out every way spear-wise; and the whole mob displayed girdles and yellow shoes. They dressed the Goddess in a silk-vestment, and placed her upon my back. Then swinging oversized swords and axes, with their arms bared shoulder-high, they frolicked and bounded in maddened ritual-dance to the inciting flute-accompaniment.

After performing before several cottages, they arrived at a rich man's villa; and screeching their tuneless threnes from the moment they saw the gates, they rushed frantically inside. Bending their heads, they twisted, writhed, and rolled their necks to and fro, while their long hair swung round in circles. Every now and then they dug their teeth

[1] 'Stag, etc.': Iphigenia at Aulis.

181

into their own flesh; and as a finishing effect each man slashed his arms with the two-edged sword that he flourished. There was one of them pre-eminently ravished with religious ecstasy. Panting out deep sighs from his heaving breast as if filled to bursting with the divine breath, he acted the part of a raving lunatic– as though the presence of gods did not raise man above himself but depressed him into disease and disorder. However, you will see that heavenly providence had the last word in sending these rascallions their deserts. With a babbling parade of inspiration the fellow began testifying against himself, pouring out a deal of idiocies about the way in which he had sinned the Inexpiable Sin, and calling upon his own hands to take vengeance upon him. He thereupon snatched up one of the scourges which figure among the properties of these half-men, and which have several long lashes of twisted wool strung with sheeps-knucklebones; and with this knotty contraption he flogged himself cruelly, bearing the pain of the blows with astonishing fortitude. You could see the ground thickly sprinkled with the epicene blood that gushed from the sword-cuts and the whip-weals. This spectacle of blood spouting from wounds on every side made me feel very queasy lest the Goddess's belly might crave for ass's blood, as some men's for ass's milk.

When they wearied at last, or felt that they had flagellated their sins sufficiently, they desisted from this shambles-show. Then the audience vied with one another in showering coins (not only copper but silver also) into the opened folds of the performers' gowns; and they heaped up winecasks, milk, cheeses, barley, and wheaten meal – not to mention barley for myself the depositary of the Goddess. All these presents the priests greedily smuggled at once into bags kept ready for such alms; and the bags were festooned about my back – so that, doubly burdened, I was simultaneously walking Temple and Barn.

One day, feeling cheerful at the amount of booty which a certain town had forked-out, the priests decided to have a jovial supper party. They wheedled a very meaty ram from a farmer by means of some fortune-telling roguery, telling him that they would sacrifice it as supper for the hungry Goddess. When all the preparations were concluded, they went off to the Baths and returned later with a lusty young rustic, obviously chosen for his goodly proportions; and before the first course of a few herb-dishes had been fully dispatched, they lewdly fetched out in front of the table all the bawdy apparatus for the perfect perpetration of privy perversions. Gathering round the young fellow, naked and variously supine they turned upon him a steam of horrid solicitations.

Unable to bear such a sorry sight a moment longer, I did my best to shout 'Help here!' but finding myself deprived of articulation, I could manage to produce no more than 'Hee . . . haw . . .' That much was clear, resounding and appropriate to an ass, however unfortunate in the circumstances. For a crowd of young men of the neighbourhood, who were in search of an ass stolen the night before, chanced to be prying and snooping into all the inns roundabouts. They heard my penetrating bray and thought that I was their ass concealed inside the house. Marshalling their ranks, they burst through the doors precipitately into the room and took the priests in flagrant filth. They at once called in everybody within hearing; and with a wealth of ironical compliments belauding priestly chastity, they disclosed the wicked scene that they had interrupted.

Dismayed at this exposure, which was rapidly rumoured round and which aroused the people's dislike and contempt, the priests collected their belongings and made a sneaking exit from the town about midnight. A fair distance was covered before the first sparkle of day; and we arrived shortly after sunrise in a deserted region where my owners held a long murmuring together and then girded themselves for my slaughter. They removed the Goddess from my back and laid her on the soil; they took off all my trappings and fastened me to a tree; and then they swung their whips tasselled with sheeps-knuckles and beat me till I was on the brink of passing-out. One of them threatened to cut my hamstrings with his hatchet, because I had infamously brayed his snow-white chastity away; but the others voted that I should be spared – out of consideration for the Goddess, not for me.

They therefore restored the load to my back; and cursing me on with blows from the flat of their swords, they proceeded till they reached a fine city. One of its chief citizens, a very religious man with a partiality for the Goddess, heard the clash of the cymbals, the thumping of the timbrels, and the mollifying drone of the Phrygian music. He hurried out to meet us and to offer his pious protection to the Goddess; and lodging us within the walls of his magnificent mansion, he courted divine favour with humble homage and sacrifice-de-luxe.

Here, however, I endured the greatest of all the dangers that I can remember. A certain farmer had sent to our host (his landlord) the fat thigh of a full-grown stag as a toll on his hunting. The venison had been negligently hung rather low behind the kitchen-door; and a dog, intruding for a sniff, pulled it down and made off with it in glee. The cook, on noticing his loss, blamed himself with a wailing waste of unavailing tears and at length, when the master asked for supper to be served, the cook, devastated with grief and terror, gave a farewell-kiss to his small son, picked up a cord, and prepared to hang himself in place of the meat. But his loving wife got wind of her husband's sad fix and arrived in time to seize the fatal noose with both her hands.

'What's this?' she cried. 'Has an accident terrified your senses away? Don't you behold the lucky substitute that the gods' providence has provided? If this whirlwind of fate hasn't dizzied you out of your wits, rouse yourself and lend an ear. Take this new arrival of an ass to some lonely spot and cut his throat. Hack from his carcass a haunch like the lost one, cook it and baste it in the most piquant savoury sauces you can invent, and then serve ass up to your master disguised as stag.'

The heartless jailbird grinned at the notion of saving himself at my cost; and verbosely praising his better-half's shrewdness, he began whetting his knives for the proposed butchery.[1]

---

[1] The whole of this chapter and the next shows how acutely an observer like Apuleius was aware of the social decay of the Empire under the fine show. In a sense the odyssey of the ass is a journey into the causes of that decay, with the growth of brigandage and of misery in the countryside – with the "oppressive landlord."

BOOK THE NINTH

T H U S did this vile slaughterer arm his impious fists against me. But the danger was too pressing to permit of long deliberation over counter-measures. I determined to escape the imminent knife-blade by flight. Accordingly, I snapped the halter by which I had been tied, and galloped off helter-skelter, flinging my hooves out left and right to clear the way. I launched myself safely through the first passage, and dashed unhesitatingly into the dining-room where the master of the house was reclining with the priests of the Goddess among the sacrificial meats. In my hurry I upset and damaged a large portion of the supper-materials as well as the tables themselves; and the owner, irritated at this disgraceful havoc, commanded one of the servants to remove the 'nuisance of a frisky beast' and to lock me up straitly in some strong place which would prevent me from making a second wanton interruption upon the peace of his meal. Delivered from the grinding knife of my enemy by this astute manœuvre, I was only too glad at the thought of having the walls of my prisons as bulwarks to keep him out.

But certainly, while Fortune remains lowering, it little profits mortal man to make a clever move; and not all the wise counsels and far-seeing efforts on earth can direct or alter the fatal dispositions of divine providence. This very trick of mine, which seemed to have afforded me a passing deliverance, procured me another great peril which all but wiped me out. For a slave-boy came hurtling into the dining-room with a staring gasted face – as I later learned through the gossipping servants – and he blubbered out that a mad dog had been seen foaming into the house through the back door which opened on to the lane; that this invader had gone furiously for the hounds; that he had then rushed into the stables, where he had savaged the greater part of the beasts; and that, lastly, he had not even left men alone – for he had torn with his bites Myrtilus the

muleteer, Hephaestion the cook, Hypataeus the chamber-
lain, and Apollonius the physician, as well as several others
of the household who had tried to chase him away; and
already a number of the bitten and contaminated beasts
were showing signs of rabies.

At once everybody jumped to the conclusion that my wild
behaviour had been caused by the same infection; and
taking up any weapons that they could see, they declared
to one another that I must be got rid of instantly as a
menace to the community – though in point of fact the
madness was all on their side of the fence. Without a doubt
they would have shredded me into mincemeat with the
lances and hunting-spears (plus a battle-axe or two) which
the servants thrust into their hands; but I scudded before
the storm broke into the bedroom where my masters were
lodged. The pursuers at once slammed and barred the doors
behind me, and then besieged the room. Having no desire
to force a hand-to-hoof fight, they preferred to wait till I
should be overpowered and worked-off by the resistless
ferment of the deadly inoculation.

But I, at last free to follow my own wishes, took full
advantage of my unembarrassed state. Lying down on a
properly made bed, I slept the sleep of a human being as I
had in the times long past.

Broad daylight arrived. I awoke to find my weary limbs
refreshed by the soft bed, and heartily hurdled out on to
the floor. Then I heard the people who had kept night-long
watch over the state of my health, arguing outside about
what I was up to.

'Are we to believe,' asked one, 'that this sad ass can go
on raging everlastingly? Surely not. The virus must be
exhausted by now, and the ass recovered from his fit.'

As they all held different opinions, there was nothing to
do but find what was actually the case. So they peeped in
through a crack and saw me standing there at my ease, sane
and sound as ever. At that they ventured to open the door
wider to test out my tameness; and one of them (sent by
heaven to be my saviour) suggested a sure means of learning
whether I was mad or not. This was to place a basin of fresh
water before me: If I lapped fearlessly in my usual splashy
way, then they might take it as proved that I was perfectly
untouched by the distemper; but if I shrank at the sight

and winched from wetting my whistle, then it was evidence that I was still in the grip of the infection – for that was how experience taught (so the old books said) that the malady could be detected.

This plan was at once adopted; and a huge vessel, full of crystal-clear water drawn from the nearest spring-head, was set in the doorway by the shying servants. I forthwith advanced straight towards it; and as I was very thirsty, I thrust my whole head into the vessel and drained the contents: a very salutary morning-draught indeed. Then I patiently submitted to being patted, and handled, and rubbed on the ears, and led by the halter, and put through any trial that they liked –till my mild demeanour shamed them one and all for their overeasy assumption of madness.

I thus succeeded in dodging a double danger; and on the next day I was laden once more with the baggage of divinity, and led away to the clatter of cymbal and castanet, to continue our mendicant meanderings. After tapping a number of villages and towns, we turned into a certain hamlet which (so the folk affirmed) was built on the ruined foundations of a once-flourishing city. We lodged at the first inn that we sighted; and there we heard a jolly pretty story about A Poor Man Who Was Cuckolded by His Wife. This is the story that I mean to tell you now.

The Tale of the Wife's Tub

THERE was once a hard-up labouring-man who lived a life on his wages as a journeyman-carpenter. He had a wife as poor as himself, a little slip of a thing but (so scandal had it) incurably lecherous. One day when the carpenter had gone off to his work after breakfast, the wife's lover sidled warily into the house. But while the adulterers were amorously parleying together and imagining themselves quite secure, the complaisant husband (without any suspicion of what was going on) unexpectedly returned. Finding the doors locked and bolted, he thought nothing but praise for his wife's careful chastity; and he knocked and whistled to announce his arrival. The cunning wife, well-schooled in all naughty guiles at once loosed her lover

187

from her serpenting embraces and secreted him in an old empty tub that was half sunk in the corner of the room. Then, throwing open the door, she ushered in her husband with a nagging welcome.

'So you've come back empty-handed,' she cried, 'a gentleman of leisure with your arms folded! What are we to live on if you can't keep a job? Where's the food coming from, I'd like to know? Here I am, wearing myself away, day and night, with twirling on my spindle, or there wouldn't be even a lamp to give us a drop of light in our poky room. Ah, how much happier is my next-door neighbour Daphne who wallows in food, drink, and fornication, from early morning to bedtime.'

'What's all this noise about?' answered the abused husband. 'Although the foreman gave us a holiday, being called into town on some market-business, yet I drove a bargain myself to make sure of a sup tonight. Do you see that old tub? It's no use, and it takes up such a deal of space that it's only a stumbling-block and nuisance in our little shanty. Well, I sold it to a fellow for fivepence. He'll be here in a moment to pay me and cart it away. So tuck up your skirts and lend me a hand, till I lug it out and hand it over to the new owner.'

Always ready with a suitable lie, the woman gave an insolent laugh. 'A fine husband!' she exclaimed. 'And what a business-head he has. Why, he's gone and sold at such a low price the very article that I (only a woman, of course) had just sold for sevenpence without setting foot out-of-doors.'

Delighted to hear of the extra tuppence, 'Who is it,' asked the husband, 'that paid so high for it?'

'You boob!' she replied, 'he's been down in the tub, testing and sounding it this long while.'

The lover took his cue from this remark and instantly popped up. 'Look here, my good woman,' he cried, 'do you want to hear the truth? Your tub is old, and cracked in I-can't-count-how-many places.' Then turning to the husband as to a stranger, 'Why don't you bring me a light, squab, whoever you are?' he went on. 'I want to scrape off the dirt that's crusted inside, and find out if the tub is any use at all. Hurry, unless you don't think I've come honestly by my money.'

The excellently keen-witted husband, suspecting nothing, fetched a light. 'But come out, my friend,' he said. 'Stand aside, and let me make that tub spick and span for you.' With these words he stripped, took up the lamp, and set hard to work chipping away the hardened dirt on the decayed sides.

While this toil was proceeding, the delightful lad of a lover bent the wife over the tub on her belly, and then crouched down out of sight to do some other kind of tinkering. The woman had her head thrust down into the tub; and she amused herself by guying her husband with her harlotry-jokes. She kept pointing out with her finger spots to be rubbed, saying, 'There . . . here . . . there . . .' until both jobs were finished. Then the cuckolded carpenter was paid his sevenpence and told to carry the tub on his shoulders to the adulterer's house.

.   .   .   .   .

After delaying a few days in this town, stall-fed at the public expense and crammed with cash gained by their prognostications, these ascetic priests ferreted out a new way of getting-rich-quick. They composed an Oracular Response adaptable to every occasion; and with this they bubbled a number of people, who came with varying inquiries. The response was as follows:

The Oxen yoked make furrows in the earth,
the seeds come forth in glad enriching birth.

Now, for instance, if someone interrogated as to his matrimonial chances, then the response clearly advised that he should marry on the spot and beget a large crop of children. If the inquirer was worried about a land-purchase, then the oxen yokes and richly harvested fields solved his problem. If the gull wished to find how heaven smiled upon a proposed journey, then his success was clearly indicated by the yoking of the most ungrumbling of quadrupeds, and his profit by the germinating seeds. If the fellow was considering his luck in battle or in police-work against some robber-band, then the verses clearly presaged an undoubted triumph, since he would bring the necks of his enemies

189

under the yoke or he would reap a fat and fertile harvest of booty from the thieves.

The priests raked together a tidy heap of money by this cheating method of interpretation; but when they were at last exhausted with continually cutting all answers to one pattern, they again took the road – a road incomparably worse than that of the preceding night. How was that? It was slashed with ruts and gutters, pitted in places with pools of stagnant water, and elsewhere deep with muddy slush, and slippery. I bruised all my legs as I slid and stumbled and tumbled, until after a fair distance of this slithering we debouched into some meadow lanes.

Then all of a sudden there appeared a troop of pursuing horsemen, armed to the teeth. They were riding so angrily that they almost rode us down; but pulling up in time, they gripped Philebus and his companions by the throats, and pummelled them all with their fists, calling them sacrilegious dirty rascals. Then they handcuffed the whole party and menaced them loudly.

'Cough up the golden cup,' they cried. 'Cough up the evidence of your iniquity. You sharked it from the very altar of the Mother of the Gods when you shut yourselves up in the temple under pretence of doing things too holy to be seen. And then you bunked out of the town in the grey light without rousing anyone, as if you thought you could get away with such a wickedness.'

Meanwhile one of the posse was groping in the goddess on my back. Discovering the gold-cup dropped in her bosom, he drew it out before the whole company. But even this undeniable proof of guilt could not abash or dash the spirits of the villains. They tried to lie the affair away into a joke. 'What an unforeseeable affront! How often are the innocent brought under the shadow of calamity! Here are the faithful servants of heaven arrested on a capital charge, and all because of a single little cup which the Mother of the Gods presented to the Syrian Goddess as a parting gift!'

But disregarding all this balderdash of excuses, the rustics marched them back and threw them fettered into the town jail. The cup and the image that I carried were bestowed in the treasure-chamber of the temple with all due solemnities; and on the following day I was led out and offered for sale by the crier. A baker from the next town bought me for sevenpence more than Philebus had paid for me; and placing on my back a huge load of corn for which he had been bargaining, he led me by a bumpy root-infested road to his mill and bakehouse.

There I found a large number of labouring-beasts yoked in the tramping roundabout that produced the flour – and not only by day; for all night long also they toiled by lamplight, tugging the creaking millworks in an eternal grind. But in order to break me gradually into this hard life, my master entertained me as a notable stranger. He gave me the whole first day as a holiday, and he strewed my manger with a first-class ass's dinner. But this blessed existence of leisure and good cheer lasted only one day; for on the morrow I was harnessed early in the morning to turn what appeared to be by far the biggest millstone of them all. My eyes were blinkered; and I was sent treading a circular path that time had worn into a trough. Here I was to wander perpetually chasing my own tail round and round in aimless keeping-to-the-beaten-track.

But I had not so far forgotten my foresight and sagacity as to accept this new bondage without an effort to malinger. Accordingly, although I had often seen horse-mills of this kind rotating in the days when I acted a human part, I now stood stone-still, feigning to be stupefied, unable to understand this newfangled and complicated mechanism. For I thought that when they saw me unused and clumsy they would appoint me to some lighter labour or put me out to graze like a gentleman. But instead of aiding me, my cunning only brought me more trouble. For several men armed with waddies surrounded me as I was standing with my eyes covered and thinking no harm; and suddenly, at an uttered signal, they bellowed at the tops of their voices and belaboured me like mad. I was so demoralized by the roar that I abandoned all my plans of obstruction; and straining at the traces with might and main, I paced the ring briskly. Indeed, my conversion was so abrupt that it drew a general shout of laughter.

The day was almost done, and I was on my last legs, before they untied the rush-ropes, released me from my drudgery at the mill, and attached me to the manger. But although I was overwhelmingly tired, badly in need of recruiting my energies, and perishing with hunger, yet I was so solicitously drawn by my undampable interest in life that I neglected the food set out before me and observed with a sort of pleasure the routine of the wretched mannikins I saw. Their skin was striped all over with livid scourge-scars; their wealed backs were crusted rather than clothed with their patchwork rags; some had no more covering than a bit of dangled apron; and every shirt was so tattered that the body was visible through the rents. Their brows were branded; their heads were half-shaved; irons clanked on their feet; their faces were sallow and ugly; the smoky gloom of the reeking overheated room had bleared and dulled their smarting eyes; and (like boxers who fight befouled with the dust of the arena) their faces were wanly smeared with the dirtied flour.

But how shall I describe the beasts, my comrades? What superannuated mules and enervated geldings! They drooped their heads around the manger as they munched the heaps of straw; their necks were frotted with bleeding and putrefying sores; they coughed continuously and wheezed through their feeble nostrils; their chests were raw from the rubbing of the rush-ropes; their sides were split by the ceaseless cudgelling till their rib-bones showed; their hooves were crushed out broad and flat by their never-ending tramp in the mill-round; and their hides were scarified all over with mange and emaciation.

Dismayed at the graveyard-state of these animals (perhaps foretelling my own future), I recalled the happy days when I was Lucius; and hanging my head I mourned for this my final degradation. There was no relief whatsoever for my tormented existence, except to indulge my inborn curiosity; for everyone acted or spoke as he pleased, without even noticing that I was there. Justly the Divine Author of the ancient poetry of the Greeks, desiring to depict a man supremely wise and humanly perfected, sang of him who had visited many cities and known many people. I therefore gratefully recall to mind the times when I was an ass, because, hidden under the ass's skin, I experienced all life's variety and acquired much knowledge if little wisdom. Thus I picked up a neat and pleasant story which I shall shortly relate. It happened like this:

The baker who had put down my purchase-money was a

more or less respectable and sober citizen; but he endured the worst of household-hells through having married a woman who was miles ahead of all other wives on the road of wickedness. Indeed, I often offered up a quiet groan of sympathy over his misfortune. For there wasn't any known fault lacking from this woman's composition; every kind of vice had flowed into her heart as if that were a general cesspool of devilry. She was lewd and crude, a toper and a groper, a nagging hag of a fool of a mule. She was grasping in mean thefts, riotous in vicious living, an inveterate liar and whore. She scorned and spurned the gods of heaven; and in the place of true religion she professed some fantastic blasphemous creed of a God whom she named the One and Only God. But she used her deluded and ridiculous observances chiefly to deceive the onlooker and diddle her wretched husband; for she spent the morning in boozing, and leased out her body in perpetual prostitution.

This woman persecuted me with curious malice. As she lay in her bed before dawnlight she would call out and bid the men yoke the new ass to the mill; then, as soon as she had risen and come out, she would insist that I should be whacked unmercifully before her eyes; and lastly, when the other beasts were unyoked for their feed, she would see that I was the last to get near the manger. These cruelties greatly increased my natural curiosity as to her way of life; for I noted that a young fellow was for ever prowling into her bedroom, and I was extremely keen to catch a glimpse of his face. But the bandage across my head had taken away the use of my eyes. Had it not been for this I should have had the wit to devise some method of unbaring the vices of this profligate woman.

A certain old creature (the confidante of her intrigues, and the bawd of her bitcheries) was with her all day like a shadow. The two of them breakfasted together, and then sat and sipped neat wine. After the first cup-clinking skirmish, they spent their time in plotting and contriving new shifts for the husband's undoing. Now without extenuating the miserable mistake of Fotis in turning me into an ass instead of a soaring bird, I may admit that there was one consolation in my state to set against the obvious disadvantages. Being supplied with long ears, I could hear all that was going on even at a good distance.

Thus, one day the following speech of the stewed old woman was wafted to my ears. 'Decide yourself what you want to do with him, mistress. It was against my advice that you took up with this dull dog, this lily-livered lover. He quails at the least frown wrinkling up the forehead of that graceless stinkard your husband; and his cowardice leaves you all hot-and-bothered as if you've been nailed on your cross instead of seduced. How preferable is Philesitherus! Young, and handsome, and generous; quick off the mark, and more than a match for the silly snares of husbands. By Hercules, he ought to be the sole man taken to bed by all the ladies of the land; for he's the sole man that deserves to wear a golden crown on his head – even if it were only for that fine trick he lately played the jealous husband. Listen now and see how different this lad is from your lover. You know that Barbarus the decurion[1] of our town, the man who's nicknamed Scorpion because of his spiteful stinging ways? He's married to a real lady who's well known for her good looks; and he keeps her locked up at home as carefully as can be.'

'Of course,' said the baker's wife, 'I know her very well. You're speaking of my schoolfellow, Arete.'

'Then you know the whole story about Philesitherus?' asked the old woman.

'Not a word of it,' replied the other. 'But I long to hear it, mother. So please unravel the yarn from the very first thread.'

Instantly the old woman (an insuppressible chatterer) began the tale:

The Tale of the Jealous Husband

THIS Barbarus was once obliged to take a trip; and he sought out every means of stopping up the possible gaps in his wife's chastity. So he imparted his fears secretly to his slave Myrmex, whose fidelity had been long proved, and ordered him to keep an unflinching watch upon his mistress. He threatened him with prison, with loaded chains, with tortures and a shameful death, if a single man

[1] 'Decurion': Decurions were the senators or town-councillors of the Roman municipia or free-towns.

so much as grazed her with a fingertip in passing; and he confirmed the threats with heaven-shaking oaths. Leaving Myrmex convulsed with terror to act as the wife's guardian, he then set out on his travels with a mind at rest.

Painfully nervous about his charge, Myrmex refused to allow her to go out alone. He kept her shut up all day spinning wool, and never left her; and during her necessary journeys to and from the Baths in the evening, he stuck like grim death to her side, holding the hem of her skirt in his hand and faithfully attending to every detail of his commission. The beauty of the lady could not escape the roving amorous eye of Philesitherus; but what piqued and inflamed him most of all was the noise of her impregnable chastity and the infinite zeal of her warder. Prepared to do or suffer anything, the lad summoned all his energies to the task of besieging the house in which she was so rigorously enclosed; and convinced of the frailty of human nature, convinced of the power of gold to blast all obstacles and to bore a hole through adamantine gates, he bided his time till he had a chance of approaching Myrmex alone. Informing the slave of his passion, he besought him to relieve the anguish of a crucified heart; for his death was marked on the calendars of fate unless he very soon possessed his desire.

'And as for yourself,' he said, 'what I ask is easy, and you have nothing to dread. Let me creep alone and unseen into your house at dusk, under cover of friendly darkness, and remain there only for a moment.'

These persuasive remarks he followed up by an application of the wedge that he had chosen for the purpose of splitting the stubborn rind of the warder's faith. He stretched out a fistful of gleaming freshly-minted goldpieces, and said that twenty of them were for the lady and ten for the slave's free spending.

Horrified and unable to believe his ears, Myrmex fled without waiting to hear more. But the glitter of the yellow coins refused to cease troubling his eyes; and though he had left the gold far behind, and was soon panting inside the doors of his house, yet the lovely lustre of the money danced before him and his hands opened to clutch the phantom bribe. Tossed on the stormy main of dissentient motives, the poor fellow was blown distractedly from one decision to another. Faith against greed; pang against pleasure. At last the lust for gold defeated the terror of death. The more he thought of the beautiful coins, the less he could fight the wish to own them. Greed like a plague infested his dreams with anxiety; and next day, when the echo of his master's threat bade him stay at home, the image of the gold lured him forth. Gulping down all shame, and making no more bones about the matter, he carried the message to his mistress; and she (a woman) was true to her whore's nature. She instantly accepted the bid, and sold her virtue for accursed metal.

So Myrmex hurried out, sweating with joy at the downfall of his fidelity, and yearning not merely to pocket but even to finger the gold which it was his ruin to have seen. With tremulous glee he announced to Philesitherus that after immense difficulty he had managed to settle the affair; and then, demanding his promised payment in spot-cash, he suddenly found himself the master of a handful of gold – he, Myrmex, who had never before called a copper his own!

When night arose, leading the lively lecher alone to the house with face muffled in the approved fashion, Myrmex introduced him into the lady's bedchamber. But just as the couple were completing the first shy oblations to Love (like naked recruits on their first campaign in the wars of Venus) the husband knocked at the door to everyone's surprise – for he had selected a night-arrival on purpose. He knocked long and loud; he shouted his name; he banged the door with a stone; and growing more and more suspicious at the tarrying, he menaced Myrmex with dire reprisals. The slave was so gravelled by this unexpected misfortune that his bewildered wits betrayed a sad poverty of invention. The only excuse he could frame was that he had been unable to find the key in the dark, as he had hidden it with particular care. Meanwhile, Philesitherus, recognizing the voices, smuggled himself into his clothes and hastened out of the bedroom; but in his confusion he forgot to slip on his shoes.

Then Myrmex fitted the key into the lock and opened the door. His master, still bawling out round oaths, shoved past and dashed straight for the bedroom, thus enabling Myrmex to let Philesitherus out unnoticed. Once the lover

196

was safely gone, the slave closed the door again and retired to bed, feeling secure.

But when Barbarus got up in the early morning, he saw under the bed some strange shoes (those which Philesitherus had worn when he came to the rendezvous). At once he suspected the truth; but without publishing the discovery to his wife or to any of the servants, he unobserved took out the shoes and hid them in the folds of his gown. Then, ordering Myrmex to be gyved and marched off to the Forum, he proceeded in the same direction, groaning inwardly and convinced that he would be able to identify the adulterer by his lost shoes.

Now, as Barbarus walked the street with rage-swollen visage and knitted brows, the shackled Myrmex was hustled along in the rear. He had not been caught red-handed; but he was stricken with a guilty conscience, and he howled out such sobs and complaints that he moved the fruitless compassion of all who heard. Luckily Philesitherus crossed the track of these lamentations on a business-errand; but though he was shaken by the unexpected spectacle, he suppressed his dismay. For, recalling the error of his haste and at once inferring its consequences, he acted with his usual witty presence of mind. Shouldering aside the guard of servants, he assaulted Myrmex, roaring indignantly and hitting him (gently) in the face with clenched fists.

'Scoundrel and perjurer!' he cried, 'may your master and all the gods in heaven, by taking whose name in vain you doubly damn yourself, pitch you into pitiless pits of perdition! You're the man that stole my shoes yesterday from the Baths. You deserve, by Hercules, to wear these chains out and to pine for ever in a dark dank dungeon!'

Fooled by the prompt stratagem of the bold lad, raised out of his dumps, and dropped back into his old complacency, Barbarus returned home; and summoning Myrmex, he handed the shoes over to him with sharp instructions that they should be returned to their rightful and injured owner.

.   .   .   .   .

The old trickster had no sooner ended her tale than the baker's wife exclaimed, 'Happy is the woman with the free use of such a stickfast lover! while I, poor thing, have fallen into the hands of a fellow who shivers at the mere creak of the mill-wheel or the hoodwinked face of that scabby ass yonder.'

'Well, I'll go bail for myself,' replied the old woman, 'that I'll fetch you the brisk boy in no time; and he'll come aware what's expected and ready for action.' Then, arranging to return at dusk, she hobbled out of the chamber.

The chaste wife at once set about preparing a banquet fit for a priest's appetite. She strained some costly wines, made fresh savoury dishes, and laid out a lavish supper, yearning for the advent of the fornicator as if for some god. Her husband, it conveniently happened, was dining out at the fuller's next door.

When the sun was nearing his goal, I was loosed from the mill and let go unmolested to feed. But, by Hercules, it was not my release from toil that delighted me, but the fact that as my eyes were no longer bandaged I could freely over-look all the crafty doings of this mischievous woman. At last, when the sun (sunk through the ocean) was lighting up the Antipodean zones, I beheld the bold bad lecher stride in with the bawdy old woman hanging on his arm. The fellow looked hardly more than a boy, with his smooth flushed cheeks – handsomely liable to attract lechers him-self. The baker's wife welcomed him with a ready supply of caresses, and bade him lose no time as the supper was on the table. But as soon as the youth had taken one gulp of the wine and lifted the first of the hors d'oeuvres to his lips, the husband was heard returning hours earlier than he was looked for. Thereupon his affectionate wife cursed him heartily and asked heaven why the fool didn't break his legs; and concealing the palely scared youth under a wooden bin (used for corn-sifting) which chanced to lie handy, she turned with a face of ingenuous surprise to her entering husband. Why, she asked, had he so soon deserted the entertainment of his dear friend?

The baker fetched out a sigh that betokened a heavy depression. 'I made my excuses,' he said, 'because I couldn't bear the impudent behaviour of his abandoned wife. Good gods! what a trustworthy and respectable mother-of-a-family she seemed, and yet how foully she blemished herself. I swear by yonder holy Ceres that I can scarcely credit my own eyes when they testify against such a woman.'

The unconscionable wife, excited by this speech, was all of an itch to hear what had occurred. She importuned her husband to relate the whole story; and she refused to cease scolding till he agreed and had begun to unfold his neighbour's dishonour, meanwhile never guessing his own.

The Tale of the Fuller's Wife

THE wife of my old pal the fuller always seemed a woman of the choicest morals, and folk said that she ruled the roost in her husband's house most virtuously; but she burst out at last in a muffled love-affair with a young fellow. Now, as they met as often as they could squeeze-in an unsuspected embrace, it came about that when the fuller and I returned from the Baths to supper, there were the two of them fast-hugging.

Startled by our premature arrival, the woman could improvise no better method of concealment than to push her lover under a high wicker-cage draped round with clothes that were being exposed to the bleaching fumes of sulphur. Thinking that he was snugly hidden, she sat blithely down to share the supper with us. All this while, however, the young man was drawn to inhale the suffocating clouds of acrid vapour given off by the burning sulphur that surrounded him; and (the usual effect of that lively sublimate) he could not resist repeatedly sneezing. The husband who sat facing his wife heard this sound come from behind her and thought it was her product. So he exclaimed, 'Lord save you!' as is usual in such circumstances.

Then came a second sneeze, a third sneeze, and a whole volley of sneezes – till at last, astonished at this excessive sternutation, he began to realize the facts of the case. Pushing back the table, he knocked the cage over and revealed the man panting for breath and almost strangulated. Furiously indignant at this outrage, he roared for his sword and would have cut the throat of the swooning fellow had I not after a struggle restrained him from a deed which would have brought the law down upon us all. I asseverated that his injurer would soon perish from convulsions without involving us in any guilt. Softened not so much by my arguments as by sheer necessity, he dragged this choking young man into the next alleyway. While he was doing this I pressed his wife and at last persuaded her to leave the shop for a period, and to shelter herself with some friends until time had cooled her husband's hot blood. For I had no doubt that in his choleric fit of madness he would inflict some terrible damage upon himself and his wife.

By this time I had sampled more than enough of my friend's entertainment; and so I decided to come home.

·   ·   ·   ·   ·

While the baker was recounting this experience, his spouse with pert effrontery kept interrupting him to curse and abuse the fuller's wife, calling her a shameless whore and strumpet, the one great blot upon the name of woman, a wretch who put her chastity behind her, who trampled upon the duties of her nuptial-bed, who turned her husband's house into an infamous brothel, who discarded the dignity of a matron, and who had written herself down as punk. Such females (she added) ought to be burned alive.

Mindful, however, of her own sore point and the sewers of her conscience, she suggested to her husband that he should go to rest early. For she wished to release her rakehell as soon as possible from the pins-and-needles of his confinement. But the baker, cheated of his meal with the fuller, had come home fasting; and he now civilly asked his wife to lay the table. She quickly but ungraciously served him up the supper which she had meant for another. Meanwhile my very bowels were tormented when I compared the late lewderies and the present two-faced wickedness of this woman; and I deliberated sedulously whether I could not find some method of doing my master a good turn and disclosing her practices, and whether I could not reveal the young adulterer by kicking over the bin under which he was flattened like a tortoise.

But while I hesitated (racked on a cross of indecision), heaven aided me at last. For a lame old man, who had charge of all our stabling-concerns, perceived that it was time to give the beasts water; and he came to herd us all away to the nearest pond. This supplied me with a most excellent chance of revenge. As I passed, I noted that the adulterer's fingers were sticking out under the edge of the bin; and so, pressing down the point of my hoof upon them, I crushed them badly. He uttered a moaning scream, unable to control the spurt of anguish; and then, lifting and throwing off the bin, he exposed himself to the general gaze and laid bare the schemes of that deboshed woman.

The baker, however, showed no great commotion at the revelation of his wife's infidelity. With a placid brow and a smile of reassurance he addressed the wan and worried lad in soothing tones. 'Fear no harsh treatment from me, my son,' he said. 'I am no barbarian, nor am I a country-bumpkin with uncouth manners. Nor shall I take example from the fuller to strangle you with the death-dealing fumes of unpleasant sulphur. Nor shall I put so handsome and promising a lad into the hands of the police, to see him suffer the cruel penalties enacted against adultery. Rather, I shall negotiate with my wife for a share and thereby settle this dispute over ownership. Not that I mean to sue for a division of property. No, I should prefer a partnership-agreement, so that without squabbles and dissension we three might come to reciprocal terms in bed. I have always lived comfortably with my wife on the simple and sane principle that what she likes I like; but common equity will not permit the wife to wield more authority than the husband.'

After suavely jesting in this way, he conducted the shying but undenying lad to his chamber, and closing the door in his chaste wife's face, he exacted an agreeable requital for his soiled marriage-couch. But when the glinting chariot wheel of the sun had ushered in the day, he called for two of the heftiest labourers; and these men hoisted the lad while the baker himself birched his bottom.

'What's this!' he cried. 'You so soft and tender, you a mere boy, you scorn the lovers of your own budding age and run after full-grown women, free-born women, eh? You want to feel you're breaking a marriage-bond and setting yourself up precociously as an Adulterer, is that it?'

After rating him soundly and castigating him as he

deserved, he chased him out of the house; and thus did that most gallant of adulterers scamper away in tears, escaping more easily than he had hoped, but nevertheless bearing a snowy bottom sadly the worse for wear. The Baker then sent word to his wife that she was divorced and given instant notice to quit. Her naturally malicious temper was vehemently exasperated by this insult (merited as it was); and she turned for help to the trumperies and familiar tricks of incensed women.

She expended much time and care in ferreting out a certain aged slyboots of a woman who was believed to be able to work anything whatsoever with her sorceries and drugs. She loaded this wretch with presents and deafened her with prayers. 'I want one of two things,' she said, 'reconciliation with a forgiving husband, or (if that can't be worked) some ghost or demoniacal visitation to scare him out of his life.'

The wise-woman, who was capable of tapping the springs of divine power, at first used only the lighter forces of her black art. She endeavoured telepathically to influence the husband, to mitigate his feelings of injury, and to draw him back to his former affection. When, however, her results did not come up to expectations, irritated against her controls and goaded by a sense of their mockery (as well as resentful at losing the reward promised for success) she began to make attempts upon the life of the unfortunate man. She obtained contact with the ghost of a woman who had died a violent death; and she set about using this ghost to murder the baker.

But perhaps at this point some pernickety reader will interject a sneer and the following objection: 'How could you, O crassest of asses, be aware (as you assert) of what these women were secretly doing, when you were enclosed all this while within the bakehouse-bounds?' Hear then how I, a very inquisitive man who was wearing at the time the shape of a beast-of-burden, chanced to learn all that was being performed to blast this baker of mine.

About midday there suddenly appeared in the bakehouse a woman hideously melancholy and criminal-looking. She was clad in patched mourning-garb; her feet were shoeless; her woe-begone face was sallowed to the colour of boxwood; and her scattered greying hair, dirtied with ashes, hung over her brow in a fringe that hid half her face. This person, taking the baker softly by the hand, drew him aside into his chamber as if she had something urgent to tell him privately. Shutting the door, they remained closeted for some time.

At last all the wheat which had been measured out to the workmen was ground, and it became necessary to procure more. So the servants went to the chamberdoor; and calling to their master they explained that their wheat-supply was exhausted. But no master answered, though they clamorously repeated their demand and knocked more trenchantly. Discovering that the door had been carefully bolted, they began to fear some tragic dénouement; and making a mighty rush they burst the door off its hinges and entered. There was no woman to be found; but they saw their master hanging from a rafter with the last spark of life extinct. Loosening the noose from round his neck, they took him down; and then with a great expense of lamentation and weeping they washed the corpse, performed the customary offices for the dead, and laid the baker in his sepulchre. The funeral was thickly attended.

Next day his daughter came hurrying from the nearby town where she had lately settled after being married. She showed all the signs of grief, shaking her tousled hair and beating her bubs with her fists. For she knew the whole story, though no mortal had brought her word of the family's distress. The pitiable form of her father had obtruded upon her sleep with his neck still haltered; and the dead man had disclosed to her the wicked work of her stepmother (the infidelity and the use of spells), and told her how he himself had been haunted by a spirit off the earth.

When the daughter had hung on a daily cross of grief, she was persuaded by the combined entreaties of her friends to put an end to her mourning. Consequently, when the last of the funeral rites were duly completed before the tomb, on the ninth day as sole heiress she held an auction of all the slaves, furniture, and beasts. Thus did capricious Fortune by the chances of sale scatter here, there, and everywhere, the property that one man had gathered as his own.

A hard-up gardener bought me, when my turn came, for fifty pence. 'Too much,' he said, 'but the two of us together,

I trust, will help each other to keep alive.' So here now
I launch into the description of my experiences as a
gardener's hack. Every morning my master used to drive
me to the nearest market with a load of vegetables; and
after he had sold these to the retailers he returned home
to his garden, sitting on my back. But while he was digging
and watering and bending over this or that task, I was left
to take things easy and enjoy a restful day. When, however,
the inenarrable motions of the stars and the slow succession
of days and months had brought the year towards its close
– when we degenerated from the vintage-luxuries of
autumn into the wintry frost of Capricorn[1]– then I was
racked on a cross of stiffness with the continuous rains and
night dews; for my roofless stable lay open to all the airs
of heaven. My master through extreme poverty could not
purchase for himself, let alone for me, any straw or cheap
bedclothes; and he had no choice but to rest content with
the thatch of his hut as sole protection against the weather.
Moreover, in the mornings I had to force my way with
unshod hooves across the rough frozen mire and the jagged
blades of ice; and I never even got my old bellyful of food to
hearten me. For both my master and myself had meals equal
in size and substance. Meagre meals they were, consisting
of ancient unattractive lettuces which had run to seed and
looked like so many brooms: rotten lettuces in which the
juice was bitter and smelt nasty.

One night a householder of the next village lost his way
in the glooms of a moonless night. Drenched to the skin
with rain, he turned his tired horse into our little garden;
and being hospitably received (all things considered) he
was provided with a night's rest (the necessity he craved)
though with no dainty extras. However, out of a grateful
wish to remunerate his host, he promised to despatch from
his farm some corn and oil, with two casks of wine.

My master accepted the invitation without waiting to
be asked twice; and he set out for the aforesaid farm
(which lay about seven and a half miles from the garden)
seated on my back and carrying with him a sack and some
empty wineskins. After covering the distance, we knocked
at the farm door; and my master was immediately welcomed

[1] 'Capricorn': The sun enters the sign of Capricorn at the beginning
of winter.

in by the jovial farmer to share a mouth-watering collation.

But while they were pledging each other, a most extra-ordinary scene occurred. One of the hens in the poultry-division, roaming about the middle of the yard, kept cack-ling busily as if she meant to lay. On this the farmer took a look at her. 'Well, my good and prolific pullet!' he exclaimed, 'for a long time now you have stuffed us with your daily output; and now, I see, you are about to provide a tasty morsel for the table.' Then he called to one of the servants, 'Boy! fetch the laying-basket and put it in the usual corner.'

The boy did as ordered; but the hen, scorning her wonted nest, brought forth before the very feet of her master an offspring premature in itself but for us the ominous progenitor of calamity. She produced, instead of the common-or-garden egg, a fully formed chicken which at once began cheeping after its mother. Then an even worse prodigy broke out, a thoroughly hair-raising one. Under the very table on which lay the scraps of the repast, the earth split to its foundations and a gushing fountain of blood glittered forth – the plentiful drops of which spattered the table with gore. At that same moment, as the company stood transfixed with wondering dismay before these super-natural presages, a servant bolted up from the wine-cellar with the news that the wine (which had been racked-off a good while) was boiling up in the jars as if a large fire was bubbling beneath. In the meantime some weasels were seen outside the house dragging along a dead snake; and out of the jaws of the sheepdog there leapt a small green frog. At once a ram that stood near by came charging at the dog and killed him with a fierce grip on his throat. These various omens struck the farmer and all the household with a numbing sense of terror. They were at a loss what was the first or last action to take; what was the best or the worst; what they ought to avoid in order to placate heaven; and how many sacrifices and what kind would make atone-ment. While all were standing about in torpid expectation of some terrible event, a servant came running in with tidings that meant the utter wreck of all the agriculturist's hopes.

The Tale of the Oppressive Landlord

THIS man was the proud father of three sons now come to manhood, well-educated and decently behaved lads. The trio were old acquaintances of a poor farmer who lived in a cottage on the borders of a vast teeming estate owned by a wealthy and powerful young man. This landlord, however, made a bad use of the influence accruing to his long-descended line. He was master of an army of servants; and he was never called to account in the city for his high-handed ways. He objected to his poverty-stricken neighbour most vehemently, slaughtered his cattle, reived his oxen, and trod down his corn while still in the ear. Already he had spoiled all harvest hopes, and the next step which he aimed at was to eject the man from his holding. The big landlord therefore raised some legal fribble about boundaries and claimed the whole of the land.

The rustic, naturally a law-abiding fellow, seeing himself disinherited through a rich man's greed, anxiously collected all his friends with the intention of determining the precise boundary-lines; for he desired to keep at least six feet of his ancestral ground to be buried in. Among the friends were the three brothers, who came to offer him what small assistance they could muster in his hour of need. But the bully was not in the least daunted, or even affected, by the presence of so many fellow-ratepayers. So far indeed was he from any intention of surrendering his robber's-claim that he could not even control his tongue. When they expostu-lated moderately with him, and sought to restrain his blusterous temper with pacifying speeches, he interposed with blood-curdling oaths and swore by his life and all that was dear to him that he didn't give a fig for all the inter-fering arbitrators in the world. In fact (he declared) he meant to settle the matter in his own way by ordering his servants to take the recalcitrant farmer by the ears, hurl him out of the cottage, and get rid of him once and for all.

These words aroused a lively animosity in the minds of the audience; and one of the three brothers told him plainly, on the spur of the moment's anger, that it was in vain for him to rely on his wealth and to utter such tyrannical menaces, since the impartial protection of the law stood between even the poorest of men and the rich oppressor.

What oil is to flame, what brimstone is to a burning house, what the whip is in the Furies' hand, such was the stimulus of this declaration to the landlord's ungovernable temper. Enraged to the brink of insanity, he bade the whole company go and hang themselves, and take their laws away at the same time. Then he commanded the shepherd-dogs to be loosed, as well as the farm-bandogs – savage and burly brutes, accustomed to gorge themselves on the carcasses that were thrown out into the fields, and to set upon and maul the passing traveller. Now, excited to the pitch of frenzy by the familiar booing of the shepherds, the dogs rushed upon the men, rasping their eyes with a barking babel of horror, rending and ripping them. Not even when the men ran did the dogs cease from the massacre; rather, they leaped upon them the more cruelly.

In the midst of this trampling scene of chaotic bloodshed the youngest of the three brothers bruised his toes against a stone and fell sprawling to the ground. At once he was seized upon by the ravening dogs, who began intently tearing him to pieces and quarrelling over their prey. The other brothers recognized his dying cries. They ran agonized to his aid, wrapped their cloaks round their left hands, and sought to drive away the dogs by pelting them with stones. But they failed altogether to quell or even to disturb the preying beasts. The mangled and miserable youth died, entreating with his last breath that they would avenge his death on the swaggering capitalist.

The surviving brothers (not so very much, by Hercules, in desperation as in scorn of living safely unavenged) made an immediate attack on the rich man, flinging stones with ruthless courage and inexhaustible energy. Then that bloody man, calling up his murderous oft-used skill-in-arms, hurled a lance which passed clean through the breast of one of the brothers. Yet, wounded to his death, the lad remained upright; for the lance had pierced him so violently that the greater part of its length had come out on the other side and been driven into the earth, and the dying body stood sustained by this strong and yet-quivering prop.

At the same time one of the murderer's retinue, a tall

sturdy fellow, took a part in the game of hurling a stone from a distance at weapon-arm of the third brother. The stone merely grazed the fingertips and skidded hurtless to the ground, though it seemed to the onlookers to have done its work. The quick-witted lad realized how this lucky escape could be turned to full advantage; and hugging his hand as if it were fractured, he thus addressed the oppressor:

'Exult in the destruction of our family. Quench your insatiable lust with the blood of three brothers. Complete your glorious triumph over your fallen fellowmen. But bear in mind that after you have robbed this poor man of his fields, after you have extended your boundaries farther and yet farther, there will always be some neighbour beyond. And this hand of mine with which I had resolved to strike off your head hangs impotent! Such is the injustice dogging the lives of men.'

Infuriated by these words, the snarling thief drew his sword and rushed eagerly upon the defenceless youth, meaning to slay him; but he had misjudged his antagonist. The youth showed unexpected resistance, feinted, and grasped the other's wrist; then freeing his own sword, he plunged it again and again into the tyrant's body, and put an end to the other's evil existence. After that, perceiving himself ringed round with the hurrying attendants, he cut his own throat with the sword that still streamed with the blood of his enemy.

These were the events foreshadowed by the mysterious omens; and these were the events which the servant unfolded to his stricken master. The old man, environed by such a tangle of misery, could not so much as speak a single word or shed a single tear; but seeing the knife with which he had been helping his guests to cheese and other viands, he slashed his throat several times, thus following the example of his ill-starred son. Falling face down upon the table, he washed away with the streams of his own blood the gouts of that earlier portentous gore.

The gardener, shaking his head over the catastrophic fate of his friend's house and deploring his own bad luck, had nothing but his tears to lick after all; and so, continually clapping his empty hands together, he mounted upon my back and set off to retrace our steps.

But trouble met us half-way. A tall fellow (a legionary,

as his clothes and oaths demonstrated) encountered us and asked the gardener in an offhand over-bearing tone where he was taking the unladen ass. My master, stunned with sorrow and ignorant of Latin, went to pass on without replying. At this the soldier could contain his brim-high insolence no longer; and considering the gardener's silence to express contempt, he knocked him from his seat and struck him with a vine-rod[1] that he carried in his hand. The gardener humbly explained that he had not understood what was said as the language was strange. The soldier thereupon repeated the question in Greek.

'Where are you taking that ass?'

'To the next village,' answered the gardener.

'But I happen to want him,' said the soldier, 'So I'm commandeering him for the baggage-train that is needed in yonder hamlet to transport the trunks of my commanding officer.'

With that, seizing my halter, he began to lead me off. But the gardener, wiping the blood that trickled from the switch-wounds in his head, again requested the soldier to treat him more decently and civilly, and begged his consideration by all the hopes he had of heaven smiling upon him.

'For this ass,' he said, 'is very lazy; and worse than that, he's affected with the falling-sickness. He's not worth your trouble. It's as much as he can do to carry a few strings of vegetables from my garden over there. Even that takes the wind out of him. So he's no use whatever for heavier bundles.'

Soon, however, he found that no prayer could touch the hard-hearted soldier who merely became every moment more maliciously pleased; and noticing the man shift his hold on the vine-rod (meaning to break the suppliant's skull with the knob on the end), he realized that there was only one way out. Under pretence of clasping the soldier to move his compassion, he bent submissively down, pulled the other's legs from under him, and flung him heavily on his back. Then, jumping upon his prostrate foe, he assailed face, arm, and ribs with fist, elbow, teeth, and a paving-stone.

The soldier lay helpless on the ground all this while.

[1] 'Vine-rod': Only a centurion should have been carrying one.

unable to do anything but threaten that he would chop the gardener into sausage-meat as soon as he was on his feet again. The gardener, warned by these jabberings, snatched the sword from the fellow's belt; and throwing it aside he once more began thumping, this time even harder, till the soldier, flat on his back and weakened with his wounds, was compelled to lie as if he were dead in order to keep alive.

The gardener then salvaged the sword, mounted my back, and set off with all speed towards the town. Preferring to neglect his garden for the time being, he wended his way to the house of a close friend of his. There he recounted the whole episode and entreated the man not to desert him in his perplexity but to yield him and his ass a temporary refuge; for in two or three days the trouble (a crucifying matter) would doubtless have blown over. Staunch in his friendship, the man welcomed him into his house; and tying my four legs together they dragged me up the stairs into the attic. Then the gardener crept into a chest in the shop-store below; and closing the lid, he retired into hiding.

The soldier (as I afterwards ascertained), like a man bleary from a heavy drunken drowse, made his tottering way to the town, sore and stiff with his smarting wounds, and staggering onwards with the aid of his staff. Ashamed to spread abroad the tale of his own defeat and downfall, he silently digested his sense of injury until he came across some fellow-rankers, to whom he told the whole story. They decided that it would be as well for him to confine himself to his quarters (for besides the disgrace, he dreaded being called to account for the loss of his sword, which amounted to a breach of his military oath never to fail the Emperor) while they, taking down the description of myself and the gardener, searched everywhere till they poked us out of our holes and avenged the army. And sure enough, there was a villain of a neighbour who lost no time in informing against us.

The soldiers at once made application to a magistrate, falsely alleging that they had lost on the road a very valuable silver cup, the property of their commander, and that a certain gardener had found the cup but refused to restore it. This man (they said) had hidden himself in a friend's house. When the magistrate heard this story (capped as it was with the name of an officer whom he knew by repute), he proceeded at once to the doors behind which we had taken refuge; and with a loud voice he announced to our host that it would be better for him to deliver up to justice the criminals indubitably concealed on his premises than to involve himself with a risky business. But our undaunted friend was still as resolved as ever to aid the man whom he had taken under his wing; so he declared that he knew nothing about us and that he had not seen the gardener for several days. Against this the soldiers, invoking the Genius of the Emperor, swore that the wanted man was laired in that house and none other.

At last the magistrates decided to prove the householder a liar by closely searching the house; and they bade the lictors and other officers of the law make forcible entry and ransack every room. But, after a lot of peering about, the sergeants reported that there was not a man to be found, no, not even an ass. The dispute then grew in violence on both sides. The soldiers swore vociferously by Caesar that we were certainly there, while our host swore obstinately by the Gods that we weren't.

Hearing this contentious clamour, I (in general an ass of restlessly inquisitive morals) craned my neck out of a little window-slit to discover what was causing all the uproar; but one of the soldiers, chancing to look in the direction of my shadow, excitedly pointed out to the others what he had seen. Instantly a tremendous hullabaloo arose; and several of the soldiers rushed up the steps, grabbed hold of me, and led me out like a prisoner-of-war. At the same time a stricter search of the house was instituted; every cranny was investigated; the chest was opened; the poor gardener was discovered, dragged out, carried before the magistrates, and thrown into the town jail to await the death penalty. But the others were unable to desist from joking and laughing at the idea of an ass looking out of a window. From this episode the famous proverb[1] sprang. The Peeping Ass, and his Shadow.

---

[1] 'Proverb': There are two old proverbs here telescoped, both referring to a great fuss over nothing; 'all about an ass's shadow', 'just because an ass looked in the window'.

BOOK THE TENTH

WHAT happened to my master the gardener next day I
do not know. But the soldier who had been so handsomely
walloped for his flabby behaviour unfastened me from my
manger and led me off, without anyone saying him nay.
He took me to what I judged to be his barracks, and then
out into the highway, laden with his baggage and furnished
with full military trappings. For he placed on my back a
luminously polished helmet, a shield even more dazzling,
and a spear with a fine long shaft. The spear he carefully
fixed on the top of my pack (which he had disposed in the
form of a trophy) not so much as a matter of routine for
the purpose of impressing the startled wayfarer. Passing
through a plain by an easy enough road, we came to a town
where we lodged not at an inn but at the house of a
decurion. After handing me over to the ministrations of one
of the servants, the soldier bustled off to report to his
captain, who was in charge of a thousand men.

A few days after our arrival, I remember, a particularly
atrocious crime was committed in this town; and I have
made a written account of what I heard, so that you may
read it here.

The Tale of the Wicked Stepmother

THE master of the house had a son, a youth well-versed
in literature and consequently conspicuous for his piety
and quiet nature – the son, in short, of every parent's dream.
When the mother of this youth had been dead for several
years, the father had again ventured into matrimony; and
this second wife had borne a son who was now just past
his twelfth birthday. But the stepmother, who held the
dominating position in the household by reason of good

looks rather than of good morals, cast eyes of lust upon her stepson – either through natural lewdness or the vicious compulsion of fate. Know, therefore, gentle reader, that you now embark on a tragic and not a comic narrative and that you must for the moment climb from the sock to the buskin.

Now, while the baby Cupid was sucking his first drops of milk, the wife managed to keep him quiet; she repressed the first blush of her desire; and sat in silence. But when Love, nourished into madness, revelled within her sweltering soul and curled into every cranny of her flesh, then she surrendered to the cruel god: she feigned physical illness and lay in bed to hide the disorders of her mind.

Everyone knows that the morbid changes in condition and appearance are alike in those who are sick and those who love. To wit: an unpleasing paleness, languid eyes, weak knee-joints, broken sleep, and sighs which are the deeper because the pain burns slowly. You would have diagnosed her trouble as the restive pangs of fever, had it not been for her tears. Alas, for the callow intelligence of the doctors! What meant that skipping pulse, that sudden burning flush, that difficulty in breathing, those incessant tossings and turnings from side to side? Good gods! how easy is it for the man who knows nothing of medicine but who has experienced the symptoms of amorous ague to read the malady of a person who burns without reason for the heat.

Overmastered by the stress of passion, the woman at last broke her long silence by asking to see the elder son – a name which she wished could be for ever obliterated, since every use of it reminded her of her shame. The young fellow hastened to obey the request of his (love) sick parent. With a brow that sorrow and not age had furrowed he went duly respectful into the bedroom of the woman who was his father's wife and his brother's mother. She, wearied out by the cross of silence on which she had long writhed, was now run aground on a second shoal of hesitations. After rejecting every word which she had carefully recited in the mental rehearsal of the interview, and finding her indecision intensified by shame, she could not bring herself to utter the first word. But the unsuspecting youth with downcast eyes asked her unprompted what was the cause of her ailing condition. Thus, proffered the pernicious opening which she could not make of her own will, she summoned all her boldness; and weeping copiously she faltered out the following brief speech, her head hidden in her nightdress:

'The cause of all my pain, the beginning and the end of it, the remedy as well, the only chance of life now left me, is you, you. It is your eyes. They looked into my eyes; and that look went deep into my bowels and kindled consuming fire in the marrow of my bones. Take pity on me then; for I die because of you. Have no scruple on your father's account. Kiss me, and keep his wife alive; for otherwise he'll lose her. There is nothing wrong about my love, since I see his face in yours. We are alone, with nothing to disturb us. You have full opportunity to save my life; and a thing secretly done is hardly done at all.'

The youth was confused by this sudden onslaught; but though he recoiled from the committal of such a forbidden act, yet he thought it as well not to infuriate the woman with a flat refusal or incautious rebuke. So he compromised with a soothing promise intended to postpone the subject indefinitely. He unreservedly agreed that if she would pull herself together, take nourishment, and look to her health, he would fall in with her wishes when his father should be next called abroad. He then withdrew from the troubling presence of his stepmother; and considering that this family crisis needed the fullest analysis, he went straight to his tutor (a sage old man) and told him the tale. They reviewed the situation at length and decided that the only hope of safety lay in instant flight from the region of this moral earthquake.

The woman, however, fidgeting over every hour of delay, cunningly fabricated a pretext for persuading her husband to undertake a hurried visit to some distant farms of his. No sooner had he departed than, frantically eager for the promised consummation, she solicited her stepson to redeem his word. The youth made one excuse after another to avoid her contaminating vicinity, till at last she saw by the multifarious apologies that he was totally reneging. At once (so fickle is lust) her wicked worship of his person was transformed into an ever intenser loathing. She called a villainous slave of hers (part of the dowry); and she took him into the councils of her treacherous breast. The conclusion they reached was that the wretched youth must die; and so the rogue of a slave, ready for any mischief, was sent out post-haste to purchase a deadly poison. This, when procured, she carefully diluted in wine with the intention of removing the sinless stepson.

But it so happened that while the guilty pair were discussing how they should administer the poison, the younger boy (the whore's own son) came home after his morning at school. Feeling thirsty from the food he had eaten, he discovered the cup of wine in which the venom lurked; and unaware of the noxious ingredients he drained the cup. No sooner had he quaffed the death prepared for his brother than he fell speechless to the ground. The schooling-slave, horrified at the boy's collapse, aroused his mistress and the whole household with his clamouring grief; and quickly enough the cause of death was traced to the poisoned draught. But none could guess rightly at the identity of the poisoner.

The female, however (a perfect specimen of the ruthless stepmother), was in no way diverted from her vengeful purpose by the shocking death of her son, or by the knowledge of her own instrumentality, or by the misfortune of the house, or by the grief that her husband would feel. No, she grasped at her son's death as the very bludgeon she wanted, and at once despatched a messenger to inform her travelling husband of the house's visitation. Then, when he hurried home, she boldly declared that her son had been poisoned by his half-brother. And there was this much truth in the statement: the boy had died because his brother had escaped dying. But she pretended that the stepson had deliberately done away with his brother because she had refused to respond to his incestuous advances. Nor was she satisfied with such a complete reversal of the truth; for she added that she had been menaced with a sword because she had threatened to expose these practices.

Passionately did the unhappy father bow his head beneath this mighty storm of sorrow, mourning for two lost sons; for he saw with his own eyes one lad already laid-out, and he knew that the other would as surely be condemned to die for incest and fratricide. Moreover, he was stimulated into grievous hatred of the latter by the feigned lamentations of his beloved wife. Scarcely, therefore, had the funeral rites and burial of the younger son been concluded when the broken old man (wetting his cheeks with tears, plucking his white ash-grimed hair) rushed from the sepulchre to the Forum; and there, weeping, beseeching, even embracing the knees of the decurions, he loosed all his pent emotions in striving for the destruction of his remaining son. Ignorant of the cheat put upon him by his wife, he accused the lad of committing incest in his father's bridal bed, of plotting his brother's murder, and of threatening to slay his stepmother. In short, his misery moved not only the assembly but the populace also to such pity and indignation that all tedious formalities were waived, the accusation was taken as proved, and all the web of legal inquiry was dispensed with. One and all, they shouted that the crime was so horrid a social offence that society should take vengeance into its own hands and the criminal should be stoned to death.

Meanwhile the magistrates grew privately apprehensive lest from the small seed of righteous uproar some riot might arise subversive of civic order and the interests of the state. So they proceeded, appealing to the decurions on one side and quieting the people on the other, to argue that the trial must continue along the usual time-honoured lines, that all allegations must be scrutinized, and that sentence must be pronounced in a legal manner; for they would be imitating brutish barbarians and lawless tyrants if they insisted that any man should be condemned unheard. Worse, they who were blest with a reign of peace, would be leaving posterity a precedent fraught with ugly possibility.

This sound advice carried the day. At once the crier made proclamation that the senators were requested to assemble in the Senate House. That building was at once filled, each man taking his wonted seat in order of rank and dignity. The crier then again made proclamation; the accuser came forward; the prisoner was called and led into court; and then the crier (following the usage of Attic law and the Areopagite process) announced that the advocates must speak without preambles or pleas for pity. That this was the procedure adopted I learned from overhearing various comments and discussions; but as for all the bitter charges of the accusing lawyer, and all the excuses of the accused, and all the harangues, and all the cross-examinations, I have nothing to say. For as I cannot recount what I never knew, I shall only write here what I can myself vouch for as fact.

As soon as the speeches were over, the senators voted that the charges must be established by sure proof, and that suspicion and conjecture would not suffice in so serious a prosecution. They further stated that the slave, who was alleged to be the only person with any evidence bearing on the case, should be questioned in court. Nor was that cross-ripe rogue in the least scared, either by the doubtful chances of so important an inquisition, or by the presence of all the listening dignitaries, or by his own guilty conscience; for he began at once confidently to prate and state all kinds of lies as the solemn truth. He swore that the young man, indignant at being repulsed by the stepmother, had called him and ordered him to murder her son in revenge for that affront; that he had promised him a large reward as the price of his silence, and that he had threatened him with death in punishment for disobedience; that he had mixed the poison with his own hand and bidden him administer it to his brother; and that finally, suspecting that his orders had not been executed and that the poison was being kept as incriminatory evidence, he had administered the poison in person.

When this knavish fellow with a great display of agitation had uttered this plausible set of lies, the trial ended; and not one of the senators remained disposed to express any doubt of the youth's guilt. The prisoner was therefore condemned to be sewn in the Leathern Sack; and the unanimous verdicts were about to be committed to writing (according to the old custom) and then dropped into the brazen urn – after which, the die being cast, no alteration of the sentence could be accepted, and the prisoner passed into the hands of the common crucifier. But at this juncture an aged member of the senate (a physician, than whom none had a higher reputation or wider influence) covered with his hand the mouth of the urn to prevent anyone from slipping in his billet unadvisedly. Then he addressed the court as follows:

'I am happy, sirs, that through all the days of my life I have enjoyed your good will; and I may not permit a

217

manifest homicide to be perpetrated by the false incrimination of an innocent man. Nor may I permit you to violate your judicial oaths by hearkening to the lying testimony of a slave. I myself may not unlearn my reverence for the sanctions of religion, or deceive my conscience, by pronouncing an unjust verdict. Learn from me therefore the true facts of the matter. This varlet approached me some time ago and offered me a hundred gold crowns for a quick and sure poison. He told me that he was acting on behalf of a sick friend who was suffering unbearably from an incurable disease, and who wished to release himself from the crucifixion of life. Remarking the clumsy and disconcerted nature of the villain's babble, and feeling sure that he intended some mischief, I gave him the potion; but as a precaution against any future inquiry. I did not at once accept the proffered price. I said to the man, "Lest any of these goldpieces that you produce should turn out to be lightweight or base-metal, put them in this bag and seal it with your own seal, till they are examined tomorrow by a competent banker."

'He agreed, and sealed up the money. As soon, therefore, as he appeared in this case I bade one of my servants hurry home and fetch the bag from my laboratory; and here I now exhibit it before you. Let him look, and identify his own seal. Now, how can the brother be held on a charge of giving the poison which this fellow purchased?'

An immediate trembling-fit seized the villainous slave; his natural colour disappeared under a deathly pallor; and a cold sweat oozed from every pore. He shifted and shuffled; he scratched one side of his head and then the other; he twisted and screwed his mouth as he stuttered unintelligibly – till there was no observer who had any reasonable doubt of his culpability. Restored at length to his craftiness, he began stoutly to deny the charge and to call the doctor a liar. The latter, wishing to vindicate both his jury-oath and his impugned veracity, replied with increased earnestness to the villain's rebuttal, until at last the officers of the court, by order of the magistrates, grasped the slave's hand, revealed the iron ring, and compared it with the impression on the bag. The comparison corroborated all that the doctor had said; and the Rack and Wooden Horse were accordingly requisitioned (in the Greek manner). But, resolute in his bold denials, the wretch defied the stripes of the scourge and the blisters of the fire.

Finally the doctor exclaimed, 'I won't allow it, by Hercules, no, I won't allow it. Neither shall this guiltless youth receive an unmerited sentence, nor shall this rogue make a scorn of our judgement and escape retribution. I shall produce absolute proof of my story. When this hell-hound came worrying me for a poisonous drug, I decided that it would be a betrayal of my profession to supply any-body with the means of murder, since medicine was meant to be used for preservation, not the destruction, of mankind. Yet I feared that an untimely refusal would provoke him to devise some other way of carrying out the nefarious project on which he was clearly determined – either by buying poison elsewhere, or by having recourse in desperation to the knife or some such weapon. So I gave him a drug, but a sleeping-drug compounded of mandragora: a herb esteemed for its numbing effect which can hardly be dis-tinguished from the repose of death.

'So it is no marvel that this doomed caitiff, sure of bring-ing down upon his head the worst errors of the law if convicted, can lightly brave these milder crucifixions. But if the boy has really swallowed the poison that came from my pharmacopoeia, then he has never died. He lies in suspended animation; and as soon as his leaden trance is shaken off, he will return to the light of day. If, however, he has indeed been murdered, if he has passed away, then you must search out some further explanation of his death.'

After the old man had delivered this speech, all assented to his test. At once the assembly hastened to the tomb where the boy's body was deposited. Not a single senator, not a single dignitary, was missing from the wondering throng. And lo, the father himself, removing with his own hands the lid of the coffin, discovered his son rising that moment from the dead, with the last effects of the drug dissipated. Embracing him tenderly, struck dumb with relief, he led him forth before the people; and the boy was brought into court just as he was, swathed and draped in his cere-cloths.

The truth now stood naked before all; and the villainy of the unscrupulous slave and of his sinful mistress was fully established. The woman was condemned to exile for life; the slave was crucified; and by general consent the gold crowns were presented to the worthy physician as a reward for his providential drug. Thus did the remarkable and ripe romance of the father find an end worthy of divine justice; for in a moment of time, in the mere twinkling of an eye, he found himself blessed with two fine young sons while he was in the midst of bewailing his childless destiny.

.　.　.　.　.

But now it is time that I told you about the waves of fortune on which I was being tossed. The soldier who had taken unquestioned possession of me without paying a farthing, was instructed by his tribune to carry letters to the great Potentate of Rome. He therefore sold me for elevenpence to two brothers, servants of a nearby land-owner who was extremely wealthy. One of these men was a confectioner who baked sweet-breads and dainties; the other was a cook who specialized in appetizing messes succulently seasoned with mixed herbs. These two, living in common, bought me for the purpose of loading me with the abundant vessels that were needed for their master's use during his travels. I was thus received as a kind of third brother; and in all my metamorphosed peregrinations I never had such a good time as now. For in the evening after supper (which was always a luxurious affair) my masters usually brought home to their little apartment a toothsome head of scraps. The cook brought large slabs of roast-pig, chicken, fishes, and other good meats. The confectioner brought rolls, pastries, tartlets, hook-cakes, lizard-loaves, and all kinds of honeyed flawns. Then, after they had fastened the chamber door and departed to refresh themselves at the Baths, I crammed my guts with these heaven-sent delicacies; for I was not such a fool of an ass as to neglect these most delicious foods and to jar my teeth upon dry prickly hay.

For a long time my artful thefts succeeded beautifully. For I pilfered cautiously and frugally, taking only a small proportion; and the brothers did not suspect an ass of being such an epicure. But after a time habit begot boldness; and I gobbled up all the choicest scraps, nosing through the heaps for the best oddments and leaving only the least desirable. Then a growing suspicion entered the minds of the brothers, and they made diligent efforts to detect the agent of their daily loss; but me they never suspected. At length they began to believe each other guilty of playing a mean trick; and keeping a shrewder eye open, they counted and noted the dishes that they brought.

Finally, dropping all reserve, one of them accused the other outright. 'Now look here,' he said, 'this isn't fair, it isn't like a man, to sneak the finest eatables aside, to sell them on the sly for your private profit, and then to insist on a full half-share of what's left. If you're tired of our partnership we can still be brothers as far as things in general are concerned, but we can drop this share-and-share-alike idea. For I can see that if this kind of thing goes on getting worse and worse, we'll end up bitterest enemies.'

'By Hercules,' answered the other, 'I certainly do admire your brazen cheek. Here you have been stealing the food day after day, and then you get in first with a complaint, while all this long time I've been submitting in sorrowful silence rather than face the fact that my brother was a scurvy sneak-thief. It's a good thing that the subject has been broached between us and a stop can be put to this leakage. Otherwise we'd have brooded ourselves into a grudge as bad as Eteocles.'

After they had thus exchanged reproaches for a while, they both of them seriously took an oath that they had stolen nothing whatsoever, not a single surreptitious mouthful; and they decided that they must try every conceivable trap for the thief who was embroiling them in this common loss. It was impossible (they said) for the ass, who was shut in the room alone, to fancy such food; yet daily the best morsels disappeared. Flies could not be the culprits, since only flies as large as the Harpies that plundered the banquet of Phineus could have removed the articles; and no such flies penetrated the room.

Meanwhile, liberally fed and farced with human food, I found that I was plumply filling out, larding and suppling the hide, and showing a sleek glossy coat. But this bodily grace was the cause of my discredit. For the brothers' suspicion was stirred by my uncommon breadth in the beam; and when they had further noticed that the hay remained daily untouched, they directed all their attention towards me. They shut the door as usual at the hour for the Baths, and peeped in at me through a hole in the door as I began busily chewing the scattered scraps. At the sight they forgot all about the havoc I was creating; they stared in wonderment at the unnatural sweet-toothed ass and split their sides with laughter. They called one and then another of their fellow servants, and then a whole tribe of them; and they gave them each a peep at the memorable monster, the beast with a refined appetite. Indeed, so loud and infectious a mood of laughter seized them all that the sound reached their master who was passing near. He inquired what jest was amusing the household. Being informed what it was, he came himself and put his eye to the hole. At once he laughed broadly until his very entrails quaked; and then, opening the door, he approached and inspected me at close quarters. For my part, beholding the face of Fortune benignantly smiling upon me, I continued eating at my ease without turning a hair, encouraged by the applauding merriment.

Charmed by the novelty of the spectacle, the master of the house ordered me to be led (nay, led me with his own hands) to the dining-room; and as soon as the meal was served he bade all kinds of solid victuals and untasted dishes to be laid before me. Although I had eaten a pretty bellyful already, I wished to make myself socially agreeable and to ingratiate myself with my host; so I appreciatively champed every delicacy that was offered. The diners racked their wits to think out every dish likely to be unpalatable to an ass, and offered them to me to test my manners: things such as vinegared beef, peppered pullet, and exotically pickled fish. And all this while the banquet-chamber was one roar of laughter.

Finally the buffoon of the party suggested, 'Give our friend a sip of wine.'

'All joking apart,' answered the host, 'I have a notion that our fellow-diner would not refuse a cup of honeyed wine. Here, lad,' he went on, 'give that golden cup a good rinse, fill it with honeyed wine, and present it to my guest – and at the same time say that I have pledged him.'

A thick hush of expectation filled the room as I unconcernedly emptied the trough-like cup at one draught, gathering up my lips into the shape of a tongue and airily acting the part of boon companion. There was a yell of laughter, and the company with one accord toasted my health.

The master, rapturously enchanted, summoned the two servants who had bought me, and gave orders that they should receive four times my purchase-money. He then handed me over to a certain man (a favourite freedman who was in easy circumstances) and asked him to take good care of me. This man treated me with all humanity and civility; and to earn the praises of his diverted patron he took great pains to teach me a repertoire of tricks. For instance, he taught me to recline at table, leaning on my elbows; to wrestle and dance with lifted forefeet; and (a specially admired attainment) to converse by raising my head as a sign of Yes and by lowering it as a sign of No. He also taught me to look towards the cupbearer, when I was thirsty, and to wink first with one eye and then with the other. In all these acquirements I displayed myself a ready-learner, since I could have done them all without any lessons. But I was afraid that, if I showed knowledge of the human routine without being first taught, people would think that some horror was portended and that I should have my head amputated and my carcass thrown out to feast vultures.

Meanwhile the tale spread rapidly far and wide; and my marvellous exploits had consequently made my master an illustrious personage. 'There goes the man,' folk said, 'who dines with an ass at his table, a wrestling ass, a dancing ass, an ass that understands human speech and answers with signs.'

But I must now mention (as I should have at the beginning) who this man was, and whence he came. Thiasus (that was the name by which he went) was a native of Corinth, the capital of the province of Achaia. Gradually climbing the ladder of civic success, as his worth and birth warranted, he arrived at nomination to the office of five-yearly magistrate. Then, to show himself equal to the calls of that position, he promised to finance a three-day gladiatorial display. Munificence could go no further.

It was, in fact, his zeal to please the public which had brought him to Thessaly; for he was now engaged in collecting troupes of genuine wild beasts and prominent gladiators. When his dispositions and purchases were completed satisfactorily, he arranged for the homeward journey. But scornfully repudiating the glittering chariots and luxurious coaches which, some covered and some open, were herded along in the rear – ignoring his Thessalian steeds and his Gallic gennets, whose flawless pedigree demonstrated their valuable rarity – he rode affectionately upon me – me, trimmed with trappings of gold, bearing a painted saddle, hung with purple, bridled with silver, girthed with embroideries, and prinked with tintinnabulating bells. As we went he spoke to me confidentially. Among other remarks I remember him expressing his delight at possessing in me at one and the same time a nag and a nob.

At last after travelling by land and sea we arrived at Corinth, where the citizens streamed jostling out to greet us, not so much to pay their respects to Thiasus as to catch a glimpse of me. For my fame had preceded me so loudly that I was the source of considerable profit to my keeper. When he perceived that crowds of people were enthusiastically keen to see me amusing myself, he shut the gates and admitted the populace one at a time, charging a stiff price for the privilege. The daily gate-money soon amounted to a fair sum.

Among the visitors there was a rich and respected lady who after once paying for a view was so tickled by my manifold gambols that her flustered wonder drifted into a wondrous lust. Unable to cool her turbulent blood, she took heart at the example of Pasiphae and decided to act the she-ass. In short, she won my keeper over, by a heavy bribe, to surrender me to her mercies for a single night; and the corrupt servant, considering his own gain more than my amenities, assented.

Therefore, when I had supped as usual with my master, we left the parlour and went up to my bedroom. There we lighted upon this woman, whose nerves were already ragged with awaiting us. Good gods! how lordly were the preparations. Four eunuchs strewed the ground with mattresses of down and air-filled bolsters. The coverlet was of cloth-of-gold and broideries of Tyrian dye; and the pillows were small but wide enough for their purpose, and soft like those on which delicate ladies lay their lazy cheeks or necks. The eunuchs, anxious not to delay the pleasures of their mistress a moment longer, closed the bedroom-doors and went away; but there were tall wax-candles that banished every shadow from the glowing room. Then the woman stripped full-length (even to the band that upheld her darling breasts) and standing close to the light she rubbed herself from top to bottom with balmy unguents. After that she turned to me and anointed me likewise all over, expending particular care in scenting my nose.

That done, she gave me a lingering kiss; not the kind that you met in the stews, in the whore-shops and the open markets of venery. No, it was a sisterly and sincere salutation, accompanied with such remarks as 'I love you', 'I want you', 'You're the only one in the world', 'I can't live without you', and other phrases of the kind that women use to lead-on their lovers and to express their emotions. Then she took me by the neck-rope and placed me on the bed; and as she was a very beautiful woman, and as I was flushed with excellent wine and soused in fragrant ointments, I had no difficulty in meeting her half-way.

But I was deeply harrowed, uncertain how I could embrace so flower-like a lady with my clumsy legs; or how I could touch her gleaming tender milk-and-honey body with my coarse hooves; or how my enormous slavering jaws and rows of teeth like stones could kiss her small and scarlet lips dewed with ambrosia; or (to sum up) how she, who was still a woman even if she were itching to the very tips of her little fingernails, could manage to receive me. 'Woe's me,' I thought, 'if I hurt this fine lady, I shall be thrown out for the beasts of prey to devour.'

But, looking on me with burning eyes, she redoubled her enticing nicknames, assiduous kisses, and sweet moans, till at last, crying, 'I take you, I take you, my dovelet, my heart's sparrow,' she demonstrated that all my fears were falsely grounded. She embraced me successfully; and so far from finding her ass-journey troublesome she it was who set the pace and showed that she had no timidities or doubts as to the final destination. Indeed, I soon discovered that the only apprehensions I needed to entertain were on my own account; and I thought that the mother of the Minotaur knew what she was doing when she chose a lowing lover.

At last this laborious and sleepless night was concluded; and the woman, to avoid the eye of day, left me in haste – not neglecting, however, to contract with my keeper for another night later on at the same price. The fellow was willing to fall in with her schemes, partly because of the large sums she offered, and partly because of the chance he saw of providing a new side-show for his master. He, therefore, incontinently disclosed the whole episode to the latter, who, after richly rewarding him, decided to put the act on as a public spectacle. But as my winsome wife could not be employed for the job on account of her social position, and as no one else would volunteer, a certain debased woman (whom the prefect had condemned to be eaten alive by wild beasts) was procured to mate with me in the arena before the populace. Of this woman I heard the following story:

The Tale of the Jealous Wife

SHE had a husband whose father had been once called away from home. Before leaving he gave strict injunctions to his wife (the young man's mother) whose belly was swelling roundly, that if the babe turned out to be one of the frailer sex it should at once be strangled. While he was still absent, the wife gave birth to a girl; but overcome by the impulses of mother-love she disobeyed her husband and arranged for a neighbour to rear the child. Then on the husband's return she admitted that she had borne a daughter but said that it had been duly destroyed.

When, however, the girl had grown to a nubile age, the mother realized that she was unable to give her a dowry suitable to her birth without the father knowing; and in desperation she told the whole tale to her son. A further reason for this step was the fear that he might in the heats of youth fortuitously seduce the girl, since neither knew of the relationship. The young man, who loved his mother ardently, religiously followed her suggestions, acted in brotherly fashion, and kept the family secret so well that he seemed to any observer merely a good friend to the girl. But he undertook to fulfil his obligations by receiving her into his house as if she was an orphan girl from the neighbourhood who needed parental protection; and he proposed to marry her soon to a beloved and trusty friend of his,

226

after settling a liberal dowry upon her out of his own estate.

But these excellent and innocent dispositions could not escape the distorting rancour of Fortune. They sowed the seeds of bitter jealousy in the household and drove the wife to the crimes for which she was later condemned. For the wife first suspected the sister to be a rival who had ravished her husband from her; next she hated her; and finally she resolved to murder her with the cruellest tortures. In pursuance of this she devised the following trap. She stole her husband's signet-ring and went to a farm of theirs in the country. Thence she despatched a servant of hers (a faithful villain who deserved death for such fidelity to inform the girl that the husband was come to the farm and wished to see her alone as soon as possible. To remove any doubts that might breed delay, she gave the messenger the stolen ring as a token of the message's truth.

The girl, obedient to her brother's request (for she was the only other one in the secret of her birth) and convinced by the signet which was shown her, instantly set out unaccompanied for the farm. When she had been thus basely lured into the wife's clutches, the latter goaded by lustful frenzy stripped her naked and madly flogged her. In vain the screaming girl confessed the truth; in vain she declared that she was the husband's sister. The wife was too overcome by jealous rage to listen; she considered the confession mere trumped-up evasion; and thrusting a burning brand between the girl's thighs, she cruelly murdered her.

When the brother of the dead girl (and spouse of the murderess) heard what had happened, he hastened to the scene of the crime. Deeply affected, he saw to all the burial arrangements; and then, distracted by the girl's unhappy death at the hands of the woman who should most have cherished her, and racked through and through with regret, he fell into a dangerous fever. Some medical attention was clearly indicated; and the wife (if we can still give her that honourable title) went straightway to a notoriously corrupt doctor, who, victor in many a stricken field, could boast (if he so wished) of the golden trophies reared upon his palm in consequence. Meaning to remove her husband, she offered fifty goldpieces for guaranteed effective poison.

No sooner said than done. She and the doctor pretended that they were about to administer a drug (called Sacred by the learned) which was never known to fail in alleviating intestinal trouble and carrying off the bile. But the drug which they poured out was one Sacred to the needs of the Lady of Death. Before the assembled household and a number of friends and relatives, the doctor himself sagely stirred the cup and offered it to the sick man; but the relentless woman, planning to get rid of her accomplice and to save the money that she owed him, stayed his hand.

'My dear doctor,' she said, 'you must not give my beloved husband the potion without taking a good pull at it your-self. How do I know that there isn't poison in it? I'm sure that you as a sensible and well-read man won't be offended if I as a true-hearted wife take every rightful precaution for my husband's safety.'

The doctor, quite demoralized by the woman's truculent assurance, was deprived of all power of thought by the necessity of decision at so short a notice. If he showed any signs of doubt or fear, he would at once be suspected; and in his dilemma he drank deeply. The husband thereupon confidently received and drained the cup.

That part of the business completed, the doctor was making-off as fast as he could, in the hope of finding an anti-dote at home to counteract the fatal effects of the poison; but the persistent woman, determined not to be beaten, refused to let him get a nail's-breadth away till the potion was digested and its results apparent. However, after he had prayed and protested, she at length relented so far as to dismiss him.

But the virulent poison had already tainted his blood and was fast gnawing at his vitals. Walking in a trance of anguish he just managed to totter home and tell his wife what had happened (instructing her not to forget to claim the fee for this twin-murder) before he died in convulsions. Such was the violent end of this notable doctor.

Nor did the husband survive him many hours. He died of the same complaint, amid the fictitious tears of his false wife. After a few days (taken up by the performance of the obsequies) the doctor's widow came to demand the fee owing for the duplicated deaths; but the other relict, con-sistently deceitful, answered with a pretence of open honesty and friendliness and with promises that she would pay the agreed sum without further demur if the other on her side would complete the pact by handing over a small additional quantity of the drug.

So that's that. Duped by the woman's fraudulent assurance, the doctor's widow readily assented. She hurried home in her eagerness to curry favour with the wealthy woman, and returned at once with the whole box of poisons. The murderess, now possessed of the potent means of destruction, spread her bloody web further abroad for victims. She had borne a young daughter to her lately poisoned husband; and she was annoyed that the laws should make this child the heir to the estate. As the child stood between her and this property, she resolved to remove the child. Ascertaining that a widow inherits what is left her child under such circumstances, she showed herself as worthy a mother as she had been a wife. For, preparing breakfast one day, she grasped an opportunity to poison both her own daughter and the doctor's widow.

The child, being young and frail, died at the first shock of the encroaching venom; but the woman, feeling the powerful virus coagulate in her lungs, immediately suspected the truth. She knew her life was choking fast away; but faster she fled to the house of the provincial governor, screaming that she had horrible mischiefs to reveal. Her protesting voice attracted a large crowd, and the governor admitted her to an instant audience where she exposed the career of the infamous woman in all its atrocious details. That done, a sudden dizziness clouded blackly over her mind; her mouth, opened to speak, closed with a click; she ground her teeth furiously; and then she dropped dead at the governor's feet.

The capable official did not allow the horror of the accursed poisoner's multiple crimes to languish by delay. He forthwith ordered the chambermaids to be summoned; by torture he extracted the truth from them; and then, as a punishment less than her deserts but at least worse than any other he could invent, he sentenced the woman to be thrown to the wild beasts.

．　　．　　．　　．　　．

This was the woman with whom they decided to join me publicly in wedlock. It was therefore with the severest mental anguish that I anticipated the day of the Shows. Several times, indeed, I determined to die by my own hand rather than be stained by contact with such a foul woman and made a shameless public-show into the bargain. But destitute of human hands and fingers I was altogether foiled in my efforts to unsheathe a sword with my rounded and shapeless hoof. One ray of hope alone gilded my pitch darkness. Spring was returning; the countryside would be embroidered with gem-like buds; the meadows would be invested with a brightening flush; the roses would break forth from their thorny retreats, exhaling fragrance; and by means of the roses I should become Lucius once more.

At last the day appointed for the Shows arrived; and amid shouts of applause, escorted by a long train, I was escorted to the ampitheatre. During the opening items on the bill, which consisted of merry dances executed by the players, I was halted outside the gate. There I was pleasantly able to crop some lush grass that grew around the path, and to delight my curious eye with a fine view of what was going on beyond.

Beautiful boys and girls in the bloom of youth, gorgeously clad, moved with gesturing elegance through the charming patterns of the Greek pyrrhic dance. Now they tripped round in a circle; now, deploying they entwined in slanting line; sometimes they formed into a wedge with hollow square; then they broke into two troops – and so on, until the blast of a trumpet bade them unravel, once and for all, these tangling intricate figures. Then a screen was lowered; the hangings were drawn; and a dramatic scene was exhibited.

There was a wooden mound representing that far-famed Mount Ida of which the soothsayer Homer sang. An erection of great height, it was covered with turf and verdant trees up to the very crest, whence by the artificer's skill a fountain gushing sent its waters brawling down the slopes. A handful of she-goats were browsing among the grasses; and a young man, finely arrayed in flowing barbaric drapes, and wearing a golden tiara, acted the part of Phrygian Paris, seemingly absorbed in his pastoral work. A comely boy then appeared, naked except for the ephebic mantle that swung from his left shoulder. His hair was brilliantly yellow; and from the midst of it there issued a pair of little golden wings which together with the wand in his hand labelled him Mercury. He danced forwards, holding out an apple of gold which he presented to Paris, conveying at the same time by his gestures the command of Jove; and then he gracefully danced off.

A girl with a noble cast of features next entered, impersonating Juno; for she had a white diadem upon her head, and she carried a sceptre. Another girl came out behind her, whom you knew at a glance was Minerva; for she wore a gleaming helm encircled with an olive-wreath, and she raised her shield and darted her spear like that goddess in battle-wrath. Thirdly, there appeared a girl who far surpassed the others in all the paraphernalia of beauty; and her ambrosially tinted charms proclaimed her Venus, but Venus when a virgin. She was rather unclad, and the grace that her nakedness uttered had no flaw. Unclad she was, save for a gauzy silken scarf which shadowed her admirable loins, and which sometimes lifted at the gay twitch of the lascivious wind to show how truly young she was, and sometimes clung the closer to delineate more deliciously the moving contours of her body. The hues of her presence were twain; white were her glistening limbs, because she had descended from heaven; azure were her silken vestments, because she had arisen from the sea.

The virgins who were acting as goddesses were accompanied by their proper servants. First, Juno, attended by two player-lads miming Castor and Pollux with round pointed helmets and spangled crests of stars, advanced with a calm and unaffected air to the harmonies of the flute and promised the shepherd with becoming gestures that she would see him crowned King of All Asia if he handed her the prize of beauty.

The girl who was panoplied as Minerva was followed by two armed youths (squires of the Lady of Battles) named Tear and Terror, who now danced before her with drawn swords. Behind her a piper played a warrior-tune, mingling shrill piercing notes with deep roaring tones in order to stir the vigorously nimble dancers as the trumpet stirs the battle-line. Next, with animated head and with quick menacing eyes, the goddess herself began to dance, intimating to Paris with her quickened pulsating gestures that if he adjudged her the victor of the beauty-contest she would give him valour and trophied fame by her patronage.

Thereupon, welcomed with tumultuous applause, Venus advanced with a sweet smile and posed gracefully in the middle of the stage surrounded by a throng of merry little boys – such plump and milky babes that you would have sworn them authentic Cupids who had that moment flown from heaven or the sea. They had tiny wings and arrows, and all the rest of the equipment; and they waved glittering torches before their mistress, as if to light her way to a nuptial feast. Behind them pressed a lovely choir of maidens (the darling Graces and the charming Hours) who danced congruous measures and strewed the path of the goddess with loose or woven bouquets of flowers, propitiating the Queen of Pleasure with the tresses of the Spring.

Presently the flutes began sweetly to harmonize in the honeyed Lydian modulations, which thrilled and relaxed the audience. But that was nothing to the thrill when Venus began to dance quietly in tune with the music, making slow delaying steps, sinuously bending her body, and moving her gracious arms. Every delicate movement that she made was answered by the warbling flute – one moment her eyes were gently drowsy; the next moment they flashed passionately; and sometimes she seemed to dance with her eyes alone. As soon as she had come near the umpire, she was perceived to promise by her tokening arms that if he selected her as winner she would grant him as wife the most beautiful woman in the world – a woman like Venus. Gladly then did the Phrygian youth hand her the golden apple, the symbol of her unconquerable beauty.

O why do you wonder after this if those dregs of humanity, those forensic cattle, those gowned vultures, the judges now sell their decisions for cash? Even at the world's infancy a bribe could corrupt judgement in a question agitated between gods and men; and a young fellow (a rustic and a shepherd) appointed judge by the counsels of great Jove sold the first judicial decision for the lucre of lust, thereby entailing damnation on mankind. Aye, by Hercules, and another such judgement was given later by the noble generals of the Grecian host when Palamedes (famed for wisdom and learning) was condemned on a lying

232

charge of treason. And a similar injustice was done when the trifling soldier Ulysses was preferred to great-heart Ajax who excelled in war. And how may we describe the judgement enforced by those illustrious lawyers the Athenians who had mastered all knowledge? Was not that divinely wise old man (pronounced by the Delphic god the wisest of mortals) conquered by the lies and envy of a pack of villains who called him a corruptor of the youth when he was the bridler of excess? Was he not murdered by the deadly juices of a hellish herb, leaving his death as an indelible blot upon the state? For to this very day the most distinguished philosophers select his doctrinal teachings as supreme, and in their topmost aspirations toward happiness it is by his name that they swear.

However, to prevent the reader from reprehending my righteous indignation by muttering to himself, 'How long are we to endure this philosophizing ass?' I shall pick up my narrative at the point where I left it. After the judgement of Paris was concluded, Juno and Minerva retired from the stage in melancholic fury, revealing by their gestures how resentful they felt at being the losers. But Venus, gaily rejoicing, testified to her satisfaction by dancing with full choir. Then wine tinged with saffron spurted out from the mountain-crest through a privy pipe; and streaming down in scattered rivulets it besprinkled the browsing goats with odoriferous spices and dyed their whiteness with the richer tint of yellow. Finally, when the whole theatre was pervaded with the sweetness, a chasm opened and gulped down the wooden mountain.

One of the soldiers at once was detached, in response to the shouts of the eager populace, to fetch from her cell the woman who (as I have related) was condemned to the wild beasts as a penalty for her manifold crimes and appointed to me in much-discussed nuptials. The couch meant to serve us was already carefully laid out. It was gaudy with Indian tortoise-shell, bulgy with feather cushions, and adorned with a coverlet of silk. But as for me, beyond the shame of my public prostitution, beyond the horror of contact with that polluted woman, I felt the terrors of death gathering about me. For I was thinking that if some wild beast should be sent in to eat the woman while she and I were entangled in our share of the performance, was it likely that that wild beast would be so extraordinarily well trained and intelligent, so restrained and abstemious, as to tear my partner to pieces and yet spare me as a guiltless individual not included in the sentence?

I was therefore perturbed not merely for my moral character but for my very life. So while my master was engaged in superintending the preparation of the couch, and while all the servants were absorbed either in getting ready for the hunting event or in staring at the grand show, little by little I quietly edged away. For no one thought that so tame an ass needed very attentive watching, and I had been left to look after myself. As soon as I passed the nearest city gate, I galloped on at a great speed, till after six miles of fast travelling I arrived at Cenchreae, a town considered the noblest of the Corinthian settlements and bordered by the Aegean and Saronic Seas. Here there is a harbour with a safe anchorage for ships, and consequently the streets are full of people. Avoiding the crowded quays I found a sequestered nook by the shore, hard by the foam of the billows; and there I stretched out my weary body on the cradling lap of the sand. The chariot of the sun had reached the end of his course; and surrendering myself to the peaceful dusk I was soon rocked in sweet slumbers.

BOOK THE ELEVENTH

About the first watch of the night I was aroused by sudden panic. Looking up I saw the full orb of the Moon shining with peculiar lustre and that very moment emerging from the waves of the sea. Then the thought came to me that this was the hour of silence and loneliness when my prayers might avail. For I knew that the Moon was the primal Goddess of supreme sway; that all human beings are the creatures of her providence; that not only cattle and wild beasts but even inorganic objects are vitalized by the divine influence of her light; that all the bodies which are on earth, or in the heavens, or in the sea, increase when she waxes, and decline when she wanes. Considering this, therefore, and feeling that Fate was now satiated with my endless miseries and at last licensed a hope of salvation, I determined to implore the august image of the risen Goddess.

So, shaking off my tiredness, I scrambled to my feet and walked straight into the sea in order to purify myself. I immersed my head seven times because (according to the divine Pythagoras) that number is specially suited for all ritual acts; and then, speaking with lively joy, I lifted my tear-wet face in supplication to the irresistible Goddess:

'Queen of Heaven, whether you are fostering Ceres the motherly nurse of all growth, who (gladdened at the discovery of your lost daughter) abolished the brutish nutriment of the primitive acorn and pointed the way to gentler food (as is yet shown in the tilling of the fields of Eleusis); or whether you are celestial Venus who in the first moment of Creation mingled the opposing sexes in the generation of mutual desires, and who (after sowing in humanity the seeds of indestructible continuing life) are now worshipped in the wave-washed shrine of Paphos; or whether you are the sister of Phoebus, who by relieving the pangs of child-birth travail with soothing remedies have brought safe into the world lives innumerable, and who are now venerated in the thronged sanctuary of Ephesus; or whether you are Proserpine, terrible with the howls of midnight, whose triple face has power to ward off all the assaults of ghosts and to close the cracks in the earth, and who wander through many a grove, propitiated in divers manners, illuminating the walls of all cities with beams of female light, nurturing the glad seeds in the earth with your damp heat, and dispensing abroad your dim radiance when the sun has abandoned us – O by whatever name, and by whatever rites, and in whatever form, it is permitted to invoke you, come now and succour me in the hour of my calamity. Support my broken life, and give me rest and peace after the tribulations of my lot. Let there be an end to the toils that weary me, and an end to the snares that beset me. Remove from me the hateful shape of a beast, and restore me to the sight of those that love me. Restore me to Lucius, my lost self. But if an offended god pursues me implacably, then grant me death at least since life is denied me.'

Having thus poured forth my prayer and given an account of my bitter sufferings, I drowsed and fell asleep on the same sand-couch as before. But scarcely had I closed my eyes before a god-like face emerged from the midst of the sea with lineaments that gods themselves would revere. Then gradually I saw the whole body (resplendent image that it was) rise out of the scattered deep and stand beside me.

I shall not be so brave as to attempt a description of this marvellous form, if the poverty of human language will not altogether distort what I have to say, or if the divinity herself will deign to lend me a rich enough stock of eloquent phrase. First, then, she had an abundance of hair that fell gently in dispersed ringlets upon the divine neck. A crown of.interlaced wreaths and varying flowers rested upon her head; and in its midst, just over the brow, there hung a plain circlet resembling a mirror or rather a miniature moon – for it emitted a soft clear light. This ornament was supported on either side by vipers that rose from the furrows of the earth; and above it blades of corn were disposed. Her garment, dyed many colours, was woven of fine flax. One part was gleaming white; another was yellow as the crocus; another was flamboyant with the red of roses.

236

But what obsessed my gazing eyes by far the most was her pitch-black cloak that shone with a dark glow. It was wrapped round her, passing from under the right arm over the left shoulder and fastened with a knot like the boss of a shield. Part of it fell down in pleated folds and swayed gracefully with a knotted fringe along the hem. Upon the embroidered edges and over the whole surface sprinkled stars were burning; and in the centre a mid-month moon breathed forth her floating beams. Lastly, a garland wholly composed of every kind of fruit and flower clung of its own accord to the fluttering border of that splendid robe.

Many strange things were among her accoutrements. In her right hand she held a brazen sistrum, a flat piece of metal curved like a girdle, through which there passed some little rods – and when with her arm she vibrated these triple chords they produced a shrill sharp cry. In her left hand she bore an oblong golden vessel shaped like a boat, on the handle of which (set at the most conspicuous angle) there coiled an asp raising its head and puffing out its throat. The shoes that covered her ambrosial feet were plaited from the palm, emblem of victory.

Such was the goddess as breathing forth the spices of pleasant Arabia she condescended with her divine voice to address me.

'Behold, Lucius,' she said, 'moved by your prayer I come to you – I, the natural mother of all life, the mistress of the elements, the first child of time, the supreme divinity, the queen of those in hell, the first among those in heaven, the uniform manifestation of all the gods and goddesses – I, who govern by my nod the crests of light in the sky, the purifying wafts of the ocean, and the lamentable silences of hell – I, whose single godhead is venerated all over the earth under manifold forms, varying rites, and changing names. Thus, the Phrygians that are the oldest human stock call me Pessinuntia, Mother of the Gods. The aboriginal races of Attica call me Cecropian Minerva. The Cyprians in their island-home call me Paphian Venus. The archer Cretans call me Diana Dictynna. The three-tongued Sicilians[1] call me Stygian Proserpine. The Eleusinians call me the ancient

[1] 'Three-tongued Sicilians': The islanders changed from Sicilian to Greek to Latin. The Arii are of Parthian Aria.

goddess Ceres. Some call me Juno. Some call me Bellona. Some call me Hecate. Some call me Rhamnusia. But those who are enlightened by the earliest rays of that divinity the sun, the Ethiopians, the Arii, and the Egyptians who excel in antique lore, all worship me with their ancestral ceremonies and call me by my true name, Queen Isis.

'Behold, I am come to you in your calamity. I am come with solace and aid. Away then with tears. Cease to moan. Send sorrow packing. Soon through my providence shall the sun of your salvation arise. Hearken therefore with care unto what I bid. Eternal religion has dedicated to me the day which will be born from the womb of this present darkness. Tomorrow my priests will offer to me the first fruits of the year's navigation. They will consecrate in my name a new-built ship. For now the tempests of the winter are lulled; the roaring waves of the sea are quieted; and the waters are again navigable. You must await this ceremony, without anxiety and without wandering thoughts. For the priest at my suggestion will carry in the procession a crown of roses attached to the sistrum in his right hand; and you must unhesitatingly push your way through the crowd, join the procession, and trust in my good will. Approach close to the priest as if you meant to kiss his hand, and gently crop the roses. Instantly you will slough the hide of this beast on which I have long looked with abhorrence.

'Fear for no detail of the work to which I once put my hand. Even at this moment of time in which I appear before you, I am also in another place instructing my priest in a vision what is to be brought to pass. By my command the crush of people will open to give you way; and despite all the gay rites and ferial revelries not one of my worshippers will feel disgust because of the unseemly shape in which you are incarcerated. Neither will any one of them misinterpret your sudden metamorphosis or rancorously use it against you.

'Only remember, and keep the remembrance fast in your heart's deep core, that all the remaining days of your life must be dedicated to me, and that nothing can release you from this service but death. Neither is it aught but just that you should devote your life to her who redeems you back into humanity. You shall live blessed. You shall live glorious under my guidance; and when you have travelled your full length of time and you go down into death, there also (on that hidden side of earth) you shall dwell in the Elysian Fields and frequently adore me for my favours. For you will see me shining on amid the darkness of Acheron and reigning in the Stygian depths.

'More, if you are found to merit my love by your dedicated obedience, religious devotion, and constant chastity, you will discover that it is within my power to prolong your life beyond the limits set to it by Fate.'

At last the end of this venerable oracle was reached, and the invincible Goddess ebbed back into her own essence. No time was lost. Immediately snapping the threads of sleep, and wrung with a sweat of joy and terror, I wakened. Wondering deeply at so direct a manifestation of the Goddess's power, I sprinkled myself with salt water; and eager to obey her in every particular, I repeated over to myself the exact words in which she had framed her instructions. Soon the sun of gold arose and sent the clouds of thick night flying; and lo, a crowd of people replenished the streets, filing in triumphal religious procession. It seemed to me that the whole world, independent of my own high spirits, was happy. Cattle of every kind, the houses, the very day, all seemed to lift serene faces brimful with jollity. For sunny and placid weather had suddenly come upon us after a frosty yesterday; and the tuneful birdlets, coaxed out by the warmths of the Spring, were softly singing sweet hymns of blandishment to the Mother of the Stars, the Producer of the Seasons, the Mistress of the Universe. The trees also, both those that blossomed into fruit and those that were content to yield only sterile shade, were loosed by the southerly breezes; and glistening gaily with their budded leaves, they swished their branches gently in sibilant sighs. The crash of storm was over; and the waves, no longer mountainous with swirling foam, lapped quietly upon the shore. The dusky clouds were routed; and the heavens shone with clear sheer splendour of their native light.

By this time the forerunners of the main procession were gradually appearing, every man richly decked as his votive fancy suggested. One fellow was girded about the middle like a soldier; another was scarfed like a huntsman with hunting-knife and shoes; another, wearing gilt sandals, silken gown, and costly ornaments, walked with a woman's mincing gait; another with his leg-harness, targe, helm, and sword, looked as if he had come straight from gladiatorial games. Then, sure enough, there passed by a man assuming the magistrate with fasces and purple robe, and a man playing the philosopher with cloak, staff, wooden clogs, and goat's beard; a fowler with bird-lime elbowing a fisherman with hooks. I saw also a tame she-bear dressed as a matron and carried in a sedon-chair; an ape with bonnet of plaited straw and saffron-hued garment, holding in his hand a golden cup and representing Phrygian Ganymede the shepherd; and lastly, an ass with wings glued on his back ambling after an old man – so that you could at once have exclaimed that one was Pegasus and the other Bellerophon, and would have laughed at the pair in the same breath.

Into this playful masquerade of the overflowing populace the procession proper now marched its way. Women glowing in their white vestments moved with symbolic gestures of delight. Blossomy with the chaplets of the Spring, they scattered flowerets out of the aprons of their dresses all along the course of the holy pageant. Others, who bore polished mirrors on their backs, walked before the Goddess and reflected all the people coming-after as if they were advancing towards the Image. Others, again, carrying combs of ivory, went through the various caressive motions of combing and dressing the queenly tresses of their Lady; or they sprinkled the street with drops of unguent and genial balm.

There was a further host of men and women who followed with lanterns, torches, waxtapers, and every other kind of illumination in honour of Her who was begotten of the Stars of Heaven. Next came the musicians, interweaving in sweetest measures the notes of pipe and flute; and then a supple choir of chosen youths, clad in snow-white holiday tunics, came singing a delightful song which an expert poet (by grace of the Muses) had composed for music, and which explained the antique origins of this day of worship. Pipers also, consecrated to mighty Serapis, played the tunes annexed to the god's cult on pipes with transverse-mouthpieces and reeds held sidelong towards the right ear; and a number of officials kept calling out, 'Make way for the Goddess!'

Then there came walking a great band of men and women of all classes and ages, who had been initiated into the Mysteries of the Goddess and who were all clad in linen garments of the purest white. The women had their hair anointed and hooded in limpid silk; but the men had shaven shining polls. Terrene stars of mighty deity were these men and women; and they kept up a shrill continuous tingle upon sistra of brass and silver and even gold. The chief ministers of the ceremony, dressed in surplices of white linen tightly drawn across the breast and hanging loose to the feet, bore the relics of the mighty gods exposed to view. The first priest held on high a blazing lamp – not at all like the lamps that illumine our evening suppers; for its long bowl was gold, and it thrust up from an aperture in the middle a fat flame. The second priest was similarly vestured, but he carried in both hands model altars to which the auxiliary love of the supreme Goddess has given the fitting title of Auxilia. The third priest grasped a palm-tree with all its leaves subtly wrought in gold, and the wand of Mercury. The fourth priest displayed the Symbol of Equity; a left hand moulded with open palm (since the left hand seemed to be more adapted to administer equity than the busier, craftier right hand). The same man also bore a vessel of gold rounded into the shape of a woman's breast, from which he let milk trickle to the ground. The fifth priest had a winnowing-fan constructed with thickset sprigs of gold; and the sixth priest had an amphora.

After these came the Gods themselves (deigning to walk before our eyes on the feet of men). First we saw the dreadful messenger of the gods of heaven and hell, Anubis, with his face blackened on one side and painted gold on the other, lifting on high his dog's head and bearing his rod in his left hand. Close upon his heels followed a Cow (emblem of the Goddess that is fruitful mother of all) sitting upright upon the proud shoulders of her blessed worshipper. Another man carried the chest that contained the Secret Things of her unutterable mystery. Another bore in his beatified bosom a venerable effigy of Supreme Deity, which showed no likeness to any bird or beast (wild or tame) or even to man, but which was worthy of reverence because of its exquisite invention and originality: a symbol inexpressible of the true religion that should be veiled in

Deep Silence. This effigy was of burnished gold, made as follows: a small urn was delicately hollowed out with a round bottom: the strange hieroglyphs of the Egyptians covered its outside; the spout was shaped rather low but jutting out like a funnel; the handle on the other side projected with a wide sweep; and on this stood an asp, stretching up his scaly, wrinkled, swollen throat and twining round the whole length.

At last the glorious moment which the presiding Goddess had promised me was at hand. For the priest, adorned exactly as she had described, neared with the instrument of my salvation. In his right hand he carried the Goddess's sistrum and a crown of roses. Ah, by Hercules, a crown indeed it was for me, since by the providence of the over-mastering gods, after so many toils of experience, I was now to find my efforts crowned with victory over Fortune, my cruel foe.

However, though shaken with up-bubbling joy, I did not dash immediately forwards; for I did not want the peaceful order of the holy procession to be disturbed by an unruly beast. Instead, I nosed through the crowd with a polite all-but-human tread and a sidelong twist of my body; and, as the people (clearly by the Goddess's dispensation) disparted to let me through, I slowly approached the flowers. But the priest (as was obvious to me) recollected his admonitory vision of the night. He at once stopped stock-still; and spontaneously raising his right hand, he held the bunch up to my mouth. Trembling, with a thudding heart, I seized the crown in which some fine rose blooms were brightly woven; and greedily I masticated the whole lot.

Nor did the heavenly promise fail. At once my ugly and beastly form left me. My rugged hair thinned and fell; my huge belly sank in; my hooves separated out into fingers and toes; my hands ceased to be feet and adapted themselves to the offices of my erected state; my long neck telescoped itself; my face and head became round; my flapping ears shrank to their old size; my stony molars waned into human teeth; and my tail (the worst cross of my ass-days) simply disappeared.

The populace stood in blinking wonder; and the devotees adored the Goddess for the miraculous revelation of her power in a metamorphosis which partook of the shifting pageantry of a dream. Lifting their hands to heaven, with one voice the beholders rendered testimony to the loving-kindness of the Goddess thus signally declared. As for me, I remained nailed to the spot in mute stupefaction; for my wits were scattered by the shock of joy, and I was quite at a loss. What was the right utterance with which to begin my new life? Where was my voice to come from? How was I most auspiciously to employ my newborn tongue? What phrases could I choose to express my gratitude to so great a Goddess?

But the priest (who by advertisement knew the whole tale of my misfortunes) though wonderstruck at the miracle recovered himself so far as to signify with gestures that I should be handed a linen garment. For from the moment that the ass stripped me of his wretched skin I had been doing my naked best to hide my privities with the sole naturally-supplied veil (the hand), while compressing my thighs. At once one of the initiated pulled off his upper tunic and wrapped me in it; and then the priest, smiling kindly but still staring at my quite-human countenance, thus addressed me:

'At last, Lucius, after the long days of disaster and the heavy storms of fortune you have reached the haven of peace and the altar of mercy. Neither your high lineage, nor your pride of place, nor your learning, profited you one jot. You gave yourself to the slavery of pleasure in the lewdness of hot-blooded youth; and you have reaped the reward of your unprospering curiosity. Nevertheless, blind Fortune, persecuting you with horrors and snares, has led you in her shortsighted malice to this beatitude of release. Let her go now and rage as madly as she will; but let her seek another object for her hate. For terror and calamity have no power over him whose life the majesty of our Goddess has claimed for her service.

'What benefit has furying Fortune gained from the robbers, from the wild beasts, from the servitude, from the unending hardships of the way, from the daily fears of death? You are now received into the protection of Fortune, but of Fortune who is open-eyed and who lightens even the other gods with the splendours of her light. Let your face be joyous therefore. Let it be such a face as accords with

243

that white gown you wear. Follow in the train of the Goddess your Saviour with steps of triumph. Let the scoffer behold. Let him behold and be shamed, saying in his heart:

' "Lo, here is Lucius who rejoices in the providence of mighty Isis. Lo, he is loosed from the bonds of misery and victorious over his fate."

'Yet, that you may be the safer and the surer, enrol your name in this army of holiness, to which you were but a short time past pledged by oath. Dedicate yourself to the service of true religion, and voluntarily bend your neck to the yoke of this ministry. For when you have begun to serve the Goddess you will feel the full fruitfulness of your liberty.'

When the worthy priest, labouring hard to breathe under the pressure of inspiration, had concluded this speech, I joined the ranks of the religious and followed the procession. All pointed or nodded at me, and cried aloud: 'This day has the august power of Almighty Goddess restored him that you see there to human form. Happy, by Hercules, thrice blessed is he who by the purity and faith of his past life has merited such particular patronage from above! For it is as though he had been set apart from the moment of his second birth for the ministry of heaven.'

Among these ejaculations and the hum of happy prayers, we moved slowly on till we approached the sea. The spot chosen was the very beach where on the preceding day (while yet an ass) I had stabled myself. First, the images of the gods were orderly disposed; and then the high priest dedicated and consecrated to the Goddess a nobly built boat (scribbled all over with the peculiar Egyptian marks) after purifying its torch, flame, egg, and sulphur, and pouring solemn prayers from his sanctified lips.

The shining-white sail of this blessed ship bore a broidered inscription repeating the words of the prayer for this year's prosperous navigation. The mast, when raised, was seen to be a rounded pine-tree of great height with a glittering top that drew all eyes. The prow was curved to represent a goose-neck[1] and covered with flaming gold-plates, while the whole of the polished keel consisted of rich citronwood.

[1] 'Goose-neck': The goose was sacred to Isis.

All the people (initiate or lay) zealously piled up winnowing-fans with aromatic scents and other such offerings, and threw libations of milk mixed with crumbs into the sea, until the ship, cargoed with plentiful gifts and auspicious devotions, was let slip from her anchoring ropes. She put out to sea with a mild breeze; all her own; and after she had sailed out of sight into the distance on her course, the bearers of the holy things reassumed their burdens and began a lively return journey to the temple in the same order and propriety as they had come.

On arrival at the temple, the high priest, those who bore the divine figures, and those who had been admitted into the inner light of the cult, collected in the sanctuary of the Goddess. First they put back the breathing images into their right places; then a man (whom all entitled the scribe) took his stand in a high pulpit before the doors, and the Society of the Pastophori[1] (such is the name of the sacred college) was convoked. The scribe thereupon read out of a book a set of patriotic prayers for 'the great Prince, the Senate, the Equestrian Order, the Roman people, and all sailors and ships which come under the jurisdiction of Rome'. After that he pronounced in the Greek tongue and manner the words *'Laois aphesis'*. The people were dismissed.

The shout that followed showed the popular approval of the day's proceedings; and the congregation began to file out, beaming with joy, carrying boughs of olive and other votive wreaths, and garlanded with flowers. As they left the precincts, they one and all stopped to kiss the feet of a silver image of the Goddess that stood on the steps. But my emotions would not allow me to stir a single inch away from the place. With my eyes fixed upon the image I brooded over my past miseries.

Winging rumour, however, let no moss grow on her feathers. The tale of the Goddess's adorable goodness and of my curious adventures very soon had reached my native city; and my servants, friends, and those near to me in blood, at once discarded the sorrow into which the false tidings of my death had plunged them. Overjoyed and surprised, they hastened to visit me with various gifts, looking upon me as a man divinely raised up out of death. I who had shared their grief now shared their pleasure but

[1] 'Pastophori': The priests that carried the shrines of the gods.

gratefully refused their gifts, particularly as my servants had luckily taken care to bring me more than enough of clothes and money. Therefore, after I had met these acquaintances politely and told them the full story of my past pains and present prospects, I once more returned to what had become my chief source of delight: the contemplation of the Goddess. Renting a temporary apartment within the temple enclosure I took part in all the services, frequenting the company of the priests and becoming a constant worshipper at the shrine. Nor did a single night pass without some vision visiting my sleep and commanding me to be initiated into the priesthood, to which vocation I had long since been destined.

But though I profoundly desired to take this step, yet a religious qualm held me back. For after careful inquiry I had learned that a consecrated life was full of snags, that the requisite chastity was difficult to observe, and that only the most unrelenting discipline could save the priest from casual pollutions. Turning these doubts over and over in my mind, I kept delaying my initiation, though every day brought me closer to the final decision.

One night I had a dream. I thought that the high priest came to me with his bosom full of something or other. I asked him what he was offering me, and he answered, 'presents from Thessaly, for that Snowy Servant of yours has arrived from that province.'

When I awoke I pondered over the meaning of this vision, especially as I was sure that I had never had a servant of that name. However, I concluded that something to my advantage was portended by the priest offering me presents. Thus, worried and yet hopeful, I awaited the opening of the temple in the morning. At last the white curtains were drawn, and we offered up our prayers before the holy face of the Goddess. The priest went the round of the altars, performed the sacred ceremonial with solemn supplications, and poured out libations of water from the sanctuary-spring. When all these rites were completed, the worshippers saluted the rays of dawn and announced in clear voices that the day had begun.

Then lo, some men who had been in my employ arrived from Hypata, where I had left them on the day when Fotis by her wicked error fitted me for a halter. Accosting them

I found that they had brought back my old horse, which had been recovered after changing hands several times and which I indentified by a mark on his back. At once I realized how admirably prophetic was my dream; for not only had it foretold gain in a general way but it had actually described the recovery of the horse, my snowy servant.

After this I applied myself even more diligently to attendance on the temple-services; for I considered that the Goddess had vouchsafed sure token of future blessings by her present benignity. Besides, my desire to enter the priesthood increased by bounds every day. Accordingly I had frequent interviews with the high priest, during which I earnestly besought him to initiate me into the mysteries of the Holy Night. But he, a serious-minded man who was noted for his strict observance of his unevangelical religion, checked my implorations with gentle friendliness, as parents get rid of children who come bothering at the wrong moment. At the same time he was careful to soothe me with hopes for the future.

For (he said) the initiation date for each aspirant was given by direct sign from the Goddess; and the officiating priest was selected by the same process – as also the precise sum to be expended on the ceremony. All these details must be awaited with uncomplaining patience, since it was necessary on every count to avoid either forwardness or contumacy, and neither to be slothful when called nor precipitate when not called. Not indeed that there was a single man among them who was so lost to common sense or so foolhardy that he would dare in rank blasphemy to undertake the ministries of the Goddess, which without her consent would be an invocation of destruction. For the gates of shadow as well as the bulwarks of life were under the Goddess's control; and the act of initiation had been compared to a voluntary death with a slight chance of redemption. Therefore the divine will of the Goddess was wont to choose men who had lived their life to the full, who were coming near to the limits of waning light, and who yet could be safely trusted with the mighty secrets of her religion. These men by her divine providence she regenerated and restored to strength sufficient for their new career. Consequently I must await the celestial token, although I had already been manifestly indicated as destined for the blessed ministry. Meanwhile I should abstain from all profane or forbidden foods like the other devotees, that I might hasten the more uprightly into the secret bosom of the faith.

Thus spoke the priest; nor did impatience fret my obedient days. For I ambitiously performed the daily tasks of the ministry, intent upon preserving a serenity of soul and a laudable silence. Nor did the mindful love of the Goddess desert me or nail me on a cross of long delay; for there was no darkness in the visions that admonished the darkness of my sleep. She appeared and told me that the day of my desire had arrived, the day which would fulfil my dearest wishes. She also stated the sum of money to be spent on the ceremonial, and appointed the high priest Mithras to preside over my initiation; for (she said) he and I had our destinies mingled by a conjunction of our stars.

Elated by these and other divine commandments of the supreme Goddess, I threw off the coverlet of my sleep, although light was just greying. Hastening straightway to the retreat of the high priest I greeted him just as he was leaving his bedchamber. I had resolved to press my initiation as a thing now due; but the moment that he saw me he began speaking:

'O Lucius, what a happy and blessed man are you, whom the august deity has selected for such direct honours. O why,' he cried, 'do you stand there idle? Why do you delay a moment? The day that you have so constantly desired is come. You are to be initiated into the holy mysteries by these hands of mine in accordance with the divine mandate of the many-titled Goddess.'

Thereupon the old man took me by the hand and led me towards the spacious temple; and after he had duly performed the rituals of opening the doors and of making the morning-sacrifice, he produced from the secret recesses of the shrine certain books written in unknown characters. The meaning of these characters was concealed, at times by the concentrated expression of hieroglyphically painted animals, at times by wreathed and twisted letters with tails that twirled like wheels or spiralled together like vine-tendrils – so that it was altogether impossible for any peeping profane to comprehend. From these books the high priest interpreted to me the matters necessary for my mystic preparation.

That done, I set about purchasing, partly at my own cost and partly with the aid of friends, all the required commodities. This I did on a larger scale than I had been bidden; and then, at the time that the priest had appointed as most suitable, I was led to the Baths, surrounded by a crowd of devotees. There, after I had taken the usual bath, Mithras himself washed and sprinkled me with pure water, invoking first the pardon of the gods.

Then he led me back once more into the temple and sat me down at the very feet of the Goddess. Two parts of the day had now gone; and after giving me some secret charges (too holy to be uttered) he bade me aloud to fast for the next ten days, eating no flesh and drinking no wine. This fast I reverently observed; and then at last the day arrived when I was to pledge myself to heaven. The sun swung down and drew the evening on; and lo, hosts of people came eagerly from every direction, each man honouring me with various gifts according to the ancient rite. Then, after the uninitiated had withdrawn to a distance and I had donned a new linen gown, the priest grasped my hand and conducted me into the Holy of Holies.

Perhaps, curious reader, you are keen to know what was said and done. I would tell you if it were permitted to tell. But both the ears that heard such things and the tongue that told them would reap a heavy penalty for such rashness. However, I shall not keep you any longer on the cross of your anxiety, distracted as you doubtless are with religious yearning. Hear therefore and believe what I say to be truth.

I approached the confines of death. I trod the threshold of Proserpine; and borne through the elements I returned. At midnight I saw the Sun shining in all his glory. I approached the gods below and the gods above, and I stood beside them, and I worshipped them. Behold, I have told my experience, and yet what you hear can mean nothing to you. I shall therefore keep to the facts which can be declared to the profane without offence.

Morning arrived; and after the due solemnities I came forth sanctified with twelve stoles, an habiliment of deep religious import, but which the bonds of my obligation do not keep me from mentioning, as I was seen by many by-standers. For, by order of the priest, I climbed a wooden pulpit which stood in the middle of the temple before the image of the Goddess. I wore a vestment of linen embroidered with a flower-pattern; a costly cope hung down from my shoulders to my ankles; and from whatever angle you inspected me you saw interesting new animal-shapes among the decorations – here Indian serpents, there Hyperborean griffins (which the Antipodes incubate like birds). This latter garment was what the priests commonly call an Olympic Stole. In my right hand I held a lighted torch; and a comely chaplet was wound round my head, from which the palm-tree leaves jetted like rays of the sun.

Thus decorated like the sun and draped like a statue (the curtains being whisked away) I was suddenly revealed to the gaze of the multitude. After this I celebrated the festal day of initiation (as if it were a birthday) with a sumptuous feasting and merry converse; and the third day was taken up with similar ceremonies, with a ritual-breakfast and the consummation of my priest-hood.

Lingering about the temple for several more days, I was granted the delight of viewing the Holy Face: a benefit that no grateful services can ever repay – till at length, after humbly thanking the Goddess (not as she deserved but as I was able), I received her admonition to depart home; and I reluctantly made my preparations. But I could hardly bear to break the ties of intense affection that bound me to the place. Prostrating myself before the Goddess and water-ing her feet with my tears, I addressed her, gulping back the sobs that disturbed my articulation:

'Most holy and everlasting Redeemer of the human race, you munificently cherish our lives and bestow the consoling smiles of a Mother upon our tribulations. There is no day or night, not so much as the minutest fraction of time, that is not stuffed with the eternity of your mercy. You protect men on land and sea. You chase the storms of life and stretch out the hand of succour to the dejected. You can untwine the hopelessly tangled threads of the Fates. You can mitigate the tempests of Fortune and check the stars in the courses of their malice. The gods of heaven worship you. The gods of hell bow before you. You rotate the globe. You light the sun. You govern space. You trample hell. The stars move to your orders, the sea-sons return, the gods rejoice, the elements combine. At your nod the breezes blow, clouds collect, seeds sprout, blossoms increase. The birds that fly in the air, the beasts that roam on the hills, the serpents that hide in the earth, the monsters that swim in the ocean, tremble before your majesty.

'O my spirit is not able to give you sufficient praises, nor have I the means to make acceptable sacrifice. My voice has no power to utter what I think of you. Not a thousand mouths with a thousand tongues, not an eternal flow of unwearied declaration, could utter it.

'Howbeit, poor as I am, I shall do all that a truly religious man may do. I shall conjure up your divine countenance within my breast, and there in the secret depths I shall keep divinity for ever guarded.'

I thus offered my prayer to the supreme Goddess. Then I embraced the priest Mithras (my father in Her); and clinging upon his neck and kissing him oft, I begged his forgiveness that I could not recompense him adequately for the benefits he had heaped upon me. After expressing my sense of obligation at full length, I left him and prepared to revisit my ancestral home from which I had been so long absent.

So, a few days later (as the Goddess admonished), after hastily packing my luggage I went on shipboard and set sail for Rome. Safely and swiftly carried by a favouring breeze, we soon reached the port of Augustus. There I disembarked; and travelling by post-chariot I arrived at the Holy City on the evening of the day before the Ides of December. Nothing now mattered to me so much as to supplicate daily the supreme godhead of Queen Isis (who is propitiated in this city with the deepest veneration as Campensis:[1] a name derived from the site of her temple). In short, I became an unslackening worshipper, a newcomer to this church of hers, but indigenous to her religion.

Now the strong-thewed Sun had passed through all the signs of the circling zodiac, and the year was ended. But

[1] 'Campensis': In-the-Fields – the Campus Martius.

the loving insistence of the Goddess once more broke in upon my sleep, once more strongly speaking of mysteries and holy rites. I wondered what was the meaning of this, and what even was foreshadowed. How should I not? For I had thought myself fully initiated already.

After I had re-examined all my religious doubts in the privacy of my own conscience, I consulted a priest. I then learned a new and disturbing thing: that I was initiated into the mysteries of the Goddess, but that I knew nothing of the rites of the mighty God, the supreme Father of the Gods, unconquerable Osiris.

For though there is amity and even unity to be found between the two essences and their religious statement, yet the approach to knowledge of them is by different tracks. So now what I had to do was to await a summons from the great God to his service. Nor was I left long in doubt. During the next night I saw in a dream one of his devotees clad in linen and bearing ivied thyrsi and other objects (which I may not name). He placed his load before my Household Gods; and then, seating himself in my chair, he recited to me the articles necessary for a splendid religious feast – and, in order that I might know him again, he showed me how the heel of his left foot was somewhat hurt, giving him a slight hobble. All the mists of my doubt were cleared away by such a manifest sign of the will of the gods.

Therefore, as soon as my matins were finished, I carefully noted the priests, to see if any of them walked like the man in my dream. There he was, the very man. One of the Pastophori closely resembled my midnight visitor in stature and looks as well as in gait. His name, I later found, was Asinius Marcellus (a name asininely suggestive of my late plight). I at once approached the priest, who was not at all surprised at what he heard me say; for he had been similarly admonished as to my initiation into the mysteries of Osiris. On the preceding night, while dressing the garlands on the statue of the Great God, he imagined that the Mouth (which pronounced the dooms of all mankind) spoke to him. The message said that a native of Madaura was being sent to him and that he must impart to this man, poor as he was, the sacraments of the God – whereby through the God's providence the one would be glorified for his religious exercises and the other greatly profited.

Thus affianced to religion I was yet held back from the full consummation of my desire through the slenderness of my means. For the travel expenses had wasted the remnant of my estate; and the cost of living in Rome was far ahead of that in the provinces. My poverty thus kept interfering with my plans; and I was left stranded (as the saying goes) between the altar and the block.

Yet the mandates from the God did not weaken their pressure. They continued to goad me till I became very troubled; and then as the commands grew more incisive, I sold the clothes off my back and scraped up enough to carry on. This indeed was the course prescribed; for the God said to me: 'If you were hot after some trifle of pleasure, would you hesitate to throw your clothes away? And now, on the brink of initiation, do you shrink from a poverty that can bring no repentance?'

Everything was thus fully prepared; and now once more I abstained for ten days from eating flesh. Then, admitted with shaven head to the nocturnal orgies of the Lord of Gods, I resorted to the ceremonies with the full confidence that knowledge of a kindred ritual evoked. This occurrence consoled me for my sojourn in a foreign city and also gave me a better chance of earning my livelihood. For, favoured by the god Good-Luck, I managed to subsist on the small fees I gained in the Forum pleading causes in the Latin tongue.

But shortly afterwards I was once more molested by unexpected visionary commands; and a third time[1] I found myself yearning towards a mystery. This left me in an oppressively shaken and perplexed state of mind, uncertain what could be the significance of this new and peculiar expression of celestial will and what could remain incomplete in my dual initiation. Surely (thought I) the instructions given me by the two priests must have been either incorrect or fragmentary; and, by Hercules, I began to suspect them of bad faith. While, however, I was drifting on these stormy tides of doubt and driven to the verge of

[1] 'Third time': This initiation was into the mysteries of the Roman Isis – the first having been into those of the Achaian Isis.

distraction, the benign figure of the God appeared in dream once more.

'To no end,' said he, 'are you frightened by the continued series of religious rites, as if something had been previously omitted. Rather, you should take heart because the deities repeat the tokens of their love for you. You should exult that you will thrice achieve that which is scarcely even once given to others. And you may rightly conjecture from the number Three that you will remain eternally blessed. Moreover, you will find the ceremony indispensable if you will but realize that the stole of the Goddess with which you were invested in the province is still kept in the temple there. You are thus unable to supplicate at Rome in your stole or to be distinguished by that auspicious garment when you are bidden to don it. Therefore let my command be as glory, happiness, and health to you. Once more joyously become initiated, with the mighty gods for your sponsors.'

Thus far did the persuasive majesty of the divine vision announce what I must profitably do. So I did not neglect or weakly postpone the matter. At once I related to a priest what I had seen; and I not only submitted to the yoke of abstinence from meat but voluntarily extended the period beyond the ten days ordained by everlasting law. Then I bought all the necessary articles, considering more the measure of my piety than the narrowness of the regulations. Nor, by Hercules, was I ever sorry for my trouble and expense. And why should I? For now by the generous aid of the gods I was being decently repaid for my forensic labours.

At length, after the lapse of a few days, the Lord Osiris, the most powerful of the great gods, the highest of the greater, the greatest of the highest, and the ruler of the greatest, appeared to me in the night, now no longer disguised by deigning to speak to me in his own person and with his own divine voice. He declared that I should rapidly come to the forefront of the legal profession at Rome and that I should not fear the slanders of the malevolent who naturally disliked me on account of the learning I had studiously acquired.

In addition, to enable me to mingle with the throng of devotees and duly serve his mysteries, he appointed me a member of the College of Pastophori – and more, one of the five-yearly decurions; and so, with tonsured crown, I set about joyfully executing my duties in that most ancient society (which had been founded in the period of Sylla), not shading or hiding my baldness but freely exposing it where-ever I went.